SEXUAL ASSAULT AND THE J
A QUESTION OF ATTITUDE

This book is set against the background of the 'justice gap' in sexual assault cases—the dramatic gap between the number of offences recorded by the police and the number of convictions. It seeks to examine the attitudinal problems which bedevil this area of law and possible strategies for addressing them. Written by a professor of law and a professor of psychology, it reviews evidence from socio-legal and social cognition research and presents new data drawn both from interviews with judges and barristers and from studies with prospective lawyers and members of the public. In the final part, it considers different ways in which rape trials could be improved and suggests steps that could be taken to change public attitudes about sexual assault.

Sexual Assault and the Justice Gap: A Question of Attitude

Jennifer Temkin and Barbara Krahé

·H A R T·
PUBLISHING

OXFORD AND PORTLAND, OREGON
2008

Published in North America (US and Canada) by
Hart Publishing
c/o International Specialized Book Services
920 NE 58th Avenue, Suite 300
Portland, OR 97213-3786
USA
Tel: +1 503 287 3093 or toll-free: (1) 800 944 6190
Fax: +1 503 280 8832
E-mail: orders@isbs.com
Website: http://www.isbs.com

Hart Publishing, 16C Worcester Place, Oxford, OX1 2JW
Telephone: +44 (0)1865 517530 Fax: +44 (0) 1865 510710
E-mail: mail@hartpub.co.uk
Website: http://www.hartpub.co.uk

British Library Cataloguing in Publication Data
Data Available

ISBN: 978-1-84113-670-7

Typeset by Hope Services Ltd, Abingdon, Oxon
Printed and bound in Great Britain by
TJ International Ltd, Padstow, Cornwall

For

Adam and Lara
Charlotte and Justin

Acknowledgements

Looking at sexual assault and the justice gap from the very different perspectives of law and social psychology has proved to be a daunting but ultimately highly rewarding task. We feel that we have benefited greatly from engaging in a transdisciplinary dialogue and hope that the book reflects this experience. We have received much help and encouragement along the way which it is a pleasure to acknowledge. We are extremely grateful to the Deutsche Forschungsgemeinschaft (German Research Foundation) for the grant which enabled us to carry out the original quantitative research for this book and to the Sussex Law School and the University of Potsdam for stimulating the development of this project. We are grateful to Jacqueline Cheltenham and Richard DeFriend for their logistic support and to Jan Prescot for valuable research assistance. We are especially grateful to Anja Berger and Steffen Bieneck for their creative input into the design of the studies. Thanks are also due to the research team at Potsdam, in particular Konrad Gerbing, Cathleen Kappes, Julia Kleinwächter, Stefan Lüttke, Kaspar Schattke and Vitalij Spak, for their help with collecting the data. We greatly valued the advice and information provided by Adam Zellick, Kenneth Zucker and the Criminal Cases Review Commission. Finally, we are particularly indebted to Jenny McEwan and Gerd Bohner for their constructive comments on the manuscript.

Jennifer Temkin, University of Sussex
Barbara Krahé, University of Potsdam
October 2007

Contents

Introduction

THE PROBLEM OF rape has emerged from the shadows, encouraged by a climate in which sexual autonomy is increasingly demanded for women as well as for men. In jurisdictions throughout the world and through the medium of international criminal law and human rights law, the desire to deal with sexual coercion and to recognise the rights of victims has been demonstrated. However, legal change has yet to be demonstrably effective. Laws may have been stripped of their most blatantly misogynistic manifestations, but the processing of rape cases through the criminal justice system remains problematic.

In England and Wales, ever since the 1970s, reform of the law concerning sexual offences has continued apace. These reforms of both substantive and evidential law have influenced or have been influenced by those enacted in other jurisdictions in the common law world. Civil law jurisdictions, albeit at a slower pace, have also set about the process of law reform. At the same time, the policies and practice of the police in the investigation of rape and that of the Crown Prosecution Service (CPS) in its prosecution have altered substantially to take account of the victim's interests. In response to these developments, women and more recently men, have become increasingly willing to report sexual victimisation with the result that rape reporting rates have increased exponentially since the 1980s. However, rape conviction rates have remained relatively static. Reports rarely translate into convictions. It is this discrepancy that has been termed the *justice gap*.

Psychological and sociological research has revealed for some time that there is an attitude problem in this area. Perceptions of rape are influenced by stereotypes, bias and gender prejudice. This book will argue that it is this attitude problem which needs to be addressed if the justice gap is to be reduced. The book is necessarily therefore an interdisciplinary enterprise which draws on new psychological and legal research conducted by the authors as well as existing research in both disciplines.

It is often said that the problem in rape cases is simply the lack of evidence, or that it is frequently just one person's word against another. This suggests that the decisions made in rape cases are purely evidence-based. This book seeks to challenge that view. Within the criminal justice system, the decisions made by police, prosecutors, judges and juries are indeed normatively defined as data-driven. Decision-makers, whether lay or professional, are expected to assess the evidence in its own right without being affected by their personal feelings or biases or by extraneous information. But the reality of decision-making in sexual assault cases is not adequately explained by a purely normative understanding of the processes involved. A wealth of theorising and research at the interface of psychology and law highlights the influence of psychological processes which operate in a way that is at odds with the normative view (eg Clifford, 2003; Feigenson, 2000). The distinction between two modes of information processing, *data-based* and *schematic* processing, is of particular importance here (eg Kunda, 1999). In data-driven processing, perceivers arrive at a judgment on the basis of a careful examination of the evidence. By contrast, in the schematic mode of information processing, perceivers make sense of the data by referring to a set of abstract ideas and expectations or 'schemata', in this case their general views about rape and rape victims. There is ample evidence of the role of schematic processing in sexual assault cases, reflected in outcomes different from those suggested by the available evidence.

A SOCIAL PSYCHOLOGICAL PERSPECTIVE ON DECISION-MAKING IN RAPE CASES

This book adopts a social psychological perspective on the process of decision-making in sexual assault cases. From this perspective, decisions made in the legal context are seen as potentially susceptible to the same biases and limitations that characterise social information processing in general, such as the tendency to attend to information selectively by concentrating on what is consistent with the perceiver's pre-existing attitudes (McEwan, 2003). Despite safeguards implemented in the legal system to counteract these biases (eg legislation to restrict the use of sexual history evidence that might trigger rape stereotypes), it will be shown that they are hard to eradicate. We argue that judgments about sexual assault are skewed in the direction of low conviction rates partly because of the widely held attitudes about rape which undermine the position of the complainant and benefit the defendant.

The stereotype of the 'real rape' continues to dominate perceptions about what is a genuine rape allegation. It includes socially shared beliefs about the kinds of men who commit rape, the kinds of women who are credible victims, and the way a 'genuine' victim behaves during and after an assault. These beliefs are misguided in a descriptive sense, because only a minority of rape cases match the conditions set out in the stereotype. But the real problem is that they tend to operate as *prescriptive* norms by defining the characteristics that are thought to be necessary in order to qualify as a credible rape allegation. We argue that this discrepancy between what is widely believed to be a 'real rape' and the reality of the circumstances in which women experience sexual violence plays a critical role in the justice gap. To the extent that such generalised stereotypical beliefs interfere with the data-driven appraisal of the information given in a specific case, biased information processing is likely to result, and it is this which consistently trumps the efforts of legislators to move things on. Stereotypical views operate both at the individual level and at the institutional level of the criminal justice system, both of which are considered in this book. At the individual level, the book reviews existing research and presents new quantitative evidence on the role and impact of rape-related attitudes. At the level of the criminal justice system, it looks at the problems involved in processing rape cases as perceived by a sample of experienced judges and barristers. In addition, it illustrates how law reform which was designed in part to counter the effects of stereotyping has been undermined so that the law in action differs substantially from the law on the statute book.

As well as analysing some of the problems which lead to the justice gap, the book explores ways of narrowing it. Prevailing myths and stereotypes about rape operate towards exonerating perpetrators by shifting blame to victims. Challenging these attitudes and developing strategies for diminishing their influence may improve the position of the complainant in court and ultimately help to reduce the justice gap. The book therefore considers a variety of different methods for improving rape trials. It also looks at the steps which could be taken to educate the public about sexual assault with a view to changing both attitudes and behaviour as well as the quality of jury decision-making.

Sexual assaults are most often committed by a male perpetrator against a female victim so that the roles of complainant and defendant are divided along gender lines. This is in no way to deny the reality and traumatic effects of men's sexual victimisation by other men or by women (Krahé, Scheinberger-Olwig and Bieneck, 2003; Krahé, Schütze, Fritsche and Waizenhöfer, 2000) or indeed the operation of stereotypes in judging sexual violence against men (see Davies and Rogers, 2006, for a review). However, men's sexual violence against women is by far the most prevalent form of sexual aggression, not only in Western Europe but worldwide (see Krug, Dahlberg, Mercy, Zwi and Lozano, 2002: WHO World Report on Violence and Health). Our analysis is addressed specifically to the way in which the criminal justice system deals with male defendants and female complainants in rape cases where the whole range of beliefs and expectations about gender roles is brought to bear on the assessment of the behaviour of the two parties.

PREVIEW OF THE CHAPTERS

In writing this book jointly from the two disciplines of law and psychology, we are keen to ensure that readers from both fields have the information they need. This inevitably means that some of the legal material may be too technical for some readers, while some of the statistical detail from the quantitative studies may be hard going for others. We have tried our best to strike a balance to meet the needs of our envisaged interdisciplinary audience. Detailed discussion of some of the legal provisions surrounding rape has been confined to Appendix 1 and each chapter contains a brief summary recapitulating the main findings.

The book is divided into three parts. Part 1 (chapters one to three) considers existing research evidence on the justice gap, the role of rape stereotypes and the process of jury decision-making. It also briefly sets out the legal background. Part II (chapters four to seven) presents a series of empirical studies conducted by the authors which investigate the attitude problem underlying the justice gap, combining both quantitative and qualitative methodologies. Part III (chapters eight to ten) discusses avenues for change in terms of law reform, improving rape trials and educational interventions aimed at dispelling misconceptions about rape. The following represents a brief summary of each chapter:

Chapter one illustrates the problem of attrition in rape cases by providing information about the statistical picture in several jurisdictions. It also sets out the legal background by explaining briefly aspects of the law of rape in England and Wales and elsewhere. The legal background is discussed in more detail in Appendix 1.

Chapter two considers the real rape stereotype and how it shapes attitudes towards and assessments of situations involving rape. It looks at the concept of rape myths and reviews evidence about the extent to which these myths are accepted and applied by members of the public as well as professionals who are directly involved in the legal process. It examines factors influencing the attribution of responsibility and blame to victims of rape and seeks to explain the role of schematic and heuristic information processing in sexual assault cases.

Chapter three considers the problems raised by the jury system in sexual assault trials. It presents different models explaining how juries arrive at a verdict, discusses a variety of factors undermining the quality of jury decision-making, such as jurors' susceptibility to cognitive biases and emotional reactions, and examines the functions and effectiveness of expert testimony in rape trials.

Chapter four presents original data from two empirical studies conducted by the authors on the impact of stereotypical beliefs on judgments about hypothetical rape scenarios. The studies examine the extent to which prospective lawyers are susceptible to schematic information processing on the basis of rape stereotypes and some of the processes underlying their judgments about defendants and complainants.

Chapter five presents a third study which demonstrates the impact of rape stereotypes and schematic reasoning about rape cases in a large sample of members of the public representing the population from which jurors are drawn in rape cases. This study also includes an empirical evaluation of a recent media campaign conducted in England and Wales in order to gauge its effectiveness in influencing perceptions about sexual assault.

Chapter six presents the findings from a series of systematic, in-depth interviews with a sample of judges and barristers. It considers their views of the problems involved in processing rape cases and also their attitudes towards rape and towards the justice gap.

Chapter seven draws on the same sample of judges and barristers to analyse their understanding of and their approach to key areas of the evidential law of rape which have a bearing on rape stereotyping at the trial level, namely corroboration, sexual history and third party disclosure. The chapter sheds light on the law in action and how it contributes to the justice gap.

Chapter eight looks at ways in which the law could be strengthened in order to reduce the impact of stereotypical thinking in rape cases. In particular, it examines the role of expert evidence as an educational tool for jurors and discusses the issue of consent in alcohol-related rape cases.

Chapter nine discusses a range of options for improving rape trials, including the possibility of screening jurors, different ways of assisting the jury, and educating and training lawyers involved in rape cases.

Chapter ten examines strategies for changing public attitudes about rape. These include school-based education programmes, media campaigns and initiatives by men opposed to sexual violence.

The book ends with a brief conclusion summing up its main findings and recommendations for tackling the justice gap.

Part I

The Background

1

The Justice Gap in Sexual Assault Cases

IN MANY COUNTRIES in the Western world, attempts have been made to improve the lot of victims of sexual offences but increasing conviction rates has proved to be an elusive goal. This book is set against the background of what has been officially accepted in England and Wales as 'the justice gap' in sexual cases-the gap between the large number of cases reported to the police and the tiny number which result in conviction (see eg Office for Criminal Justice Reform, 2006). The problem has also been noted across the Western world, with a large proportion of reported rape cases dropping out as they proceed through the criminal justice system (Regan and Kelly, 2003). The present chapter presents evidence for the justice gap by documenting the process of attrition in rape cases. It goes on to summarise the law relating to sexual assault in England and Wales, comparing it briefly with that of other European countries, in order to outline the complicated relationship between law and schematic reasoning and to provide the context for the analyses which are presented in later chapters.

1.1 THE PROBLEM OF ATTRITION

There are certain facts about rape in England and Wales which are indisputable. There is the fact that each year more and more women, and now more and more men, report rape to the police. There is also the fact that few of these reported rapes ever translate into convictions. Moreover, Home Office figures show that the conviction rate in terms of the annual number of convictions as a percentage of the annual number of reported rapes is declining dramatically. In 1977 there was a conviction rate of 32 per cent (Regan and Kelly, 2003: 13). By 2004/05 it had fallen to 5.3 per cent (Home Office, 2005a: Main Volume, Table 3.12; Home Office, 2005b: Table 2.04).[1] This discrepancy between the number of reported cases and the number of those which result in conviction has been aptly

---

[1] The definition of rape changed with the Sexual Offences Act 2003 which came into effect in May 2004, so that conviction rates thereafter are not strictly comparable with those of preceding years.

described as more of a 'chasm' than a gap (Kelly, Lovett and Regan, 2005). But attrition in rape cases goes far beyond this. For studies show that many reports of rape are rejected by the police so that they never enter the figures for recorded rape. Most importantly of all, most victims never report the matter at all.

Attrition in rape cases has been the subject of a great deal of discussion and a number of high quality studies which confirm the phenomenon (for a summary, see eg Temkin, 2002a: ch 1). Some studies also demonstrate the influence of stereotypes at each stage of the process from the decision to report an offence to the police, the decision taken by the police to record a complaint as rape and to seek to bring charges, the decision of the Crown Prosecution Service (CPS) whether to take the matter to court, and finally the decision of the jury whether to convict or acquit.

Evidence from Victimisation Surveys

It is universally recognised that the number of offences recorded by the police is a small proportion of the number of rapes which actually take place. Gaining an accurate picture of the true scale of sexual assaults is a difficult task, and it requires extrapolation from a limited sample to the population at large. Despite the problems involved in this estimation process, evidence from victimisation surveys and large-scale research studies comes closest to providing a picture of the true incidence and prevalence of sexual offences and is thus part of the background to the justice gap.[2]

England and Wales

The British Crime Survey (BCS) is a population survey and a key indicator of crime trends. Unlike police recorded crime, it is unaffected by changes in recording practices. The 2001 BCS has provided the most detailed picture so far of the extent and nature of sexual assault in England and Wales (Walby and Allen, 2004). A nationally representative sample of 22,463 women and men aged 16–59 was asked in 2001 via a computerised self-completion questionnaire to answer questions relating to their experience of sexual violence, including whether they had been subject to sexual assault during the preceding year (incidence), since the age of 16 or during their lifetime (prevalence) (Walby and Allen, 2004: v). Some of the main findings are presented in table 1.1.

The figures shown in table 1.1 equate to an estimated 190,000 incidents of serious sexual assault and to an estimated 47,000 female victims of rape or attempted rape (1994 definition) in the year preceding the interviews (Walby

---

[2] Incidence refers to the total number of occasions on which sexual offences occurred in a specified time period, usually 12 months; prevalence refers to the proportion of the population that has experienced a sexual offence in a given period or since a particular age.

Table 1.1

Prevalence of sexual assault in % as reported in the British Crime Survey 2001
(Walby and Allen, 2004: 14, Table 2.1).

	Women (N = 12,226)		Men (N = 10,237)	
	Since 16	Last Year	Since 16	Last Year
Less serious sexual assault *	15.3	1.9	1.8	0.2
*Serious sexual assault***	4.5	0.5	0.5	0.1
*Rape (1994 legal definition)****	3.6	0.3	0.4	< 0.0
*Rape (2003 legal definition)*****	3.7	0.3	0.4	< 0.0

*   Flashing, sexual threats or touching that caused them fear, alarm, or distress

**   Penetration of vagina or anus with an object including fingers without their consent, including attempts

***   Penetration of the vagina or anus by the penis without consent, including attempts

****   Penetration of the vagina, anus or mouth by the penis without consent, including attempts

and Allen, 2004: vi). They show that women are considerably more at risk of sexual assault than men, and the survey also found that younger people were more at risk than older people. With respect to the relationship to the assailant, the rapist was an intimate in 54 per cent of cases which participants considered to be the worst they had suffered since the age of 16, with 45 per cent being husbands or partners and 9 per cent being former husbands or partners. A further 29 per cent of rapists were known to the woman while 17 per cent were strangers (Walby and Allen, 2004: 60).

Among women who had been subject to rape or a serious sexual assault since the age of 16, 52 per cent said that the incident they considered the worst led to them suffering depression or other emotional problems, and for 5 per cent it led to attempted suicide. Forty per cent of women told no one about their worst experience of rape suffered since the age of 16 (Walby and Allen, 2004: viii, x).

The 2004/05 and 2005/06 British Crime Surveys provide more recent figures about rape and sexual assault, based on samples of 23,584 and 24,571 participants aged between 16 and 59, respectively (see Finney, 2006, for the 2004/05 survey and Coleman, Jansson, Kaiza and Reed, 2007, for the 2005/06 data).[3] The main findings from these two surveys are summarised in table 1.2.

Again, it is evident that women are disproportionately more at risk of sexual assault than men. Additional data show that as in the 2001 survey, just over 60 per cent of the incidents of less serious assault against women were committed by strangers, whereas strangers accounted for a much smaller percentage (11 per cent)

[3] The BCS 2001 employed a different methodology so that much of the data from it is not comparable with the later surveys.

Table 1.2

Prevalence of sexual assault in % as reported in the British Crime Surveys 2004/05 and 2005/06

(Finney, 2006: Table A.1, and Coleman *et al*, 2007: Table 3.1).

	Women		Men	
	Since 16	Last Year	Since 16	Last Year
*Less serious sexual assault**				
2004/5	22.3	2.6	3.1	0.5
2005/6	22.8	2.9	3.4	0.5
*Serious sexual assault***				
2004/5	5.6	0.5	0.6	0.1
2005/6	5.7	0.7	0.6	0.1
*Rape (2003 legal definition)****				
2004/5	5.0	0.4	0.4	0.1
2005/6	5.0	0.5	0.5	0.1

*   Flashing, sexual threats or touching that caused fear, alarm, or distress
**   Penetration of vagina or anus with an object including fingers without consent, including attempts
***   Penetration of the vagina, anus or mouth by the penis without consent, including attempts

of serious sexual assaults. By contrast, more than half of the serious sexual assaults against women were committed by a partner or ex-partner (for 2004/05: Finney, 2006; 7; for 2005/06: Coleman *et al*, 2007: 61). These figures indicate that the more serious the sexual assault the less likely it is to have been committed by a stranger.

The figures and estimates from the British Crime Surveys are likely to be conservative. They do not cover those over 59 or under 16. Sexual violence tends to be under-reported in surveys like the BCS which specify they are about 'crime' in general (Schwartz, 1997; Kelly *et al*, 2005: 14–7). What is now required is a national random sample study which is geared specifically to the incidence and prevalence of rape. In Canada such a study was carried out by Statistics Canada in 1992 involving a national random sample of 12,300 women. Of these, one in three claimed to have been sexually assaulted but only 6 per cent reported the matter to the police (Johnson and Sacco, 1995; Statistics Canada, 1993).

The United States

In the United States, the National Crime Victimization Survey (NCVS) 2003 found 198,850 rapes, attempted rapes and sexual assaults of which only 38.5 per cent were reported to the police (United States Department of Justice, 2005:

Table 91). The figures include male rape and threats of rape and sexual assault. The figure for rape alone was 72,240, corresponding to a rate of 30 per 100,000 citizens over the age of 12 (table 7). The NCVS 2003 was based on interviews with 74,520 people of 12 years old and upwards, in 42,000 households, who were asked about their victimisation from crime. But, like the British Crime Survey, the NCVS is not specifically geared to rape and is likely to have underestimated the extent of it.

Large-scale research studies, conducted mostly with college students, also produce incidence rates much higher than those in official crime statistics. Fisher, Cullen and Turner (2000) surveyed 4446 female students about their experience of sexual violence since the beginning of the academic year (covering an average incidence period of seven months). Just under 2 per cent (1.7 per cent) of respondents reported experiences amounting to completed rape, a further 1.1 per cent reported attempted rape. The victimisation rate was 27.7 rapes or attempted rapes per 1000 female students. Fewer than 5 per cent of the completed rapes were reported to the police. In a study obtaining prevalence data from just under 24,000 female undergraduates, almost one in 20 (4.7 per cent) were found to have been raped (Mohler-Kuo, Dowdall, Koss and Wechsler, 2004).

Germany

In Germany, there are no regular crime surveys comparable to the BCS or the NCVS. However, a recent survey of women's experience of violence provides some relevant figures (Federal Ministry for Family Affairs, Senior Citizens, Women, and Youth, 2005). Based on a representative sample of 10,264 women aged 16 to 85 interviewed in 2003 (p 3), it was found that 13 per cent of respondents had experienced at least one incident of sexual violence since the age of 16, defined as forced sexual acts contrary to criminal law including rape, attempted rape, and sexual coercion (p 9). Of these only 8 per cent had reported the incident to the police (p 19). In about half the cases, the perpetrator was a present or former partner (p 9).

Studies show that victims of rape may be influenced by stereotypical ideas of what rape is which may affect their decision to report in two different ways. They may either not perceive themselves as true victims or they may believe that others, including the police, will fail to recognise them as such if they do not conform to the stereotype (see chapter two). Thus, victims of rape, particularly non-stranger rape, may for both reasons fail to report the matter (Hall, 1985; Russell 1984; 1990). Walby and Allen found that of those in the British Crime Survey who had an experience since the age of 16 which fell within the legal definition of rape, only 43 per cent thought of it as rape (2004: viii). Bachman found that in the United States the chances of a rape being reported increased where physical injury had been sustained or a weapon had been used, thereby reinforcing the stereotype that genuine rape victims will have sustained injury or will have been intimidated into submission by a weapon (1998: 20; see also Flowe, Ebbesen and Putcha-Bhagavatula, 2007).

Rapes Recorded by the Police

In England and Wales, there has been a dramatic increase in the number of rape offences recorded by the police in the years immediately following the Second World War until the present time.[4] In 1947 there were 240 rapes recorded by the police. By 2005/06 the figure had risen to 14,449. The vast majority (92 per cent) of reported rapes in 2004/05 and in 2005/06 were of a female (Home Office 2006b, Table 2.04). The continuous rise of reported rapes of a female is shown in figure 1.1 (see also Home Office, 2006a).

In the decade 1977–87, there was an average annual increase of 9.3 per cent in the figures of recorded rape (Criminal Statistics for England and Wales, 1987:

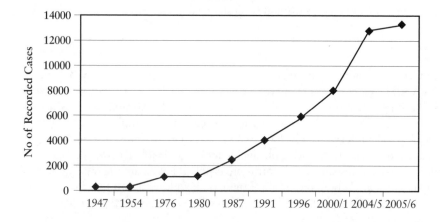

Figure 1.1 *Rape of a female – long-term trend*
(See Temkin, 2002a: 12, and Home Office, 2006b: Table 2.04)[5]

[4] The introduction of the Sexual Offences Act 2003 in May 2004 resulted in an expanded defini-tion of rape to include penile penetration of the mouth. Hence the figures after May 2004 are not strictly comparable with those for previous years. Prior to May 2004, the term rape in the criminal statistics included rape, unlawful sexual intercourse with a defective (s 7 Sexual Offences Act 1956) or a mentally disordered patient (s 128 Mental Health Act 1959) as well as attempting, conspiring to commit and aiding and abetting these crimes. For a detailed account of the annual rise in the figures for recorded rape since 1947, see Temkin (2002a: 11–13). Criminal Statistics for England and Wales from 1996 onwards are available online, at: http://www.homeoffice.gov.uk/rds/recordedcrime1.html

[5] Counting rules were changed in 1998 and 2002, accounting for some of the increase (see Home Office, 1999b: 20–22, and Home Office, 2006b: 20, for a detailed explanation).

Table 2.1). With the exception of robbery, where the average annual increase was 9 per cent, there are no figures for other crimes which are comparable. For example, the average annual increase for wounding or other act of violence against the person endangering life was 6.2 per cent. The average annual rise for all offences was 4 per cent.

Between 1987 and 1997, the average annual increase in rape offences rose to 10.4 per cent. This was surpassed only by increases in drug offences. The average increase for all offences was only 1.7 per cent. However, for more serious offences of violence against the person it was 7.9 per cent (Home Office, 1998b: Table 2.1) In the decade 1989/1990–1999/2000, the number of recorded rapes rose by almost 150 per cent. The average annual increase for rape was 9.7 per cent, exceeded only by theft from a shop which averaged 10.3 per cent. The average annual rise for all offences was 2.8 per cent (Home Office 2000b: Table 2.1).[6]

The rise in recorded rape offences is probably mainly due to a change in attitude towards rape which is less tolerant of it and to perceived changes in the way that police respond to rape, both of which encourage reporting. Improvements in police recording practices are also a factor. As from 1995, the figures have been boosted by the inclusion of male rape. The figures for this have increased annually with 231 cases recorded in 1996 rising to 600 in 1999/2000, a rise of 19 per cent over the previous year, and to 664 in 2000/2001, a further rise of 10.7 per cent. In 2005/06 the figure had risen to 1118 (Home Office, 2006b: Table 2.04).

In other countries, too, increases in recorded rape have taken place. In the United States between 1970 and 1982, reports of forcible rape more than doubled from 37,860 to 77,763 (Federal Bureau of Investigation, 1983).[7] By 1990, the figure had increased by a further 32 per cent to 102,555, rising in 1992 to a peak of 109,062. Thereafter there were annual decreases until 2000 when the figures began to rise again. In 2005, it was 93,934, dropping by 2 per cent to 92,455 in 2006 (Federal Bureau of Investigation, 2006: Table 1).[8] In 1980, 71 out of every 100,000 females in the United States reported being victims of rape or attempted rape. This represented a 38 per cent increase over 1976 (Federal Bureau of Investigation, 1980–1985). By 1990, this figure had risen to 81 and by 1992 to 84 out of every 100,000 females (Federal Bureau of Investigation, 1993). By 1999, however, the figure had dropped to 64.1 out of every 100,000 females and in 2004 it remained at 63.5, falling to 62.5 in 2005 (Federal Bureau of Investigation, 2005, 2006). The trend in the number of recorded rapes in the United States is presented in figure 1.2.

---

[6] As a result of changes in reporting and recording practices, ie changes in the counting rules introduced in 1998 and the introduction of the National Crime Recording Standard in April 2002, long-term comparisons after this date are beset with difficulties.

[7] For the purpose of these statistics, forcible rape is defined as the carnal knowledge of a female forcibly and against her will. Assaults or attempts to commit rape by force or threat of force are also included.

[8] Uniform Crime Reports from 1995 onwards are available online, at: http://www.fbi.gov/ucr/ucr.htm

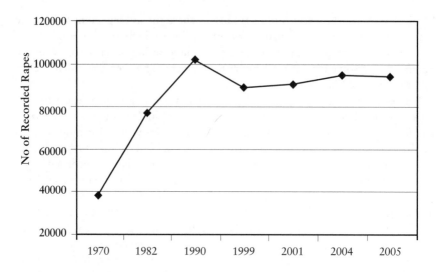

Figure 1.2 *Offences of forcible rape recorded by the police in the USA*
(Source: United States Department of Justice, 2007a).

In Germany, the number of reported offences of rape and sexual coercion has risen from 5281 in 1987 to 8133 in 2005 (Bundeskriminalamt, 2006). The pattern of change can be seen in figure 1.3.

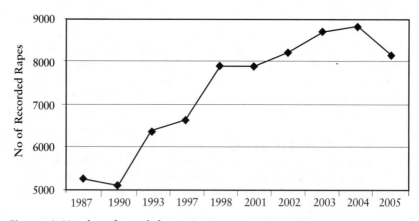

Figure 1.3 *Number of recorded rapes in Germany (§ 177 StGB).*
(Source: Bundeskriminalamt, 2006: Table 01).

Note: Data for 1987 and 1990 refer to West Germany only (excl West-Berlin), data for 1993 refer to West Germany and West-Berlin.

The rise from 1997 to 1998 will have been affected by a change in the law that now includes marital rape as well as rape of male victims.

'No-Criming'

A further reason why the official statistics of recorded rape tell only part of the story is that women who do report rape do not necessarily have their complaints accepted by the police. Alternatively, complaints which are initially recorded as rape may subsequently be afforded a 'no crime' classification so that they do not enter the official statistics of recorded crime.

Numerous studies over the past few decades testify to the overzealous and inappropriate no-criming practices of the police. In their definitive Canadian study, Clark and Lewis (1977) found that it was the classic stranger rape which was most likely to be given credence by the police. Women who had been hitch-hiking, had no injuries to show, had been drinking, or were separated or divorced were less likely to have their reports of rape classified as such by the police. What was at issue was the behaviour of the complainant rather than that of the alleged offender: 'Some reports did indicate that police officers share general prejudices about "appropriate" behaviour for women and that these prejudices affect classification of rape reports' (Clark and Lewis, 1977: 59; see also chapter two). In 1985, the Women's National Commission, an advisory group to the British Government, issued a major report on rape in which some concern was expressed about the no-criming practices of the police (Women's National Commission, 1985: para 64). This concern was taken up by the Home Office in a circular to all chief officers of police. It states:

> The only complaints which should be classified as 'no crime' are those in which the complainant retracts completely and admits fabrication. [. . .] There should be a clear distinction between unsubstantiated and false complaints. The former should remain recorded as crime whilst the latter should be recorded as 'no crime' (Home Office, 1986a: 11).

A study by Smith (1989) of two London boroughs revealed that no-criming continued to take place even where the allegation was not deemed to be false. Withdrawal of the complaint and insufficiency of evidence continued to be reasons given by the police for no-criming. A reported rape was most likely to be recorded by the police as such where it conformed to the classic rape stereotype of a violent attack by a stranger. The conclusion drawn was that it was difficult to fetter individual officers' discretion and that 'police officers are not complying with the advice which has been given' (Smith, 1989: 25).

Harris and Grace (1999) looked at nearly 500 incidents initially recorded as rape by the police in 1996. It was found that, while the no-criming rate had fallen to 25 per cent, this reduction was offset by the number of cases which had been classified as 'no further action'. Although the most common reason for no-criming continued to be that the complaint was false or malicious (43 per cent), insufficiency of evidence was the reason in 15 per cent of cases and withdrawal of the complaint in 36 per cent of cases despite the specification in the Home Office Circular (Home Office, 1986a) that withdrawal of the complaint should only be classified as no-crime where it was accompanied by an admission that the complaint was false. Thus, inappropriate use of the 'no crime' classification would appear to be a continuing problem. It was found that cases were least likely to be no-crimed where the complainant was under 13 or where violence had been used, or where there was rape by an intimate. However, rapes by intimates were likely to qualify for 'no further action'. Where violence was neither used nor threatened, cases were most likely to be no-crimed and the victim most likely to withdraw her complaint, possibly with police encouragement. Victims were less likely to withdraw complaints where violence was used. Most recently in the study by Kelly *et al* (2005: 39), 3527 cases of alleged rape were studied of which 75 per cent were reported to the police. It was found that around one quarter of reported rapes were 'no-crimed' (p xi).

It is at the police stage that the highest rate of attrition of rape cases occurs. Many victims withdraw their complaints and many complaints are no-crimed (Kelly *et al*, 2005). Indeed, Kelly et al found that in their sample 'the vast majority of cases did not proceed beyond the investigative stage' (p xi). However, attrition also occurs at the stage where prosecutors make the decision whether to take the case further.

Prosecution Rates

Studies indicate that rape allegations which conform to stereotypical notions of 'real rape' are more likely to result in prosecution (Brown, Hamilton and O'Neill, 2007; Smith 1989). Certainly, in England and Wales the number of persons prosecuted annually for rape is low compared with the number of recorded rapes, and the proportion has dropped dramatically over recent years (see Temkin, 2002a: 22–23).[9] In England and Wales the prosecution process begins with proceedings being brought against an alleged offender in the magistrates' court after which the defendant is sent for trial in the Crown Court. Of those sent for trial only a proportion are eventually tried. In 2002/03 there were 11,436 recorded offences of rape of a female and by 2003/04 the total had risen to 12,354. But in 2003, only 2621 persons were proceeded against for rape of a female in the magistrates' court. While 95 per cent of those proceeded against were sent for trial in 2003, only 1603 persons were actually tried for rape in 2003, 64 per cent of the number sent for trial. In 2004, 2516 were proceeded against for rape of a female and 97 per cent of these were sent for trial. 1636

---

[9] The *Criminal Statistics* do not record the total number of prosecutions for particular offences. Where proceedings involve more than one offence, it is only the principal offence which is recorded. For the meaning of principal offence, see Home Office 1998b: para 31, p 237. It is not possible to compare prosecution rates for different offences on the basis of the *Criminal Statistics*. This is because the reporting of principal offences only does not have a uniform effect on all crimes.

persons were actually tried for rape in 2004, 67 per cent of the number sent for trial.[10]

Concern has been expressed that the CPS is generally too concerned with acquittal rates and too prone to discontinue cases where a conviction is less than guaranteed. A joint report of the CPS and Constabulary Inspectorate into the prosecution of rape cases found some evidence of this. Generally it found that 'the prosecutor's approach too often tended to be one of only considering any weaknesses rather than also playing a more proactive role in seeking more information and trying to build or develop a case' (Her Majesty's Crown Prosecution Inspectorate, 2002: Summary, paras 30, 31). This may help to explain why the number of defendants tried for rape in the Crown Court has not increased in line with the numbers proceeded against in the magistrates' court.

Convictions and Acquittals

The official statistics show that in 1980 there were 416 convictions for rape offences in the Crown Court, and in 2005 there were 787. The number of convictions over the 25-year period is shown in figure 1.4.

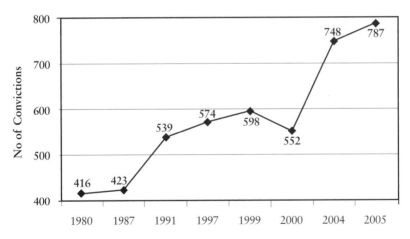

Figure 1.4 *Convictions for rape offences in England and Wales 1980–2005*

(Home Office, 1980–2000; 2005a; 2006f: Supplementary Tables vol. 2, Table S2.1(A).

Note: As a result of the changes to the definition of rape introduced by the Sexual Offences Act 2003, figures for 2004 and 2005 are not strictly comparable with previous years. The figures for 1997 onward include convictions for male rape.

[10] See Home Office 2004; 2005a: Supplementary Tables, vol 1, Table S1.1 (A) 'Defendants Proceeded Against at Magistrates' Courts by Offence, Sex and Result'; vol 2, Table S2.1A 'Defendants Tried and/or Sentenced at the Crown Court by Offence, Sex and Result'. (Those sent for trial do not necessarily come up for trial in the same year).

Given that the number of recorded rapes doubled between 1980 and 1987 and the number of those proceeded against for rape in 1987 was 50 per cent more than the number proceeded against in 1980, it would seem to be remarkable that the number of convictions between 1980 and 1987 showed virtually no increase. It is similarly worthy of comment that in 1991 the number of convictions was about 30 per cent more than the number in 1980, whereas the number of offences of rape recorded by the police was well over three times the 1980 figure. In 2000, there was actually a drop in the number of convictions to 552 from 598 in 1999, even though the number of recorded offences had risen by 184 in this period.

The conviction rate for rape as measured by the number of convictions as a percentage of reported cases in the same year is shown in figure 1.5.[11] In the period from 1979 to 2004/05, the rate of convictions for rape declined from 32 per cent in 1979 to 5.3 per cent in 2004/5. Thus, to say that convictions have not kept pace with the number of recorded rapes would appear to be a massive understatement. Home Office data quoted by Kelly *et al* (2005: 25) demonstrate that for the years 1998–2002 around one quarter of cases of rape and attempted rape of an adult which were *prosecuted* resulted in conviction.

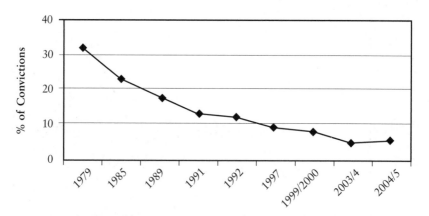

Figure 1.5 *Convictions for rape offences in the Crown Court as a percentage of reported cases in the same year*

(Based on Annual Tables of Recorded Offences: Criminal Statistics, England and Wales, Table 2.1, 1979–2004 and Supplementary Tables, vol 2 Table S2.1 (A); Home Office 1980–2000; 2005a).

Note: The figures for 1997 onward include reports and convictions for male rape.

---

[11] As from 1998, Home Office statistics for recorded crime have been presented on a financial year basis whereas figures for convictions are compiled on a calendar year basis. This means, for example, that the conviction rate for 2004 takes account of offences recorded in the first three months of 2005 and excludes those recorded in the first three months of 2004.

In 2004, 43 per cent of those who were actually tried for rape were convicted. This figure compares unfavourably with that for every other sexual offence and offence of violence against the person with the exception of 'threat or conspiracy to murder' where the conviction rate was 41 per cent.[12] Thus, for example, the overall conviction rate for 'wounding or other act endangering life' was 56 per cent, for 'other wounding' offences 71 per cent and for cruelty or neglect of children, 66 per cent. The percentage of those pleading not guilty to rape who were convicted (31 per cent) was low in comparison with most other sexual or violent offences, the only exceptions being 'wounding or other act endangering life' (31 per cent), 'threat or conspiracy to murder' (15 per cent), 'other wounding' offences (27 per cent) and cruelty to or neglect of children (29 per cent). But all these other offences had far higher conviction rates overall than the conviction rate for rape. Part of the reason for this is that the percentage of those pleading guilty to rape (18 per cent) was lower than for any other sexual or violent offence. For example, the percentage pleading guilty to 'wounding or other act endangering life' was 36 per cent, to 'other wounding' offences was 60 per cent and to 'cruelty to or neglect of children', 58 per cent. Given that a percentage of rape cases where the accused pleads guilty must involve stranger rapes where there is DNA evidence, it is clear that very few defendants in cases where consent is the issue plead guilty. It seems that such defendants would rather try their luck at a trial and, given the odds on conviction, this is not surprising.

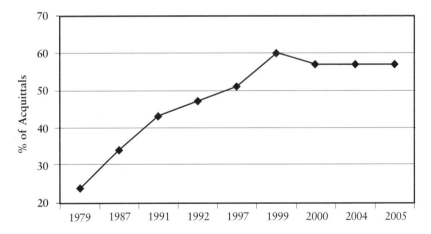

Figure 1.6 *Acquittal rate for rape offences*

(Based on Home Office, 1980–2000; 2005a; 2006f, Supplementary Tables vol 2, Table S2.1 (A)).

---

[12] These figures have been calculated using Home Office Statistical Bulletin (Home Office, 2006f: Table 2.11).

An acquittal rate for rape offences may be calculated in terms of the number of defendants acquitted of rape offences in the Crown Court each year as a percentage of the number of defendants tried for rape offences in the same year in the Crown Court.[13] On this basis, the acquittal rate for rape rose from 24 per cent in 1979 to 57 per cent in 2005, as shown in figure 1.6.

Appeals

A study of criminal appeals brought in 1996 revealed that there were more appeals in sexual offence cases than in any other offence category apart from offences of violence, and that more convictions were quashed and more retrials ordered in sexual offence cases than in other offence categories apart from offences of violence (Mattinson, 1998: Tables 14, 15). The study does not provide information on specific sexual offences but clearly suggests that the attrition of rape offences does not end at Crown Court. Furthermore, since its inception in 1997 up to November 2005, there were 1391 applications to the Criminal Cases Review Commission (CCRC) to review convictions for sexual offences out of a total of 8186 applications for offences as a whole, ie 17 per cent of the total.[14] But they constitute a far higher proportion of the number of cases which the Commission decides to refer to the Court of Appeal. In the CCRC's 2005 report, it is noted that murder and sexual offences represent the most significant category of referrals to the Court of Appeal, each accounting for approximately one-third of the total referrals for the year. The reasons for referrals in sexual offence cases 'have ranged from issues affecting witness credibility to flaws in the directions given to the jury at trial' (Criminal Cases Review Commission, 2005: 18). As of June 2007, the CCRC had referred 54 cases to the Court of Appeal involving convictions for rape, indecent assault, buggery or incest.[15] Of these, 31 applicants had their convictions quashed while some cases were still outstanding.[16]

Other European Countries and the United States

By contrast with the situation in England and Wales, many other European countries cannot even provide basic data on the numbers of reports, prosecu-

---

[13] The number of persons tried for rape is obtained by subtracting the total number of persons not tried for rape from the total for trial. See Annual Supplementary Tables vol 2 Table S2.1 (A) (Home Office, 1980–2000; 2005a; 2006f). Figures for 1997 onwards include male rape.

[14] Information provided by the CCRC. According to more recent figures provided by the CCRC, it received a total of 753 applications from persons convicted of rape from the beginning of 2002 up to 19 January 2007.

[15] In most cases those concerned had been convicted of a combination of these offences. The figure includes attempts and conspiracies but excludes cases referred for review of sentence only.

[16] The authors are indebted to the CCRC for material enabling them to provide this information.

tions and convictions of rape (Kelly *et al*, 2005; Regan and Kelly, 2003). But Regan and Kelly (2003) found that Finland, Ireland and Sweden had similar attrition problems to England and Wales. Comparison with countries with different rape laws, different criminal justice systems and different prosecution policies in criminal cases as a whole is necessarily difficult but it suggests that in some European countries, such as Germany, prosecution and conviction rates are higher than in the UK (see also Kruse and Sczesny, 1993). Certainly, in Germany the proportion of prosecutions and convictions in relation to recorded offences appears to have risen since 1997. According to the *European Sourcebook of Crime and Criminal Justice Statistics* (Council of Europe, 1999: Table 3.B.1.4) the conviction rate for rape in Germany was stable between 1990 and 1996 at 1.4 to 1.7 per 100,000 members of the population. These figures contrast with an incidence rate of reported rapes (including attempts) to the police during the same period ranging from 7.5 to 8.2 per 100,000 (Bundesministerium des Inneren, 2001: 49). This nevertheless appears to be a substantially better conviction rate than in England and Wales.[17]

In the United States, conviction rates measured in terms of convictions as a proportion of reported offences have been shown to be well below that of other violent crimes. Indeed 'the statistical data suggest that most rapes in the United States go unpunished' (Sinclair and Bourne, 1998: 576). Following 674 cases reported to a midwestern police department through the criminal justice system, Frazier, Candell, Arikian and Tofteland (1994) found a conviction rate of 12 per cent, confirming the low rate found in other studies. In addition, they found that in cases where a suspect was identified, there were much higher arrest rates in stranger than in acquaintance rapes (see also Koss, Bachar, Hopkins and Carlson, 2004).

The statistical data reported in this section document the scale of the attrition problem as sexual assault cases proceed through the criminal justice system. The attrition rate is set against a backdrop of extensive legal reform in the area of sexual offences which was intended and might have been expected to bring about an increase in conviction rates. However, it will be suggested in this book that stereotypical thinking about rape operates in a number of different ways to defeat law reform and to ensure ever increasing rates of attrition. In order to support our claim that decision-making about sexual assault is affected by stereotypical understandings which undermine the data-driven processing required by the law, the next section (1.2) provides a short overview of the legal provisions surrounding rape and other sexual offences in England and Wales as they have evolved over the past thirty years, comparing them briefly with the law in civil jurisdictions. A more detailed account of these legal developments can be found in Appendix 1.

---

[17] The narrow definition of rape in German law with its emphasis on the use of physical force may help to explain this: see below section 1.2.

1.2 THE LEGAL BACKGROUND

Legal definitions provide the normative framework for judging sexual assault allegations, specifying the criteria which need to be met to find a defendant guilty. Support for the proposition that rape complaints are susceptible to schematic processing on the basis of stereotypes can be claimed through evidence that decisions about rape cases are influenced by considerations outside or at odds with the legal definition. This would be the case, for example, if it were found that more credence was given to complaints of rape involving strangers than non-strangers since the law itself makes no such distinction. Thus, one way in which the legal background is connected to our analysis of the justice gap is that it represents a benchmark of normative decision-making against which decisions in specific cases may be interpreted. But the law itself is significant not merely for what it says but for what it does not say. Thus, for example, it will be seen that in England and Wales the law speaks only to a limited extent on the issue of alcohol consumption and its effect on consent, leaving plenty of room for stereotypical assumptions to creep in.

The legal background to sexual assault consists of more than just the legal definitions of the offences concerned. For in England and Wales evidential rules and procedures also play a vital role in the way in which events are interpreted. In order to move away from stereotypical assumptions about complainants, the evidential rules, like the law itself, have been reformed by the legislature. The new evidential rules relating to corroboration warnings and sexual history are set out below by way of background to chapter seven which demonstrates how these reforms have been undermined by negative attitudes towards them. Gaps in legislation relating to third party disclosure are also a factor in the way stereotypes are permitted to edge their way into interpretations. Third party disclosure applications will be briefly discussed as a prelude to chapter seven which considers the law in action in this area as well. A more detailed account of the law relating to corroboration warnings, sexual history evidence and third party disclosure applications is contained in Appendix 1.

England and Wales

In England and Wales, for the last three decades, ever since the decision in *DPP v Morgan*[18] first raised concerns about the law of rape and the Heilbron Committee (Home Office, 1975) reinforced these concerns, the legislature has proceeded incrementally to make changes to the law of rape and allied offences and to the evidential rules surrounding the law (see Temkin, 2002a). These legal

---

[18] [1976] AC 182, HL.

reforms may be seen as an attempt to move away from the stereotypes of rape in order to give justice to its victims.

The first important legislation was the Sexual Offences (Amendment) Act 1976 (SOA 1976) which followed on from the Heilbron Report. This attempted to tackle the problem of rape in two significant ways. First, reflecting nineteenth-century developments in the common law, it established that rape was not merely, as in the stereotypes, a crime requiring proof of violence by the perpetrator and resistance by the victim, but was quintessentially a crime which hinged on absence of consent (SOA 1976: Section 1). Secondly, in order to tackle victim-blaming attitudes and attempts to discredit complainants particularly in relation to their sexual past, the Act attempted to restrict the use by the defence of sexual history evidence (SOA 1976: Section 2).

In the 1990s, the stereotype of rape as a crime committed by a stranger was further challenged when marital rape became a crime.[19] Moreover, the idea that complainants in rape cases are more than likely to be liars and that women who allege rape are not to be trusted was subsequently addressed in legislation in 1994. This dealt with the evidential rule which required judges in every rape case to issue a solemn warning to the jury, known as the corroboration warning, that it was dangerous to rely on the word of the complainant alone. The reason for the danger was prone to be illustrated in terms which relied on negative stereotypes about women. Toner (1982: 218) quotes the following judicial explanations for the warning given in two separate cases:

Judge 1: This is a sex case. Experience has shown that women can and do tell lies for some reason, sometimes for no reason at all.
Judge 2: It is well known that in sex cases women sometimes imagine things which various ingredients in their make up tend to make them imagine.

The Criminal Justice and Public Order Act 1994 abolished the requirement that judges deliver such a warning and left it to the judges themselves to decide whether to issue one. The Court of Appeal, subsequently and supportively ruled in the leading case of *Makanjuola*[20] that such warnings should be given only if there was, on the actual evidence in the case, some reason to doubt the complainant's reliability as a witness.

More recently, several official reports have considered the problem of rape, rape law and rape trials. The Home Office Report, *Speaking Up for Justice* (Home Office, 1998a) drew attention to defects in the operation of the SOA 1976 as it applied to sexual history and the continuing difficulties faced by complainants giving evidence in court. As a result, the Youth Justice and Criminal Evidence Act 1999 scrapped the 1976 provision in favour of a much tougher regime to control the use of sexual history evidence, seeking to remove from the judges all discretion in the matter.

---

[19] *R v R* [1991] 4 All ER 481; Criminal Justice and Public Order Act 1994, s 142.
[20] [1995] 3 All ER 730.

A later report, *Setting the Boundaries* (Home Office, 2000a) focused on the inadequacy of the law relating to sexual offences in general and drew up radical plans for its transformation. It pointed out that although the 1976 Act had usefully defined rape as sexual intercourse without consent, it had failed to provide a definition of consent. As a result of this report, the whole law of sexual offences was recast in the Sexual Offences Act 2003 (SOA 2003) which came into effect in May 2004. Prior to the 2003 Act, there were two main sexual assault offences: rape and indecent assault. The SOA 2003 now contains four main offences of sexual assault: rape (section 1), assault by penetration (section 2), sexual assault (section 3), and causing a person to engage in sexual activity without consent (section 4) (see Ormerod, 2005). The offence of indecent assault has been abolished.

Rape

Prior to the 2003 Act, in order to commit rape, a man had to penetrate the victim's vagina or anus with his penis without the victim's consent. The victim could be either male or female. He must either have known that the victim was not consenting or have been reckless in the sense that he could not have cared less whether the victim was consenting or not.[21] The definition of rape has now been expanded to include penile penetration of the mouth. It remains an offence which can only be perpetrated by a man as it covers only penile penetration although women can as before be liable as accomplices. The mental element required for rape has also changed. It must now be proved that the accused did not reasonably believe that the victim was consenting. The reasonableness of the belief involves consideration of all the circumstances of the case including whether the accused took any steps to ascertain whether consent was present. The maximum punishment for rape remains life imprisonment.

Assault by Penetration

This offence is mainly designed to cover penetration of the vagina or anus with objects or parts of the body other than the penis. Again, the maximum penalty for this offence is life imprisonment.

Sexual Assault

This offence is mainly designed to cover non-penetrative acts involving sexual touching. The maximum penalty is 10 years' imprisonment.

---

[21] Criminal Justice and Public Order Act 1994, s 142; *R v Satnam and Kewal* (1984) 78 Cr App R 149.

Causing a Person to Engage in Sexual Activity without Consent

This is a new offence created by the 2003 Act. It is intended to make a clear statement that compelling others to perform sexual acts against their will is an offence. The type of conduct it covers is, for example, where the defendant forces the victim to perform acts with third parties or with animals. The maximum penalty is again 10 years' imprisonment.

Consent

A notable feature of the new Act is that it provides for the first time a definition of consent and goes on to set out the circumstances in which it may be presumed that consent is absent. All four offences require proof by the prosecution that the complainant did not consent except in the case of children under 13 where consent is irrelevant.[22] Section 74 now states that 'a person consents if he agrees by choice and has the freedom and capacity to make that choice'. On proof of any one of the circumstances summarised below, absence of consent will be presumed, and the defendant will then have to bring forward some evidence to rebut this presumption:

1. where a person uses violence against the complainant (C) or causes C to fear that immediate violence would be used against her/him;
2. where any person causes C to fear that violence was being used or that immediate violence would be used against a third party;
3. where C was unlawfully detained;
4. where C was asleep or unconscious;
5. where C has a physical disability and as a result would not have been able to communicate whether she/he consented;
6. where a substance was administered to C without C's consent which was capable of stupefying or overpowering her/him.

Nothing in the Act changes the burden of proof which remains on the prosecution. The issue of drunkenness and consent which frequently arises has not been specifically tackled save where a substance has been administered to the complainant without her consent. This is a possible shortcoming in the law given the strong stereotypes which surround alcohol and rape.

Third Party Disclosure

Although the legislature in England and Wales has been highly active in the area of sexual offences, one issue it has so far failed sufficiently to tackle in this context is that of third-party disclosure. Barristers acting for men accused of sexual offences frequently seek to obtain records from third parties, such as medical or

---

[22] See SOA 2003, ss 5–8. The Act also provides new offences to protect children between 13 and 16 years of age. The age of consent remains at 16.

school records which can be used unfairly to discredit complainants, particularly children. Although the higher courts have attempted to control this practice, there is no specific legislation geared to regulating it in sexual cases as there is in some other jurisdictions (Temkin, 2002b).

Civil Jurisdictions

In most European countries influenced by the continental legal tradition, the definition of rape focuses mainly on the use of violence or threats of violence by the perpetrator rather than purely on the absence of consent.[23] This is true, for example, of the criminal codes of France (Articles 222–22, 222–23, 227–25), Germany (Articles 177–179), Belgium (Articles 375(1) and (2)), and Denmark (Articles 216(1) and 217) as well as Hungary (Act No 4 1978, s 197 (1)), Slovenia (Article 180(1)), and the Czech Republic (Article 241(1)). This is generally augmented by reference to other coercive situations, including where the complainant is in a position of 'defencelessness' or incapacity. The German law of rape provides a typical example. There the offence of 'Sexual coercion; Rape' (section 177, Strafgesetzbuch) requires proof of coercion as manifested by 'physical force or threats involving immediate danger to life or limb or by exploiting a situation in which the victim is unprotected and at the mercy of the perpetrator's influence'.[24] It is complemented by section 179 which refers to sexual abuse of persons incapable of resisting due, for example, to mental illness or disability. Thus, the German law does not embody a simple consent standard. However, in common with the law in England and Wales, it includes marital rape within its definition and is not confined to acts of physical violence. The *mens rea* of the German offence requires both knowledge and intent so that neither recklessness nor negligence will suffice, which places severe limits on the scope of the crime.

1.3 SUMMARY AND CONCLUSIONS

This chapter has provided statistical evidence illustrating the scale of the justice gap. It has shown that in England and Wales and other Western countries, such as the United States and Germany, the number of rapes reported to the police has risen dramatically in the last fifty years. By contrast, the proportion of reported rapes that end in a conviction has markedly declined in England and Wales with other countries too suffering an attrition problem. The chapter has also summarised some of the legal developments which have taken place in relation to sexual offences in England and Wales. While entirely valuable in themselves, they have proved to be incapable of staunching the flow of cases which

---

[23] Such formulations have begun to be contested by the European Court of Human Rights: see *M.C. v Bulgaria* (2005) 40 EHRR 20.

[24] See: http://www.iuscomp.org/gla/statutes/StGB.htm#177

fall out of the criminal justice system. The following chapters will seek to show that rape-supportive attitudes and stereotypical thinking about rape are key components in this attrition process, undermining the efforts of policy makers and legislators to assist the victims of sexual crime.

2

Stereotypes, Myths and Heuristics in the Perception of Sexual Assault

CENTRAL TO THE analysis of the justice gap presented in this book is the proposition that stereotypical beliefs and attitudes about victims, perpetrators and the circumstances of sexual violence may affect the judgments of those involved at each stage of decision-making in the criminal justice process. In particular, it is argued that restrictive definitions of what is 'real rape', intuitive theories that hold women responsible for precipitating men's sexual aggression and derogatory beliefs about rape victims can impinge on judgments about individual cases reducing the likelihood that the complainant will be acknowledged as a victim of rape and that the alleged perpetrator will be convicted. Accordingly, this chapter begins by describing the widely shared real rape stereotype. It goes on to present social psychological research into the concept of *rape myths* and the role of schematic information processing based on such myths, including a review of the evidence indicative of the operation of rape stereotypes in the handling of rape cases in the criminal justice system. It then reviews a large body of evidence conducted within the conceptual framework of *attribution theory*, examining factors which influence the attribution of responsibility and blame to victims of rape. The chapter concludes by drawing on recent socio-cognitive theorising to explain the role of schematic and *heuristic information processing* in sexual assault cases.

2.1 THE 'REAL RAPE' STEREOTYPE

When asked to describe a typical rape situation, many people are likely to conjure up an attack by a stranger on an unsuspecting victim in an outdoor location, involving the use or threat of force by the assailant and active physical resistance by the victim (Krahé, 1992; Rozee, 1999; Ryan, 1988). This scenario has come to be known as the 'real rape' stereotype. It is a stereotype because it represents a generalisation that is at odds with available factual evidence (eg Fisher, Cullen and Daigle, 2005; Lea, Lanvers and Shaw, 2003). Official crime records as well as victimisation surveys reveal that the most common form of sexual assault involves some degree of previous acquaintanceship between the perpetrator and the victim, that many victims are too frightened or over-powered to fight back and that, as a result, physical injuries are often not present as evidence to support the victim's claim (see also chapter one).

The real rape stereotype is not only *descriptive*, specifying the characteristics of a typical rape, but *prescriptive* in that all too often it lays down the criteria a case must meet in order to be judged to qualify as rape. It is this prescriptive aspect which is particularly problematic because cases that fail to meet one or more of the defining features specified by the stereotype are less likely to be accepted as genuine rapes. As several studies have shown, the more a specific incident differs from the real rape scenario, the smaller the number of people prepared to consider it as rape (Burt and Albin, 1981).

This reduction of 'real rapes' to stranger assaults affects the way in which people, including those involved in the legal processing of rape complaints, eval-uate and respond to rape victims (Stewart, Dobbin and Gatowski, 1996). Victims whose experiences deviate from the real rape stereotype, because, for example, they were assaulted by an acquaintance in their own home or while under the influence of alcohol, are more likely to be blamed for the assault and less likely to receive sympathetic treatment from others (Best, Dansky and Kilpatrick, 1992; Emmers-Sommer and Allen, 1999).

The fact that the real rape stereotype is a socially shared representation means that it is also part of the victim's understanding of sexual assault. It is well doc-umented that victims who were assaulted in circumstances close to the real rape stereotype (eg by a stranger who used physical force) are more likely to report to the police than victims assaulted in circumstances not covered by the stereo-type (eg by an acquaintance where the victim was too drunk to resist; Du Mont, Miller and Myhr, 2003). Furthermore, the real rape stereotype affects women's self-identification as victims of rape. In a study by Kahn, Mathie and Torgler (1994), women who had experienced a sexual assault were asked to describe what they considered to be a typical rape situation. Those women who were found to have been raped by an acquaintance but who failed to acknowledge the fact described a typical rape as involving an unknown assailant, the use of weapons and an outdoor location. This suggests that they had not identified themselves as rape victims because their rape scripts were restricted to the stranger rape scenario (see Peterson and Muehlenhard, 2004, for similar results).

The real rape stereotype also extends to expectations about how a genuine victim will react to an assault. Victims of a real rape are expected to report the assault to the police immediately and to be visibly upset and emotional about the experience. Those who do not conform to these normative expectations are seen as less credible and as more responsible for the assault (Calhoun, Cann, Selby and Magee, 1981; Krulewitz, 1982; see also Rose, Nadler and Clark, 2006, for a general account of norms about victims' emotional reactions). In an exper-imental simulation by Winkel and Koppelaar (1991), an alleged rape victim reported the assault either in a very emotional or in a calm and composed way. Participants who saw the emotional victim regarded her as more credible, less responsible for the attack and more cautious in her behaviour prior to the assault than did participants who saw the calm and composed victim, despite the fact that the events both victims reported were exactly the same. In a Norwegian study, a rape victim who showed an incongruent emotional expression (eg smiled) when recounting her rape experience was considered by participants to be less credible and they were less inclined to return a guilty verdict in her case as compared with that of a rape victim who showed a neutral or congruent (distressed) emotional expression (Kaufmann, Drevland, Wessel, Overskeid and Magnussen, 2003). However, a subsequent study with professional judges in Norway found that they were not affected in their perception of victim credibility and defendant guilt by the congruence or incongruence of the victim's emotional expression (Wessel, Drevland, Eilertsen and Magnussen, 2006).

Beliefs about the damaging effects of rape do not necessarily benefit victims. Indeed, they can have detrimental effects on the perception of victims because they provide restrictive expectations about how a genuine victim would behave (Buddie and Miller, 2001). If a victim fails to conform to these expectations, perceivers may take this as an indication that the assault was not serious or did not happen at all. But many rape victims do not show visible signs of emotional agitation after the assault. Indeed, 'emotional numbing' is one of the defining features of the 'post-traumatic stress syndrome' (PTSD) frequently shown by victims of rape (Foa and Rothbaum, 1998). To address this discrepancy between lay persons' beliefs about typical victim reactions following rape and the empirical evidence concerning the impact of PTSD on rape victims, demands have been made for the introduction of expert testimony in rape trials to educate members of the jury about the range of victim responses to sexual assault (eg Biggers, 2003; Block, 1990). This proposal has proved to be controversial (see chapters three and eight).

2.2 RAPE MYTHS AND NEGATIVE ATTITUDES ABOUT RAPE VICTIMS

There is probably no other criminal offence that is as intimately related to broader social attitudes and evaluations of the victim's conduct as sexual assault. When confronted with an account of an alleged rape, individuals tend to respond to it against the backdrop of their personal beliefs and understandings about gender relationships in general, appropriate role behaviour for men and women, and the rules and rituals of consensual sexual interactions. For example, in a recent study commissioned by Amnesty International UK (2005) involving a representative sample of over 1000 members of the general public, 26 per cent of respondents thought that a woman was totally or partially responsible for being raped if she was wearing sexy or revealing clothes, and 22 per cent thought she was totally or partially to blame if it was known that she had many sexual partners.

Definition and Prevalence of Rape Myths

A large body of empirical evidence has shown that the attitudinal network that is accessed in forming an impression about a rape case is generally unfavourable to the victim. Public attitudes and the legal treatment of rape are shaped by widely shared misconceptions about the offence and, in particular, the victim's role in it (Burt, 1980; Schwendinger and Schwendinger, 1974). The concept of 'rape myth acceptance' (RMA) has been used to describe the endorsement of 'attitudes and beliefs that are generally false but are widely and persistently held, and that serve to deny and justify male sexual aggression against women' (Lonsway and Fitzgerald, 1994: 134). In a more recent definition emphasising the content and function of rape myths, Gerger, Kley, Bohner and Siebler (2007: 425) defined rape myths as '*descriptive or prescriptive beliefs about sexual aggression (ie about its scope, causes, context, and consequences) that serve to deny, downplay or justify sexually aggressive behavior that men commit against women*'. Rape myths are core elements of a set of stereotyped beliefs about rape referred to in the literature as 'rape-supportive attitudes' (eg Anderson, Cooper and Okamura, 1997; Anderson, Stoelb, Duggan, Hieger, Kling and Payne, 1998).

Psychologists have devised a wide range of instruments for measuring the extent to which an individual accepts rape myths. Lonsway and Fitzgerald (1994) identified no fewer than 24 different measuring scales, each of which requires respondents to indicate whether or not they agree with a series of statements encapsulating rape myths. One of the earliest measures, Burt's (1980) Rape Myth Acceptance Scale, contains 14 items each containing false ideas about rape and derogatory views about victims, such as 'Any healthy woman can successfully resist a rapist if she really wants to' and 'In the majority of rapes, the victim is promiscuous or has a bad reputation.' Two more recent measures, the *Perceived Causes of Rape Scale* (PCR) by Cowan and Quinton (1997) and the *Acceptance of Modern Myths about Sexual Aggression Scale* (AMMSA) by Gerger *et al* (2007) were used in our own studies and will be described in more detail in chapters four and five.

The vast majority of studies recording the prevalence of rape myth acceptance come from the United States and were conducted with college students. Even in this relatively educated group, some support for rape myths has been consistently demonstrated (Giacopassi and Dull, 1986). For example, 26.3 per cent of the undergraduate students studied by Johnson, Kuck and Schander (1997) agreed with the statement that 'women's reputation should be an issue', and 15.6 per cent agreed with the statement that 'healthy women can resist rape'. Medical students were found to hold significantly more negative attitudes about victims of sexual assault than about victims of nonsexual assault (Best *et al*, 1992).

American studies with groups other than college undergraduates corroborate this picture. In a large representative sample of adolescents, rape myths were not uniformly rejected (Marciniak, 1998). Other studies found levels of rape myth acceptance similar to college students among professionals (Costin, 1985) and members of the clergy from a range of denominations (Sheldon and Parent, 2002).

Findings from other countries reveal that acceptance of rape myths is common across the world. One of the few cross-national studies on the prevalence of rape-supportive attitudes was conducted by Ward and colleagues (Ward, 1995). Her team of collaborators brought together evidence from 15 countries based on the *Attitudes towards Rape Victims Scale* (ARVS; Ward, 1988). The AVRS comprises 25 items which address seven aspects of negative attitudes toward rape victims, namely victim blame, failure to resist, lack of credibility, denigration, victim responsibility, trivialisation, and deservingness. Total rape myth acceptance scores can range from 0 (complete rejection of all 25 items) to 100 (complete agreement with all items). Table 2.1 shows the overall acceptance of rape myths in the 15 countries:

Table 2.1

Summary of negative attitudes towards rape victims across fifteen countries
(Based on Ward, 1995: 55).

CountryMean	ARVS Scores (Range 0 – 100)
United Kingdom	18.3
Germany	20.9
New Zealand	21.8
United States	26.2
Australia	27.5
Canada	29.5
Barbados	30.0
Israel	32.0
Hong Kong	32.9
Singapore	36.2
Turkey	39.2
Mexico	39.7
Zimbabwe	39.8
India	40.6
Malaysia	51.6

Note: The ARVS scores are weighted by participant sex in those samples which had unequal numbers of men and women.

The findings in table 2.1 suggest two conclusions: (1) even in the countries with the lowest average ARVS scores, there was some support for rape myths. (2) There is considerable variation between the different countries in the acceptance of rape-supportive attitudes, with a difference of 33 points between the highest and the lowest scoring countries (Malaysia and the UK). In order to explain this variation, Ward (1995) linked ARVS scores to socio-structural factors in each country which were indicative of an unequal power distribution to the disadvantage of women. She found that negative attitudes toward rape victims correlated substantially with a low participation rate of women in the workforce and with a high illiteracy rate.

Individual Differences in Rape Myth Acceptance

Beyond showing the overall prevalence of rape myths, researchers have been interested in identifying variables associated with differences in rape myth acceptance (RMA) and in linking RMA to other attitudes pertinent to relationships between men and women. As far as differences in RMA are concerned, *gender* has been the most widely studied variable, and the findings are highly consistent: rape myths are more widely accepted among men than among women (eg Hinck and Thomas, 1999; Jimenez and Abreu, 2003; Morry and Winkler, 2001; Ward, 1988; see also the comprehensive review by Lonsway and Fitzgerald, 1994). The gender difference has been confirmed by Anderson *et al* (1997) in a meta-analysis involving 27 studies.[1] It was found across racial and occupational groups, including mental health professionals (eg Sapp, Farrell and Johnson, 1999; White and Kurpius, 1999) as well as across a range of countries (eg Costin and Kaptanoglu, 1993, for Turkey, England, Israel and West Germany; Nayak, Byrne, Martin and Abraham, 2003, for India, Kuwait and Japan).

In addition to gender, a range of variables has been linked to differences in the extent to which rape myths are accepted, such as traditional as against modern beliefs about gender roles, general attitudes towards violence, demographic variables such as age, race and socio-economic status, and past experience as victim or perpetrator of sexual assault. These variables will be discussed briefly in turn.

Individuals who subscribe to traditional *gender role beliefs* show greater acceptance of rape myths and adopt narrower definitions of what constitutes rape than those who do not. They hold more restrictive views about appropriate conduct for women and are therefore more likely to attribute blame to a victim who has shown behaviour at odds with those role prescriptions (Burt, 1980; Krahé, 1988; Truman, Tokar and Fischer, 1996). In a large representative sample of American adolescents, participants showed more agreement with rape

---

[1] Meta-analysis is a statistical tool for integrating the findings from a range of individual studies to provide an overall measure of 'effect size', eg an average correlation between gender and RMA or an average difference score between the mean scores of men and women on RMA measures (eg Glass, McGraw and Smith, 1981). To give greater weight to studies using larger samples, correlations or difference scores of individual studies are usually weighted by sample size for the overall measure of effect size.

myths the more they endorsed traditional beliefs about gender roles (Marciniak, 1998). Studies with university students, including all-female samples, corroborated this finding (Anderson and Cummings, 1993; Johnson *et al*, 1997). The meta-analysis by Anderson et al (1997) confirmed that the link between attitudes towards rape and gender role traditionalism was equally strong for men and women.[2] Substantial correlations between RMA and restrictive beliefs about women's social role were also found in Turkey, England, Israel and West Germany (Costin and Kaptanoglu, 1993). Moreover, attitudes tolerant of rape were significantly correlated with other beliefs detrimental to women, such as sexist attitudes towards women (eg the belief that men should dominate women in relationships) and 'macho' sex role attitudes (Bunting and Reeves, 1983; Hall, Howard and Boezio, 1986).

It has also been found that *attitudes towards violence* are significant in terms of RMA. Rape myths form part of an attitudinal network that minimises the antisocial nature of sexual violence and its consequences for the victim. The extent to which individuals regard the use of force as an acceptable means of pursuing their interests and resolving conflict in interpersonal relationships has consistently been linked to RMA. Moreover, individuals scoring high on RMA were more likely to find the use of sexual aggression acceptable under a variety of circumstances (Burt and Albin, 1981; Caron and Carter, 1997; Marciniak, 1998; Morry and Winkler, 2001).

Studies examining *age* differences in RMA have found that acceptance of rape myths declines with age (Burt, 1980). However, since most studies have been conducted with student samples, little is known about age-related differences over the lifespan. A Finnish study conducted with male participants ranging between 16 and 61 years confirmed that RMA scores went down with age (Aromäki, Haebich and Lindman, 2002). Unfortunately, the negative correlation found in this study between age and RMA does not tell us whether it is due to a developmental effect (individuals becoming less accepting of rape myths as they grow older) or a cohort effect (attitudes toward sexual coercion becoming more permissive over time, leading to higher RMA among members of the younger generation). Studies using a longitudinal design in which the same individuals are asked about their RMA at different points in their lives would be required to provide a conclusive answer to this question.

Evidence concerning differences in RMA as a function of *socio-economic status* (SES) is also limited and has generally shown only weak relationships (eg Williams and Holmes, 1981). Again, the strong reliance on student samples is a potential problem. It acts against detecting differences in relation to SES because this group is fairly homogeneous in terms of educational background, which is one of the indicators of SES. However, in a sample of adolescents from a representative range of socio-economic backgrounds studied by Marciniak (1998), SES was indirectly linked to RMA: adolescents from low SES families showed a

---

[2] For men, weighted r = .54, n = 16 studies; for women: weighted r = .59; n = 9 studies.

greater acceptance of traditional gender roles which, in turn, predicted greater endorsement of rape myths.

Evidence is limited and inconclusive with respect to *race and ethnic differences*. While some studies have found greater RMA in black than in white people, this was mainly true for men (Johnson *et al*, 1997; Marciniak, 1998). Other studies have found no differences at all (C⁻ nody and Washington, 2001). Studies comparing Caucasian and Asian students in the United States and Canada found that Asian students believed more strongly that women are responsible for preventing rape, that it is women who precipitate rape, and that most rapes are committed by strangers (Kennedy and Gorzalka, 2002; Lee, Pomeroy, Yoo and Rheinboldt, 2005; Mori, Bernat, Glenn and Selle, 1995). There is evidence to suggest that Latina women hold more negative attitudes towards rape victims than Caucasian women (Jimenez and Abreu, 2003).

Given that a key component of rape myths is the trivialisation of rape and its effects on the victim (Payne, Lonsway and Fitzgerald, 1999), one would expect little support for these beliefs among persons who have *experienced sexual victimisation* themselves. Contrary to this plausible assumption, several studies found no difference between victims and non-victims of sexual assault in their acceptance of rape myths (Anderson *et al*, 1997; Carmody and Washington, 2001; Struckman-Johnson and Struckman-Johnson, 1992; see also Kahn *et al*, 1994; Peterson and Muehlenhard, 2004).

Rape myths serve to legitimise men's use of sexual coercion and minimise their responsibility. Therefore, men who endorse rape myths can be expected to be more likely to use sexual aggression against women. Several studies show significant relationships between RMA and *self-reported sexual aggression* (eg Bohner, Jarvis, Eyssel and Siebler, 2005; Osland, Fitch and Willis, 1996; Smith, Martin and Kerwin, 2001; see also the reviews by Anderson *et al*, 1997, and Lonsway and Fitzgerald, 1994). In terms of behavioural intention rather than actual behaviour, men who are more accepting of rape myths find it easier to imagine that they might rape a woman (Chiroro, Bohner, Viki and Jarvis, 2004).

2.3 RAPE STEREOTYPES AND POLICE RESPONSES TO RAPE COMPLAINTS

Police officers' perceptions of the characteristics of typical rape scenarios have also been shown to be affected by stereotypes. When asked to list the features of a 'typical' rape, German police officers studied by Krahé (1991a) thought that it involved an attack on a young woman in the open and at night by a stranger who was psychologically disturbed. They described the features of a 'credible' rape complaint in very similar terms, except that the victim was perceived as not having drunk alcohol and as having made an attempt to escape. 'Dubious' and 'false' rape complaints were perceived very differently. In such cases, complainants were assumed to be older women (above the age of 40), who were allegedly assaulted by a friend or acquaintance in the victim's own home, were heavily drunk at the time of the assault and made no attempt to resist. Police officers' prototypes of rape were highly similar to those identified in a student sample (Krahé, 1991b), supporting other evidence that these groups show little differences in their attitudes and beliefs about rape (Brown and King, 1998).

Police officers were found in several other studies to endorse the real rape stereotype, expecting the credible rape complaint to entail a violent attack by a stranger (eg Feild, 1978; LaFree, 1981; Rose and Randall, 1982). Studying police officers, lawyers, counsellors and doctors in Singapore, Ward (1995) showed that rape myths were accepted to a significant extent in each of these professional groups. For example, the statement: 'Many women claim rape if they have consented to sexual relations but changed their minds afterwards' was endorsed by 51 per cent of the police officers and the doctors, 37 per cent of the lawyers and 27 per cent of the counsellors. Ward also explored the factual knowledge about rape in the four groups. She found, for example, that 43 per cent of the police officers failed to identify as false the statement that 'most alleged rapes involve extensive physical injury'. These findings led Ward (1995: 59) to conclude: 'On the whole, doctors, police, lawyers, and counsellors were not well informed about rape; they often held stereotyped and inaccurate expectations about sexual violence.' This conclusion is corroborated by findings from an interview study with police officers in England which revealed that more than half of the officers assumed that 25 per cent of all rapes reported were false (Temkin, 1997). On the basis of interviews with police and district attorneys, Stewart *et al* (1996) reported a widespread assumption that genuine rape victims would report to the police immediately.

The gender difference found pervasively in student samples was also confirmed for police officers in two studies where female officers tended to hold more positive attitudes towards victims than male officers (Brown and King, 1998; Schuller and Stewart, 2000). Furthermore, officers scoring high on a measure of rape empathy were more likely to believe the victim than officers low on rape empathy, but also to find the rape report of an emotionally upset victim more credible than the report of a seemingly calm and composed victim (Baldry, 1996; see parallel findings by Winkel and Koppelaar, 1991, for college students). Police officers, like students, were affected in their judgments about rape victims by information about victim intoxication. In a study by Schuller and Stewart (2000), the more intoxicated the victim was reported to have been, the more negatively she was evaluated. Similar findings were obtained with two samples of prospective lawyers in Germany (Krahé, Temkin, Bieneck and Berger, in press). Both undergraduate and graduate law students considered the defendant less legally liable and blamed the complainant more when she was unable to resist due to alcohol as compared with when the defendant used force to overcome her resistance.

Evidence of the operation of the real rape stereotype in the treatment of rape cases in the criminal justice system may also be gained from the analysis of police files. In a recent study analysing police files in the UK, only 18 per cent of the 105 cases examined eventually came to trial or resulted in a caution of the offender (Brown, Hamilton and O'Neill, 2007). By far the highest loss (74 per cent of all cases dropped) occurred at the police investigation stage. Cases referred by the police for prosecution were more likely to involve the use of violence, presence of injuries and immediate reporting. Following up their file analyses with qualitative interviews with police officers and Crown Prosecutors, Brown *et al* found both legal and extralegal considerations underlying decisions whether to drop a case. The perceptions of police and prosecutors as to the likelihood of securing a conviction at trial were crucial. These were based on consideration of whether the available evidence and the victim's presentation in court would persuade a jury. Views about what would make a convincing case were clearly informed by the stereotypes described earlier in this chapter, even though reliance on these views was attributed to juries rather than presented as personal attitudes.

This kind of anticipatory assessment, which Brown *et al* (2007) call 'down streaming', has important consequences for the social representation of sexual offences. If cases not conforming to the real rape stereotype are more likely to be dropped, those that remain in the system will shape the social perception of what genuine rape cases are like, and any cases that depart from this format are likely to be treated as suspicious from the outset. We will return to this self-perpetuating aspect of the real rape stereotype in the context of jury decision-making in chapter three.

A second study using police files was conducted in New Zealand by Jordan (2004) who analysed 164 alleged rapes. Of particular interest in the present context are the features that characterised cases which the police categorised as 'possibly true/false' or 'false'. Compared with cases considered as genuine, cases in these two categories more frequently involved a victim who was drunk or under the influence of drugs, or delayed reporting, or had previous consensual sex with the accused, or had reported rape before, or was intellectually impaired, or perceived as 'immoral'. Moreover, if the victim concealed information about the assault such as the fact that she had been drunk at the time, or if she had made a false complaint before, her case was most likely to be placed in the 'false complaint' category.

Another source of information regarding police responses to rape allegations are interviews with victims about the experience of reporting the assault to the police. These studies confirm that police responses are often perceived as unsympathetic and characterised by mistrust. Of the victims surveyed in an American study, 52 per cent described the way they were treated by the police and the criminal justice system as unhelpful and even as having aggravated their problems. Only 35 per cent found the treatment they received supportive. Assessments of treatment by medical professionals were not much better. Fewer than half of respondents (47 per cent) had perceived it as supportive. In contrast, rape crisis centres were regarded as helpful by 75 per cent of victims who turned to them for help (Campbell, Wasco, Ahrens, Sefl and Barnes, 2001).

In-depth interviews with rape victims who had reported to the police revealed both negative and positive experiences of police treatment (Frazier and Haney, 1996; Jordan, 2001; Temkin, 1999). Critically, though, a substantial proportion of victims stated they would decide against reporting if they were victimised again. When interviewed about their treatment by police doctors, some victims reported that they had felt they were being blamed for what had happened to them. Although by no means pervasive, these findings give cause for concern given the particular vulnerability of rape victims shortly after the assault to the damaging effects of this kind of 'secondary victimisation' (Temkin, 1998). The experience of secondary victimisation in the course of rape reporting can aggravate problems in coping with the assault. Perceived secondary victimisation by members of the criminal justice system was associated with a significantly higher incidence of post-traumatic stress disorder (Campbell, Sefl, Barnes, Ahrens, Wasco and Zaragoza-Diesfeld, 1999). The two forms of secondary victimisation regarded as most damaging by victims were doubts about their credibility and the assessment of their complaint as not sufficiently serious to warrant further investigation.[3]

It could be argued that rape victims have a distorted view of police and medical treatment because of the high level of stress which they experience as a result of the assault. However, when victim reports were cross-checked against reports from police officers and doctors, a high degree of correspondence was found between their respective accounts (Campbell, 2005). Interestingly, however, police officers and doctors underestimated how much victims were affected by the way they responded towards them.

Studies analysing why women decide against reporting rape to the police show that many victims expect members of the police and the judiciary to hold negative attitudes about rape victims and are likely to treat women with suspicion when they claim to have been raped (eg Fisher, Daigle, Cullen and Turner, 2003).[4] This belief prevents women from reporting rape to the police, particularly if they are raped by a person they know or under circumstances that do not conform to the real rape stereotype (Binder, 1981; Frazier, Candell, Arikian and Tofteland, 1994; Gidycz and Layman, 1996; Kerstetter and Van Winkle, 1990).

2.4 THE ATTRIBUTION OF BLAME TO VICTIMS OF RAPE

We have argued above that negative attitudes about rape victims may be part of the explanation for high attrition rates in rape cases. To support this claim, evidence is required that these attitudes actually affect the way in which

---

[3] Victims who had the assistance of a rape victim advocate (a non-lawyer) reported less distress after dealing with the legal system and also perceived the treatment they received by the police as more positive (Campbell, 2006).

[4] A Home Office study found that sexism was rampant in the police force (Foster, Newburn, and Souhami, 2005).

individuals look at and assess specific cases. Such evidence is provided by experimental studies within the theoretical framework of attribution theory. These studies identify RMA as a critical variable that affects judgments in individual cases about the causal role and responsibility of victims and perpetrators of sexual assault. Because of their very function as beliefs that serve to deny, downplay or justify sexually aggressive behaviour that men commit against women, rape myths provide a basis for shifting the blame for sexual assault from the perpetrator to the victim. Thus, these attributions influence judgments about the victim's claim and about the appropriate sanctions for the perpetrator.

A large body of evidence generated within the conceptual framework of attribution theory supports this line of reasoning. Attribution theory is based on the proposition that individuals have a basic need for causality that is rooted in their desire to understand their world of experience. They seek to attribute experiences and events to their underlying causes in order to achieve a sense of predictability and controllability in their social world (Heider, 1958; Försterling, 2001). The search for causal explanations is triggered, in particular, by events that are unexpected and those which entail negative outcomes (Weiner, 1985), two conditions that are typically met by allegations of rape.

Within attribution theory, two different modes of causal information processing have been postulated. In the first mode, individuals try to arrive at a causal judgement by examining the information available to them, ie, they engage in data-driven information processing. By contrast, in the second mode, individuals seek to reach a causal explanation by referring to their generalised beliefs and stored knowledge, ie, they engage in schema-driven information processing. Individuals are likely to engage in data-driven processing if they have sufficient knowledge about the event at hand and if they are sufficiently motivated to invest cognitive effort into this task. This may be the case, for example, when they learn that a close friend or relative was raped and they are given a detailed account of the events. In contrast, they are likely to refer to their generalised schemata if they lack sufficient information to test specific causal hypotheses and/or if they do not see the task as having personal relevance.

The predominant research strategy for studying attributions about rape cases has been the vignette methodology (Finch, 1987; Sleed, Durrheim, Kriel, Solomon and Baxter, 2002). Participants are provided with a written description of a rape and asked to make a number of judgments about the incident, including the extent to which the victim was responsible or to blame for the assault, whether or not the incident was rape, and what, if any, sentence would be appropriate for the perpetrator. In studies using the so-called 'mock jury paradigm', participants are instructed to adopt the role of jurors when making their judgments (see chapter three). Occasionally, audiotaped or videotaped accounts have been used instead of written vignettes (eg Calhoun *et al*, 1981; Tetreault and Barnett, 1987; Yarmey, 1985).

The vignette methodology has the advantage of enabling researchers to build critical variables into the rape scenarios that they expect to influence participants' judgments, such as information about any previous relationship between victim and assailant or about victim social status, while holding the remaining aspects of the case constant. Furthermore, the case material can be constructed so as to provide much less room for interpretation than would be the case in a real trial. Participants are told what happened and are not left to work out the events which occurred from the disputed accounts of the complainant and defendant. Therefore, they are presented with a much stronger set of data than in a courtroom. If it can be shown that even in this situation, which leaves little room for interpretation, participants are affected in their decision-making by rape stereotypes, then it may be concluded that the problem of schematic processing is likely to be magnified under conditions of uncertainty as they prevail in a real-life trial.

The extensive literature on attributions of blame in sexual assault cases can be summed up in terms of the key variables found to influence causal judgments about perpetrators and victims:

1. *Perceiver variables*, denoting characteristics of the persons who make the judgment, such as gender and rape-supportive attitudes.
2. *Victim variables*, comprising both stable characteristics of the victim, such as physical attractiveness, as well as behavioural information, such as whether or not the victim was drunk or behaved in accordance with female gender roles in the situation leading up to the assault.
3. *Perpetrator characteristics*, such as race, social status and physical appearance.
4. *Contextual variables*, most notably information about a previous relationship between the victim and the perpetrator.

Perceiver Characteristics

Attributions of blame to perpetrators and victims of rape are affected to a significant degree by the characteristics of the person who makes the judgment. The most widely studied variable here is gender. A large number of studies show that men are more disposed than women to blame the victim (eg Gölge, Yavuz, Müderrisoglu and Yavuz, 2003; McDonald and Kline, 2004; Ryckman, Graham, Thornton, Gold and Lindner, 1998; Wakelin and Long, 2003; Workman and Freeburg, 1999; see Pollard, 1992, for a review of earlier studies).

However, gender can only be an indicator, or marker, of differences in rape attributions, it does not have any explanatory power in itself. The crucial question, therefore, is what makes men and women differ in their perceptions of rape. One answer to this question comes from research on rape-supportive attitudes. As shown above, there is wide agreement in the literature that men endorse rape myths and other rape-supportive attitudes to a greater extent than women. This suggests that one of the reasons for the greater willingness of men to blame the victim and exonerate the perpetrator might be their greater acceptance of rape myths, including the belief that women precipitate rape through the way they behave.

Several studies have provided data on a direct link between RMA and attributions of blame to the victim when making judgments about specific cases (eg Check and Malamuth, 1985; Jenkins and Dambrot, 1987; Mason, Riger and Foley, 2004). The more individuals endorse rape myths, the less likely they are to regard a sexual assault vignette as rape and to think that they would convict the assailant (Burt and Albin, 1981; Fischer, 1986; Norris and Cubbins, 1992). Studies which considered both RMA and perceiver gender show that gender differences in the extent to which perceivers blame victims and perpetrators are due to differential subscription to rape myths by men and women.

Since, as noted above, RMA is linked to more traditional gender role beliefs, it is not surprising that a relationship has also been found between gender role attitudes and rape attributions. Perceivers holding more traditional gender role attitudes were found to be more inclined to blame the victim when assessing specific cases (Ben-David and Schneider, 2005; Howells, Shaw, Greasley, Robertson, Gloster and Metcalfe, 1984; Simonson and Subich, 1999; Snell and Godwin, 1993). Similarly, 'benevolent sexism' has been found to affect rape attributions. Benevolent sexism denotes a chivalrous attitude towards women provided that they conform to prescribed, traditional roles.[5] Benevolent sexists may think that women who get raped by a person they know have failed in their role as guardians of sexual morality. In line with this proposition, benevolent sexism predicted victim blame in an acquaintance rape scenario (Abrams, Viki, Masser and Bohner, 2003), but it did not affect perceptions of responsibility in a stranger rape scenario where the woman was more likely to be seen as the innocent victim.

In prototypical heterosexual rape scenarios, the victim is always female and the perpetrator is always male. If men are less sympathetic to the victim and more lenient toward the perpetrator, it could be argued that this is because of a general tendency to be lenient towards members of one's own sex rather than due to a devaluing of the rape victim. To address this possibility, Gerber, Cronin and Steigman (2004) used scenarios in which the victim was either male or female and was sexually assaulted by either a male or a female perpetrator. It was found that men attributed less blame to the perpetrator than women regardless of the perpetrator's gender, suggesting that men are generally more lenient. This study points to an important issue that has received insufficient attention in past research, namely whether the widely shown gender effect of men blaming perpetrators less than women is specific to the perception of heterosexual rape or rather indicates a more general difference in terms of men's greater tolerance of criminal behaviour.

[5] See http://www.understandingprejudice.org

Few studies have looked at attitudes associated with increased sympathy for a victim of rape and decreased attributions of blame. However, the concept of 'rape empathy' was developed to describe differences in the extent to which perceivers understand the traumatic nature of a rape experience and feel sorry for the victim (Deitz, Blackwell, Daley and Bentley, 1982). High empathy perceivers were found to attribute more blame to the rapist, less blame to the victim and were more likely to find the perpetrator guilty than perceivers low on rape empathy (Weir and Wrightsman, 1990).

Victim Characteristics

The kind of person the victim is perceived to be, as well as her behaviour before and during the assault, influence the way perceivers evaluate her responsibility for what happened to her. The first studies on victim blame in rape cases concentrated on *victim respectability* as a critical variable, operationalised by marital or occupational status. The evidence points overwhelmingly towards a negative relationship between respectability and victim blame. The more respectable the victim appears to be, the less she is blamed. Victim blame in a violent stranger rape case was higher when the victim was described as a shop assistant than when she was described as a school teacher (Krahé, 1985; see also Luginbuhl and Mullin, 1981; Smith, Keating, Hester and Mitchell, 1976; and Whatley, 1996, for a meta-analysis).

Of particular interest in the context of the present analysis are studies in which respectability was manipulated by information about the victim's past sexual behaviour. It has long been recognised that information about the victim's sexual history can have a powerful impact on jurors' decisions, undermining her credibility and leading to the acquittal of the defendant. The introduction of rape shield legislation is a direct reflection of this realisation (Schuller and Klippenstine, 2004; Temkin, 2003; see also chapter one). Experimental studies analysing the role of sexual history information through systematic variations of the victim's past sexual behaviour, with all other case features held constant, lend support to this view. Other studies found that the complainant was seen as less credible and more to blame by 'mock jurors' when they heard she had engaged in consensual sexual activity with the defendant previously (Cann, Calhoun and Selby, 1979; Johnson, Jackson, Gatto and Nowak, 1995; Schuller and Hastings, 2002).

A further victim characteristic found to affect attributions of blame is *race*. White perceivers saw black victims of acquaintance rape as more responsible than black victims of stranger rape but did not make a parallel distinction for white victims of stranger as against acquaintance rape (Willis, 1992). Foley, Evancic, Karnik, King and Parks (1995) showed that the rape of a black woman was perceived as less serious than the rape of a white woman. When perpetrator race was taken into account, perceivers judging an alleged sexual assault by a white man were more certain that it was rape if the victim was white rather than black. In contrast, when the alleged assailant was black, race of the victim did not make a difference (George and Martinez, 2002).

Victim behaviour is also a critical factor in attributions of responsibility and blame, relating to both what she did before the assault and how she responded in the assault situation. Victims who behave in ways which violate female gender role expectations are more likely to be blamed than role-conforming victims. For example, when a victim was portrayed as showing role-discrepant behaviour before the attack, such as drinking alone in a pub, she was held more responsible for being assaulted than a victim who had shown behaviour less at odds with the female gender role, for example, working late at the office (Krahé, 1988; Schult and Schneider, 1991).

Another behavioural cue associated with increased victim blame is alcohol consumption. If the victim is portrayed as drunk, she is perceived as less credible and the perpetrator is seen as less likely to be culpable compared with a sober victim (Stormo, Lang and Stritzke, 1997; Wenger and Bornstein, 2006). The way in which women dress is also firmly rooted in rape myths as a factor precipitating rape and increasing victim responsibility. Victims wearing a short skirt were blamed more than victims wearing a longer skirt or trousers (Gölge *et al*, 2003; Whatley, 2005).

Whether a victim actively resisted the assailant has also proved to be relevant in assessments of victim blame. In a study by Ong and Ward (1999), participants, particularly those who regarded rape as an act primarily motivated by the perpetrator's sexual needs, attributed more fault and responsibility to victims who failed to resist. Perpetrators were also judged more leniently when the woman resisted verbally but not physically (Hannon, Hall, Kuntz, Van Laar and Williams, 1995). On the other hand, physical resistance against a male attacker can be seen as role-discrepant behaviour on the part of the female victim and hence have the effect of reducing sympathy with the victim. In a study by Branscombe and Weir (1992), participants attributed less blame to the perpetrator and recommended a more lenient sentence where the victim actively fought back than where she did not physically resist. In a further study, the victim who physically resisted was viewed more negatively, particularly if she was seen as physically unattractive (Deitz, Littman and Bentley, 1984).

The findings reported so far suggest that information about the victim affects rape attributions in terms of a 'main effect', ie it shapes perceptions irrespective of other variables. Several studies, however, provide evidence of an 'interaction effect', indicating that information about the victim affects some perceivers more than others. For example, information about victim dress (short versus long skirt) had a stronger effect on attributions of victim blame in perceivers scoring high on RMA than in those low on RMA (Workman and Orr, 1996). Similarly, the information that the victim had engaged in role-conforming behaviour or role-discrepant behaviour prior to being assaulted made no difference to perceivers low on RMA. In contrast, high RMA perceivers did respond to information about victim behaviour prior to the rape and assigned more responsibility to the victim who had shown role-discrepant behaviour (Krahé, 1988).

Perpetrator Characteristics

Compared with the victim, the characteristics or behaviour of the perpetrator have received less attention as potential determinants of responsibility attributions. But in Yarmey's study, a well-dressed assailant was held less responsible for raping a woman than one who was poorly dressed, and more responsibility was attributed to the victim raped by a well-dressed than a poorly dressed man (Yarmey, 1985). Other studies found lower attributions of responsibility to a physically attractive as compared with an unattractive assailant (Vrij and Firmin, 2001). Furthermore, social status had an effect, with an assailant described as a scientist receiving less blame than an assailant described as a janitor (Deitz and Byrnes, 1981).

Physical height has been shown to play a critical role. In a study by Ryckman, Graham, Thornton, Gold and Lindner (1998), an assailant in a date rape scenario who was described as being larger than the alleged victim was held more responsible than an assailant described as being smaller than her. Similarly, victim blame was higher if the victim was described as being taller rather than smaller than the accused. Furthermore, Schuller and Wall (1998) found that a perpetrator was seen as less credible and more likely to be found guilty when he had drunk alcohol as opposed to a non-alcoholic drink prior to the rape.

Contextual Variables

Various aspects of the context in which a sexual assault takes place have been shown to affect attributions of responsibility and blame. The most widely studied contextual variable is the relationship between victim and perpetrator. The real rape stereotype posits that most rapes happen between strangers. It has been found that victims who claim they were raped by an acquaintance or a current or former partner are treated with suspicion even though the relevant law draws no distinction between stranger and other rapes. In a large number of studies, this suspicion is reflected in perceivers' reduced certainty that a rape has occurred (Bridges and McGrail, 1989; Krahé, Temkin and Bieneck, 2007; Simonson and Subich, 1999; Johnson, 1994; Viki, Abrams and Masser, 2004). It is also apparent in their attributions of increased blame to the victim and reduced blame to the perpetrator in acquaintance rapes as compared with stranger rapes. Furthermore, even if perceivers are prepared to accept that an assault by an acquaintance or an ex-partner is rape, they tend to regard it as less serious and less damaging for the victim than an assault by a stranger (Ben-David and Schneider, 2005; however, see Tetreault and Barnett, 1987, for gender differences).

One of the reasons for the reluctance to accept that an assault by an acquaintance is rape and the tendency to consider the woman's behaviour as a precipitating factor is that such cases may be seen as more ambiguous with respect to the issue of the woman's consent. Yescavage (1999) addressed this possibility by systematically varying the point in a sexual interaction at which the victim expressed her non-consent to a man's sexual advances. Later refusal after having engaged in consensual heavy petting was linked to significantly higher ratings of victim accountability, lower perpetrator accountability and lower certainty ratings that the incident should be labelled rape than early refusal after light petting (see also Kopper, 1996).

Contextual information also interacted with individual rape-supportive attitudes in influencing attributions of blame. High and low RMA perceivers responded differently to the information about a prior relationship between victim and perpetrator (Frese, Moya and Megías, 2004). The two groups did not differ in their attributions of victim responsibility in a marital rape scenario, but high RMA perceivers attributed more responsibility to the victim both in a stranger rape and an acquaintance rape scenario.

Altogether, the large body of research reviewed in this section highlights the influence of a variety of factors extraneous to the legal definition of rape on judgments about victims and perpetrators. Even though the majority of findings are based on responses from student samples, they are corroborated by studies with participants drawn from the general population (eg Howells *et al*, 1984; Krahé, 1988; Schuller and Wall, 1998; Yarmey, 1985). They show that rape cases are assessed against the background of widely shared, normative perceptions of role-conforming behaviour for men and women that restrict the range of what is considered rape and provide a basis for assigning responsibility to victims of rape. Although the findings are based on judgments about fictitious cases, they are relevant to decision-making in the legal context because they identify the impact of different information about victim and perpetrator on perceivers' judgments in a controlled and systematic fashion.

2.5 HEURISTICS IN THE PROCESS OF DECISION-MAKING ABOUT SEXUAL ASSAULT

Research in the tradition of attribution theory has focused on the *outcome* of the social decision-making process, for example, the extent to which perpetrators and victims are held responsible for an assault or the likelihood of finding the defendant guilty. Taking a closer look at the *processes* that lead to these outcomes, several studies on decision-making about sexual assault have examined the way in which information is coded, stored and retrieved to inform judgments about a case. In particular, the focus has been on perceivers' use of heuristics, ie mental shortcuts and rules of thumb, to engage in speedy and relatively effortless cognitive processing of information. When the information available is incomplete, open to interpretation or contested by the different parties, as is frequently the case where rape is concerned, perceivers may find it too difficult or cumbersome to scrutinise the evidence to arrive at data-based conclusions. In these circumstances, they are susceptible to the operation of heuristic, schema-driven interpretations of the evidence.

An important factor in information processing is the focus of the perceiver's attention. Attentional focus determines which aspects of the given information will be most salient, capture perceivers' attention and shape their impressions. Rempala and Bernieri (2005) showed that perceivers attributed more blame to whichever party they had more information about, even if the information was not directly relevant, such as the person's college major or city of residence. When biographical information was provided about the complainant, but not the defendant, just over half the participants found the alleged defendant guilty. In contrast, when biographical information was provided about the defendant, but not the complainant, 90 per cent of participants found the defendant guilty. Parallel effects were found for perceptions of victim responsibility, which were lower when biographical information was provided about the defendant rather than the complainant. By having more detailed information about a person, he or she becomes more prominent in the perceiver's awareness and is therefore a more likely candidate to be selected as responsible for the events in question.

Attentional focus also plays a role in information processing based on counterfactual thinking, another widely used heuristic. Counterfactual thinking describes the process of mentally 'undoing' events by imagining conditions under which an outcome opposite to the one observed could have been brought about. Branscombe, Owen, Garstka and Coleman (1996) presented participants with a rape scenario and asked them to generate counterfactual thoughts either about the victim (what could the victim have done differently to avoid being raped) or about the perpetrator. When participants were asked mentally to simulate alternative courses of action from the victim's point of view, they attributed greater blame to the victim. When they were asked to simulate alternative actions by the perpetrator, they attributed greater blame to the perpetrator. This is an indication that the perspective adopted by the perceiver—rather than the events themselves—guide subsequent judgments of responsibility and blame.

A related mental shortcut relevant to the processing of rape complaints is the *hindsight bias* (Fischhoff, 2002). It describes the inability of perceivers to ignore outcome information when evaluating actions that precede the outcome. For example, Janoff-Bulman, Timko and Carli (1985) asked participants to consider a scenario in which a male and a female student went out together for the evening. In evaluating the behaviour of both parties, it was found that participants overestimated the likelihood that the evening would end in rape if they were told that this is what happened, even though they were instructed to ignore this information, as compared with a control group who were given no outcome information. Furthermore, participants were more strongly of the view that the woman should have behaved differently if they were told the evening ended in rape than if they were told the woman was taken home (neutral outcome). The hindsight bias also affected memory about the information. Perceivers in the hindsight condition, who were told that the victim was raped, reconstructed the events prior to the ending in a stereotypic fashion to make them fit the outcome (Carli, 1999; Carli and Leonard, 1989).

The research discussed in this section is relevant to the justice gap in that it illuminates the cognitive processes underlying judgments about sexual assault. The effects of attentional focus, counterfactual thinking and hindsight knowledge are by no means specific to rape. They characterise general patterns of decision-making under conditions of uncertainty. What is problematic is that the type of generalised stereotypes and beliefs perceivers use to fill the information gap are likely to work to the disadvantage of the victim, as was demonstrated almost unanimously in the research reviewed in this chapter. Therefore, exploring ways in which people can be made to engage in a proper assessment of the data available rather than falling back on easy stereotypical answers that follow from rape-supportive attitudes are key objectives for research designed to improve the situation of the rape victim in the criminal justice system. We return to this theme in chapter nine.

2.6 SUMMARY AND CONCLUSIONS

An extensive body of research from social psychology and criminology demonstrates the influence of stereotypes and myths on judgments about rape. It reveals widespread endorsement of the real rape stereotype which sets restrictive criteria for the definition of rape in terms of strangers using force on victims behaving in accordance with normative expectations about female role behaviour. Since only a small proportion of rapes actually meet these defining features, the real rape stereotype effectively bars many sexually assaulted women from being acknowledged as victims of rape. Furthermore, it makes it more difficult for victims to identify their experience as rape, reducing the likelihood that they will report it to the police and seek help to cope with its aftermath.

The real rape stereotype is embedded in the wider context of generalised beliefs about rape that stress the victim's responsibility for being assaulted, minimise the seriousness of sexual assault and exonerate the perpetrator. Rape-supportive beliefs, or 'rape myths', are common in Western societies and link up with other attitudes condoning the use of sexual aggression to undermine the status and credibility of rape victims. Numerous studies have shed light on the factors, including those related to victim and perpetrator characteristics and the circumstances of the assault, which are associated with the attribution of responsibility and blame to victims of rape and the diminution of the responsibility of the perpetrator. In addition, individuals differ in their tendency to blame the victim as a function of their endorsement of rape myths, which in turn differs between men and women. Men show a stronger tendency to blame the victim, which can be explained at least partly by their greater acceptance of rape myths and stereotypes.

The findings concerning demographic and attitudinal correlates of RMA are significant as far as the makeup of juries is concerned. If juries are more or less likely to find a defendant not guilty depending on their level of rape myth acceptance, and if the level of rape myth acceptance varies between different groups as defined, for example, by age or gender, then the likelihood of a conviction may depend on factors other than those related to the case in question. The findings can also serve as a basis for identifying target groups most in need of interventions designed to challenge rape myths and replace them with more accurate views of rape and its effects on victims (eg Lonsway and Kothari, 2000; Yeater and O'Donohue, 1999).

The findings reviewed in this chapter demonstrate that some police officers and certain other professionals involved in the criminal justice system hold very similar beliefs about rape to those held by some students and members of the general public. Some police officers endorse stereotypic beliefs about rape victims and also adhere to the real rape stereotype when judging the credibility of a complaint. As a result, their responses are often perceived as unhelpful by victims who decide to report to the police. The greatest attrition in rape cases occurs at the police investigation stage, ie, before cases ever reach court. The findings concerning police officers' beliefs in rape myths and their reliance on the real rape stereotype in assessing the credibility of rape complaints point to the importance of extra-legal factors in accounting for attrition rates at the police investigation stage (Lea *et al*, 2003).

The final section of this chapter looked at decision-making about rape in terms of the underlying cognitive processes by which given information is interpreted and translated into a judgment about the victim's role. Several biases inherent in schema-driven information processing in general were shown to affect judgments about rape in particular, such as counterfactual thinking and the hindsight bias. Overall, the research reviewed in this chapter is an important source of information for identifying the causes of the justice gap in sexual assault. It also provides a basis for designing strategies directed at improving the situation of rape victims in the criminal justice system, which will be discussed in Part III.

3

The Problem of the Jury in Sexual Assault Trials

I N THE COMMON law world, rape and other serious sexual assault cases are generally decided by juries. Even in legal systems that do not rely on jury decision-making, such as the German system, lay persons have a role in the judicial process (Bliesener, 2006). Psycho-legal research has addressed the question of how well equipped juries or lay persons are to address this task. This chapter will draw on this research to present evidence on a number of aspects inherent in jury trials that may lead to biased decision-making in rape cases and thereby contribute to the justice gap. Juror decision-making is said to be biased if it is affected by factors irrelevant to the task of judging the case at hand or if factors that are legally relevant are not given proper consideration (Horowitz, Kerr, Park and Gockel, 2006). We will begin by looking at the methodology of jury studies and what they can tell us about potential problems affecting actual rape trials. This will provide the background for a closer examination of the problems arising at the different stages of the trial, starting with the presentation of the evidence and concluding with the actual decision-making phase that results in a verdict. We argue that there are potential pitfalls at each stage of the trial that can lead jurors to arrive at biased conclusions about sexual assault cases, which undermine the position of the complainant and work unfairly to the advantage of the defendant.

3.1 THE METHODOLOGY OF JURY STUDIES

The vast majority of studies on jury decision-making are based on the so-called 'mock jury paradigm' in which participants are asked to put themselves in the role of jurors and make judgments about hypothetical cases presented to them in various forms. Given that research involving real jurors is either prohibited or heavily regulated in the Anglo-American justice systems, there are few alternatives to jury simulation studies. However, critics have voiced concern about the lack of realism characterising these studies and have questioned the relevance of the findings to jury decision-making in the real world. In a detailed analysis of the mock jury paradigm, Bornstein (1999) was able to alleviate some of these concerns. He showed that mock juries composed of undergraduate students, who predominate as participants in jury simulations, did not differ in their decision-making from juries composed of citizens from the general population, who predominate in real trials. He also demonstrated that whatever the chosen method for providing the mock trial evidence, this made little difference to mock jurors' judgments. Thus, mock jurors exposed to videotapes of actual trials, which are closest to the presentational mode in a real trial, did not differ in their judgments from those who were given the same trial information in the form of audiotapes, verbatim transcripts or written summaries (for a more recent validation of mock jury studies, see Kerr and Bray, 2005).

An additional concern about mock jury studies relates to the fact that many of them are based on the judgments of individual participants and fail to include group deliberation of the evidence, thus omitting a central element of trial by jury. In fact, jurors' individual pre-deliberation views have been shown to be important predictors of the final group verdict (Ellsworth, 1993), so that this concern may not be entirely justified. On the other hand, the deliberation process can lead to shifts in individual opinion and potentially reduce the error rate in assessing the evidence (Diamond, 1997). Therefore, those mock jury studies which bring together groups of participants for simulated jury deliberations can undoubtedly answer important questions about the role of group exchanges in relation to processing the evidence and reaching a verdict.

Thus, despite its artificial nature, the mock jury paradigm has generated a body of findings relevant to understanding the process of jury decision-making in the real world. A major advantage over more realistic approaches is that it enables researchers systematically to vary the critical variables of interest (such as the sequencing of evidence or whether particular pieces of information shift jurors' judgments), while holding the remaining features of the situation constant. This provides a level of experimental control and rigour necessary to explore causal effects which could not be achieved by studying unique trials in a natural context. However, as Kerr and Bray (2005) point out, generalisations to real-life situations and conclusions about policy implications need to be made with caution.

3.2 DEALING WITH THE EVIDENCE

In this section, we will examine sources of juror bias that result from the way the evidence is presented in court and processed by members of the jury. In particular, we will discuss the inability to disregard inadmissible evidence once it has been presented, and the effects of emotions on judgments about criminal cases.

Inadmissible Evidence and the Hindsight Bias

The reasoning process which jurors employ can be conceptualised as a hypothesis-testing exercise. They examine the probability of competing hypotheses leading to conclusions about the acceptability of the complainant's account versus that of the defendant and the guilt versus the innocence of the defendant (Clifford, 2003). Once they have committed themselves to a plausible hypothesis, subsequent evidence is interpreted in that light. Carlson and Russo (2001) showed that jurors distorted new evidence unfolding in the course of a trial so as to support whichever verdict they had previously come to favour. Thus, early commitment in favour of either the defence or the prosecution is likely to bias the interpretation of subsequent evidence in the same direction.

In chapter two, we reviewed research showing that information processing about rape is affected by a number of cognitive biases, such as counterfactual thinking or the hindsight bias, that facilitate attributions of victim blame. Studies exploring mock jury deliberations further corroborate this conclusion. The hindsight bias describes the inability of perceivers to ignore outcome information when evaluating actions that precede the outcome. It is a specific example of a more general problem, namely jurors' inability to disregard information once it has come to their attention. A recent meta-analysis including 48 studies revealed that jurors are affected by the contents of inadmissible evidence in their judgments even when expressly instructed by the judge to ignore it. Evidence that was first contested and eventually ruled admissible had an even stronger effect (Steblay, Hosch, Culhane and McWethy, 2006, but see London and Nunez, 2000).

Research into the effect of inadmissible evidence on juries has mostly featured evidence concerning the defendant, however, it has a bearing on sexual history evidence in rape trials. For, despite rape shield legislation prohibiting the admission of questions and evidence about the victim's sexual history save in exceptional circumstances, the law is frequently ignored (Kelly, Temkin and Griffiths, 2006), with the result that such evidence creeps into the trial without proper application being made (see chapter seven). Schuller and Hastings (2002) found that mock jurors who were told that the complainant had engaged in sexual intercourse with the defendant in the past were less likely to find the complainant credible and more likely to blame her than those who did not receive this information. Instructions to participants to use this information only to establish whether the defendant had reason to believe in consent and not to evaluate the victim's credibility turned out to be ineffective. When jurors were told that sexual history evidence was inadmissible and should therefore be ignored, this instruction reduced the extent to which female jurors attributed responsibility to the complainant but failed to have a comparable effect on men (Johnson, Jackson, Gatto and Nowak, 1995). These findings clearly contradict the optimistic assertions of judges in a recent study by Kibble (2004) involving

77 judges in England and Wales. He states: 'The judges also pointed out the importance of giving directions to the jury to make sure as far as possible that jurors only used the evidence for proper purposes, and affirmed their belief that juries can be trusted to see the relevance of sexual history evidence and use it properly'. (Kibble 2004: 12)

What then can be done to undo the impact of inadmissible evidence on jurors' decisions or to counteract the hindsight bias? Smith and Greene (2005) explored the strategy of warning jurors about the danger of hindsight effects at three separate points in a simulated trial and found that these warnings were ineffective in suppressing the hindsight bias. Clearly, this shows that ideally evidence triggering the hindsight bias should be excluded in the first place, but this will be impossible in either a criminal or a civil trial. As far as inadmissible evidence in rape cases is concerned, the implication is that provisions preventing sexual history evidence from being introduced need to be properly enforced. Shaw and Skolnick (2004) found that mock jurors, who had attended a course on psychology and law covering potential biases against defendants in jury decision-making, were resistant to pre-trial information pointing towards defendant guilt. However, since jurors do not receive any formal training of this kind in actual trials, this finding has little practical significance under the present system.

Emotional Responses to the Evidence

The influence of current emotional state on an individual's information processing has been widely demonstrated in the psychological literature (Schwarz, 2002). Many studies have shown that when people are in a positive emotional state, superficial, schematic information processing prevails over more systematic scrutiny. By contrast, negative emotional states are conducive to careful and more accurate information processing. There is some evidence to suggest that such mood effects also affect jury decision-making. For example, in a study by Semmler and Brewer (2002), mock jurors in a reckless driving case were provided with evidence from a prosecution witness which included detailed descriptions of the victim's injuries and the emotional trauma of the parties involved. It was found that participants who were saddened by this account were more accurate in their memory of details about the case than jurors who heard a neutral account of the events without reference to injuries and psychological trauma.

Research also provides evidence of a mood-congruency effect, ie the tendency to interpret incoming information in the light of one's current mood. Jurors who were brought into a negative mood paid greater attention to negative information about the target person they were asked to judge, recalled more negative information and arrived at more negative (ie guilty) verdicts than jurors in a neutral or positive mood (Feigenson and Park, 2006). When individuals are sufficiently motivated to process information in a systematic mode, the mood congruency bias can generally be avoided. Other research suggests, however, that different kinds of negative mood states, such as anger as compared with sadness, affect information processing in different ways. Whereas sadness was found to be linked to more systematic processing, anger seems to precipitate more superficial processing (Lerner, Goldberg and Tetlock, 1998). Given the emotionally charged nature of rape cases, it is very likely that jurors will show emotional reactions to the events described in the course of the trial. The emotions elicited are likely to vary between individuals, depending on factors specific to the case, such as the extent to which they identify with the complainant or the defendant, but also on more general attitudes, such as rape myth acceptance and gender role beliefs. Some jurors may be primarily saddened by the complainant's account and angered by the defendant's actions, others may react with anger to the complainant and feel sorry for the defendant. In any case, it needs to be recognised that jurors listening to a rape charge are unlikely to be in a neutral emotional state, which in turn will affect the way they process the evidence.

Bright and Goodman-Delahunty (2006) examined the impact of gruesome evidence on jurors' decision-making. Reviewing earlier research, these authors argued that this type of graphic material is likely to elicit strong emotions in observers, leading to an increased likelihood of a guilty verdict when graphic images of the effects of the defendant's actions are shown (such as pictures of murder victims or victims of accidents caused by negligence). In their own study, they compared the effects of graphic as against non-graphic information about a murder case presented either in verbal form (written descriptions of the victim's injuries) or in the form of visual material (photographs of the victim's injuries). While the results showed no difference between the graphic and non-graphic material when it was presented in written form, mock jurors exposed to the graphic visual images were more likely to convict the defendant than those who had not seen any photographs. This could be explained, at least in part, by the fact that they experienced greater anger towards the defendant than participants who did not see any photos. It follows that in rape trials, from the prosecution point of view, photographs of injuries should be obtained wherever possible, but this frequently does not occur.

3.3 THE ROLE OF EXPERT TESTIMONY

Because of the prevalence of misconceptions about rape among the general public from which jurors are recruited and the evidence that such preconceived attitudes may well be influential in a trial context, one of the solutions advocated by psycho-legal scholars and implemented particularly in the United States is the use of expert evidence. This is seen as a tool for overcoming the problem of juror bias in rape cases. In this section, we examine expert evidence in rape cases as a legal instrument and assess its benefits and limitations.

In order to be admissible, expert evidence must not only be reliable, but should have the power to inform the jury about matters relevant to the case that are outside its experience and knowledge.[1] The expert should be someone with that knowledge and experience. It is the responsibility of the judge to decide whether these conditions are met. While it is relatively easy to determine when juries require expert evidence concerning technical or medical issues, it is more difficult to assess what kind of psychological knowledge falls outside the jury's understanding (see Zeedyck and Raitt, 1998). However, the large body of evidence reviewed in chapter two clearly shows that misguided views about rape and the veracity of a woman's claim are widespread, highlighting the need for jury education on these matters.

Rape Trauma Syndrome

Evidence about rape trauma syndrome (RTS) as a common reaction in victims of rape was the first type of expert testimony introduced into sexual assault trials in the United States in the 1980s, and it has remained controversial ever since (Frazier and Borgida, 1992). Originally, it was most often used to support the claim that sexual intercourse was non-consensual by presenting evidence that the complainant's symptoms and behaviours were consistent with those frequently shown by victims of rape. Burgess and Holmstrom (1985) described RTS as a characteristic pattern of symptoms shown by many rape victims immediately after the assault as well as in the months to follow. They distinguished between an acute phase, lasting for hours or days after the assault, and a reorganisation phase that can take several years. In the *acute phase*, victims may show strong emotional responses, such as crying or even joking, but equally they may exhibit a controlled style, appearing composed and outwardly unshaken. Regardless of their style of expression, they are likely to experience a number of adverse reactions, such as shock, numbness, embarrassment, guilt, feelings of powerlessness, loss of trust, fear, anxiety, anger, disbelief and shame. The *reorganisation phase* is characterised by strong feelings of anxiety and fear that disrupt the victim's functioning in various domains of life, including everyday routines, work and sexual relationships. These are often accompanied by anger at the assailant and disappointment at the lack of support from close others and from social agencies, including the criminal justice system.

The use of RTS as a basis for expert evidence in rape trials has been criticised on the ground that the symptoms are not sufficiently distinct and well-defined, but also on the ground that there is a danger of RTS symptoms being understood as normative information as to how a genuine victim should react (Lonsway, 2005). In response to the first criticism, subsequent research conceptualised sexual

---

[1] *Turner* [1975] QB 834. See further on this Tapper (2007, ch 11). For additional requirements in American law, see eg *Daubert and Merrel Dow Pharmaceuticals* 509 U.S. 579 (1993) and Lonsway (2005).

assault traumatisation as a specific instance of the more general construct of Post-Traumatic Stress Disorder (PTSD), as defined in the established diagnostic manuals, such as the *Diagnostic and Statistical Manual of Mental Disorders* (DSM-IV; American Psychiatric Association, 1994). Since RTS does not represent a symptomatology in its own right, experts have come to refer to PTSD rather than RTS when describing common effects of rape on the victim. The diagnostic criteria of PTSD as specified by the DSM-IV are presented in table 3.1.

Table 3.1

Diagnostic criteria for post-traumatic stress disorder (PTSD)
(Based on DSM-IV, 1994, Code-No 309.81; American Psychiatric Association, 1994).

The person

. . . has experienced or witnessed or was confronted with an unusually traumatic event that (a) involved actual or threatened death or serious physical injury to the person or to others, and (b) led to feelings of intense fear, horror or helplessness

. . . repeatedly relives the event in at least 1 of these ways:

Intrusive, distressing recollections – thoughts, images
Repeated, distressing dreams
Through flashbacks, hallucinations or illusions, acts or feels as if the event were recurring
Marked mental distress in reaction to internal or external cues that symbolize or resemble the event
Physiological reactivity – such as rapid heart beat, elevated blood pressure in response to these cues

. . . repeatedly avoids the trauma-related stimuli and has numbing of general responsiveness (absent before the traumatic event) as shown by 3 or more of the following:

Tries to avoid thoughts, feelings or conversations concerned with the event
Tries to avoid activities, people or places that recall the event
Cannot recall an important feature of the event
Marked loss of interest or participation in activities important to the patient
Feels detached or isolated from other people
Restriction in ability to love or feel other strong emotions
Feels life will be brief or unfulfilled (lack of marriage, job, children)

At least 2 of the following symptoms of hyperarousal were not present before the traumatic event:

Insomnia (initial or interval)
Irritability
Poor concentration
Hypervigilance
Increased startle response

The above symptoms have lasted longer than one month and cause clinically important distress or impair work, social or personal functioning.

In the United States, the move away from presenting evidence of RTS in favour of evidence of PTSD has resulted in symptoms specifically characteristic of traumatisation by sexual assault, such as sexual dysfunction, disappearing from expert testimony in favour of the less specific symptoms of PTSD. Thus, victims who show symptoms that are not covered by PTSD may not be recognised as traumatised. Moreover, since sexual assault is listed as one of a number of different precipitating events for PTSD in the DSM-IV, expert evidence focusing on PTSD can potentially undermine rather than support the victim's position as 'the defense may argue an alleged rape victim who exhibits PTSD symptoms may have experienced other traumatic life events but not necessarily a rape' (McGowan and Helms, 2003: 57). To resolve this problem, Boeschen, Sales and Koss (1998) suggest that expert testimony about PTSD in rape survivors should be complemented with a description of additional symptoms specifically characteristic of rape traumatisation without, however, referring to them under the label of RTS.

A general problem regarding the use of RTS or PTSD as aids to decision-making in rape cases is that the constructs are taken from a clinical context where the relevant symptoms are attributed to victims by diagnosticians without questioning their claim that they have been raped. However, the symptomatology has been presented in American courts to facilitate a decision as to whether a rape has occurred. As Faigman (2003: 380) states: 'In effect, then, a PTSD diagnosis, which partly rests on the alleged victim's statements that she was raped, is introduced to prove that very contention'. This problem can be addressed to some extent by presenting information about PTSD in general terms without relating it to the complainant in the case (Frazier and Borgida, 1992; see also Level 2 expert evidence, below).

The Varied Uses of Expert Evidence in Rape Trials

Researchers refer to five levels at which expert testimony can be given in a rape trial (Boeschen, Sales and Koss, 1998; Lonsway, 2005).

Level 1: Testimony to Address the Complainant's 'Unusual' Behaviour

Testimony at this level presents research findings showing that victims of sexual assault may show behaviours at odds with stereotypic beliefs, and that these behaviours do not suggest in any way that her complaint is unfounded. This is true, for example, for late reporting, non-emotional appearance when reporting or giving evidence in court, or not having disclosed the assault to friends or family. These behaviours have been shown in a range of empirical studies to be associated with doubts about a woman's claim of rape and the attribution of blame (see chapter two), so there is clearly a need for juries to be educated on these issues (see further chapter eight).

Level 2: Testimony on Common Reactions to Rape and the Diagnostic Criteria for PTSD

At this level, experts inform the jury about symptoms commonly found in rape survivors which are included in the diagnostic criteria of PTSD as well as those specific reactions that PTSD does not include. However, experts do not relate these findings to the complainant in the case at hand. Again, jury education on these matters is arguably necessary since there is ample evidence that jurors are ill-informed about the psychological effects of rape and are likely to endorse rape myths that trivialise them. As with Level 1, this evidence 'can help jurors to understand behaviors by the victim that might not otherwise make sense' (Lonsway, 2005: 12; see also chapter eight).

However, reiterating concerns voiced about the use of RTS evidence, some critics have warned that there is a danger of implementing just another normative standard against which the responses of an individual complainant will be judged, shedding doubt on her credibility if she does not meet the criteria of PTSD (Raitt and Zeedyck, 2000).

Level 3: Testimony on the Consistency of the Complainant's Symptoms with the Diagnosis of PTSD

This form of testimony goes beyond the provision of background information and is addressed to whether the symptoms reported by the complainant in the case match those demanded by a diagnosis of PTSD. The expert, at this level, accepts the reported symptoms at face value rather than confirming them via clinical assessment. A study by Brekke and Borgida (1988) showed that this type of evidence by expert witnesses enhanced juror perceptions of victim credibility without simultaneously reducing the credibility of the defendant. However, some American courts have disallowed this type of evidence on the ground that such boosting of the complainant's credibility is inappropriate. In England and Wales 'oath helping' is similarly disallowed.

Level 4: Testimony Stating that the Complainant Suffers from PTSD

At this level, expert testimony moves to the individual complainant, based on the expert's clinical assessment. But, as Boeschen *et al* (1998) have pointed out, there is no absolute certainty in clinical diagnoses, so the expert needs to provide a qualified appraisal, including the possibility that the symptoms may be indicative of a trauma other than the rape in question.

Level 5: Expert Opinion on the 'Ultimate Issue'

This is expert evidence used to speak directly to the question of whether or not the complainant was raped, is telling the truth, or both. This type of evidence is generally regarded as inadmissible by the courts as conclusions on these matters lie with the jury, not the expert witness.

It is apparent that within the current legal framework expert evidence is likely to be useable only at Levels 1 and 2, but the question remains even then to what extent it is likely to be helpful.

How Useful is Expert Evidence?

One key question about expert testimony is whether it has any effect on the deliberations and decisions of juries. Not many studies have addressed this issue. Nietzel, McCarthy and Kern (1999) conducted a meta-analysis including 22 studies, all of which compared the effects of different types of psychological expert testimony (eg relating to insanity, eyewitness accuracy, credibility of a child witness) against a no-expert control condition. They found a small, but statistically significant correlation between the direction of the expert testimony and the direction of jury decisions across all types of expert testimony. Looking specifically at particular forms of testimony, the largest effect ($r = .18$) was obtained for expert evidence on battered spouse and rape trauma syndromes. This finding can be translated into practical terms on the basis of a hypothetical example. Assume that in 100 cases jurors heard expert testimony supportive of the prosecution and in another 100 cases they did not hear any expert testimony. An effect size of .18 would correspond to a conviction rate of 59 cases in the expert testimony condition compared with a conviction rate of 41 cases in the absence of expert testimony, which is a substantial difference considering the consequences of a verdict on the parties involved.

Gabora, Spanos and Joab (1993) examined the effect of different forms of expert testimony on misconceptions about child sexual abuse. They found that mock jurors who heard expert evidence became less accepting of such misconceptions than those in a control condition who had not heard it. However, the type of information provided by the expert made a difference. When expert evidence was specifically directed at the case in hand, jurors were more inclined to convict and rated the defendant less credible than when they were exposed to general expert testimony. Kovera, Levy, Borgida and Penrod (1994) found that any form of expert evidence increased the likelihood of conviction in child sex abuse cases. However, syndrome evidence was less effective than evidence on child credibility.

Studying expert evidence in the context of a simulated rape trial, Marable (1999) showed that expert testimony addressing rape myths was more effective than testimony focusing on RTS in increasing mock jurors' confidence that the defendant was guilty. Schnopp-Wyatt (2000) showed that expert evidence that offered an opinion as to whether or not the complainant had been raped was more influential on verdicts than expert testimony that presented research findings or discussed hypothetical examples.

These studies show that the effectiveness of expert evidence can depend on its specific content, eg whether it focuses on syndrome evidence or on rape myths, and the form in which it is presented. But there is no guarantee that expert witnesses will clarify matters for the jury. Indeed, it is possible that they would introduce further complexity and uncertainty into an already ambiguous situation. This is true, in particular, for adversarial justice systems where the prosecution and defence introduce expert witnesses who deliver opposing messages (Brekke, Enko, Clavet and Seelau, 1991). Even where a defence expert is not used, defence cross-examination of the prosecution expert may dilute the effect on the jury of the expert's evidence. Indeed, in a study by Spanos, Dubreuil and Gwynn (1991–92), it was found that expert testimony dispelling rape myths made juries more likely to disbelieve the defendant's claim that sexual intercourse with the complainant was consensual and increased the frequency of guilty verdicts. However, this effect was obtained only when the expert testimony went unchallenged by the defence and disappeared when the expert was cross-examined by the defence.

In the United States, it has been suggested that there should be a move towards an inquisitorial use of expert evidence involving the appointment of experts by the court in an impartial role. In a study pitching testimony about rape trauma syndrome from an expert appointed by the court against an expert testifying for the prosecution, Brekke *et al* (1991) showed that non-adversarial expert testimony led to higher ratings of defendant responsibility and greater certainty that a rape had occurred than adversarial testimony, despite the fact that both experts were perceived as equally credible. Moreover, participants exposed to the non-adversarial testimony recalled more facts about the case than those hearing adversarial testimony, suggesting that the non-adversarial testimony elicited more systematic information processing.

From a psychological point of view, expert evidence must be evaluated against the background of cognitive biases and heuristic processing that affect jury decision-making. It can be effective only when it is processed systematically and has a chance to impinge on jurors' perceptions of a case before they have advanced hypotheses about the case on the basis of their general views and stereotypes of rape. Studies have shown that when the evidence is complex, jurors tend to rely on heuristic cues, such as the reputation and salary of the expert, in deciding whether to accept the information presented by the expert (McAuliff, Nemeth, Bornstein and Penrod, 2003). Thus, jurors' propensity for schematic as opposed to data-driven reasoning not only affects the way they evaluate the evidence presented to them by the prosecution and the defence, but their faith in the information provided by expert witnesses.

3.4 THE JUDGE'S SUMMING-UP AND NON-VERBAL CUES

A key element potentially affecting jurors as the trial proceeds is the judge. In England and Wales, the judge is actively involved in managing the evidence that is presented at trial. The judge's summing up of the case goes beyond instructing the jury on the law and includes a summary of and comments on the evidence that may sometimes give away the judge's views about the charge in question. This raises the question of the extent to which the jury's deliberations may be affected by their impressions of the judge's reasoning and opinions (Greene and Wrightsman, 2003: 409). Even though surveys show that jurors find the judge's summing-up useful, there is evidence that they are influenced in their verdicts by what they perceive to be the judge's stance for or against conviction (Zander and Henderson, 1993).

Beyond judges' explicit statements, research has shown that their non-verbal behaviour in the course of the trial may reveal their views on whether a defendant is guilty and, in turn, affect jury verdicts. In controlled simulations, jurors held a defendant less liable when the judge displayed pro-defendant non-verbal behaviours, such as smiling or nodding his head approvingly when turning to the defendant and shuffling his papers when the complainant's case was presented, than when he displayed such non-verbal signs in favour of the complainant (Collett and Kovera, 2003). Hart (1995) showed that jurors were influenced by non-verbal cues about defendant guilt or innocence even when asked to ignore the judge's behaviour and make up their own minds. Thus, there is reason to conclude that the judge's views about sexual assault may find some reflection in juror verdicts through both explicit and implicit forms of communication. To the extent that judges share prevalent stereotypes about rape, these can reinforce jurors' stereotypic beliefs and precipitate not guilty verdicts in cases departing from the real rape stereotype. To date, there are no systematic studies exploring judges' acceptance of rape myths and stereotypes, so it is hard to assess the seriousness of the problem. However, the interview data presented in chapter six will shed some light on this issue.

3.5 REACHING A VERDICT

The ultimate task of the jury is to reach a verdict, ie to arrive at a collective judgment about the guilt or innocence of the alleged offender. This verdict should be based on the law and evidence as it has been presented in the course of the trial and follow a process of rational decision-making. In this section, we try and shed light on the process of decision-making as conceptualised by different theoretical models. To understand the problems involved in jury decision-making about sexual assault as they affect the justice gap, it is useful to think in more general terms about the nature of the task a jury is expected to perform. Juries are typically asked to make judgments in conditions of uncertainty. They are therefore faced with the risk of error, either in convicting the innocent or in acquitting the guilty. In criminal cases, the standard of proof required for conviction is generally proof beyond reasonable doubt. Empirical studies summarised by Arkes and Mellers (2002) into what judges and jurors consider a probability 'beyond reasonable doubt' found that the average threshold was around 90 per cent, which is tantamount to the acceptance of a 10 per cent probability of convicting an innocent person. Arkes and Mellers' own study with a student sample found that the largest acceptable error rate for convictions was 5 per cent and for acquittals it was 8 per cent, indicating that people are slightly less willing to tolerate false convictions than false acquittals. While this research does not specifically address conviction and acquittal thresholds for rape charges, it may be seen as having some bearing on the justice gap. The general tendency to err on the side of false acquittals rather than on the side of false convictions may be bolstered by widely accepted attitudes that raise doubts about the guilt of an alleged offender by focusing on the question of victim blame.

Models of Juror Decision-Making

Several conceptual models have been put forward to describe the process of jury decision-making, each emphasising different ways in which complex information is integrated into a verdict. An influential psychological model explaining how jurors approach the task of reaching a verdict is the *Story Model* developed by Pennington and Hastie (1992). They argue that jurors try to make sense of the information presented in the course of a trial by incorporating it into a narrative structure, a 'story', that presents a plausible, coherent and complete account of the events in question. If the evidence is inconsistent or incomplete, competing stories may be generated. The story, or stories, are then related to the potential decision outcomes, the 'verdict' categories, that jurors are required to consider. The verdict is derived from comparing each story to the available verdict categories and selecting the verdict that provides the best 'fit' or match with the preferred story. The key elements of the decision-making process as conceptualised in the *Story Model* are presented in figure 3.1.

The model highlights the fact that jurors' decisions are the result of a complex construction process informed by both case-based and extra-legal information. If the case-based information is incomplete or contradictory, jurors draw on their accumulated world knowledge, including their general beliefs about the offence in question, their lay comprehension of the legal process and their understanding of how to construct a proper story, to infer the elements needed to make the story complete and coherent.

The *Story Model* is helpful as a framework for understanding jury decision-making in rape cases, where the information may be fragmented, disputed between the parties and focused on mental states (intentions, expectations, appraisals of the situation, consent) which jurors may find hard to infer. Depending on whether jurors give greater credence to the defence or the prosecution accounts, alternative stories result that match different verdicts. In this situation, jurors are likely to refer to their generalised views about plausible rape scenarios to decide which of the alternative stories to accept. For example, they may infer from the fact that the complainant had engaged in consensual

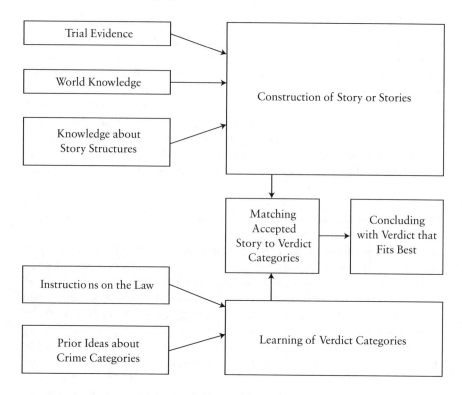

Figure 3.1 *The Story Model of jury decision-making*
(Adapted from Pennington and Hastie, 1992:191)·

sexual activities with the defendant on a previous occasion that the defendant might have reasonably assumed she consented to the sexual acts in question. The accepted story then determines which of the alternative verdicts (conviction versus acquittal) is selected. As Pennington and Hastie point out, the process of matching the story to a verdict also takes into account procedural instructions derived from the law. They found that jurors would apply the judge's instructions concerning the presumption of innocence and the requirement of proof beyond reasonable doubt to their chosen stories, returning not guilty verdicts where the story did not meet these requirements.

Olson-Fulero and Fulero (1997) applied the *Story Model* specifically to rape cases. They showed that certain undisputed facts presented in a rape trial were interpreted and utilised differently by those mock jurors who found the defendant guilty and those who found him not guilty. When asked to imagine how the events leading up to the alleged rape had unfolded, mock jurors who found the defendant not guilty mentioned the fact, confirmed by both parties, that the complainant had been drinking with the defendant earlier in the evening.

Participants who found the defendant guilty did not include this piece of information in their reconstruction of the events. The authors concluded 'that jurors come to the rape judgment situation with preconceptions and attitudes that lead them to entertain particular stories about what may have happened, that the stories are used to process the facts presented in the case, and that these stories are then used to arrive at a legal decision or verdict' (Olson-Fulero and Fulero, 1997: 418).

Findings from a study by Finch and Munro (2005a) on juror reasoning in rape cases involving intoxicants are also compatible with the *Story Model*. Using focus groups and a simulated jury trial, they found a strong tendency to blame the victim and deny that non-consensual intercourse amounted to rape, even in cases where the defendant had interfered with the woman's drink to bring about intoxication. Participants in this study constructed a story that held the woman responsible for her own safety and stressed her ability to give or withhold consent even under the influence of strong doses of intoxicants. The authors interpret their findings as showing that 'jurors frequently hold views that influence the attribution of blame and responsibility that are inconsistent with an accurate application of the law in rape cases' (Finch and Munroe, 2005a: 35).

The *Story Model* provides a general framework for explaining jury decision-making and the route through which jurors' everyday understanding is brought to bear on their decisions. Another useful conceptual framework for jury decision-making comes from the literature on persuasive communication (Bohner and Wänke, 2002), conceptualising the verdict as the result of a process of persuasive communication in which the prosecution and the defence each try to get their message across to the jurors.

Pieces of evidence presented during a trial can be seen as messages designed to persuade jurors to take a particular view of the events in question. According to dual-process models of persuasion, messages are processed in two different modes. In a *systematic* or central mode of processing, messages are carefully examined and then accepted, qualified or rejected. By contrast, in a *heuristic* or peripheral mode of processing, observers rely either on heuristic cues, such as the reputation of the source of the evidence, or alternatively on their own current mood, when evaluating the message and allow themselves to be influenced by it (Eagly and Chaiken, 1993; Petty and Cacioppo, 1986). Systematic processing requires greater cognitive effort and will only be engaged in when observers have the ability and the motivation to embark on this more demanding cognitive task. If they are unable or unwilling to devote cognitive energy to the appraisal of the information, they are likely to rely on schematic processing, following heuristic cues, such as their preconceived ideas about the offence and the parties involved. Time pressure is one factor undermining the ability to process information systematically. In a study by van Knippenberg, Dijksterhuis and Vermeulen (1999), mock jurors who were led to believe that a defendant in a criminal trial was either a drug addict with a previous conviction or a trustworthy and reliable bank employee responded to this information by finding the drug addict more likely to be guilty, but only when they were put under time pressure when reviewing the evidence. From a normative point of view, message processing in trials should be systematic, not heuristic. However, as shown above, juries were found to be influenced in their decision-making by peripheral, heuristic cues present in different stages of a trial, including their processing of expert evidence.

A final model that is useful for understanding juror judgments in rape cases is Alicke's *Culpable Control Model* (2000). According to this model, attributions of blame are not exclusively driven by cognitive assessments of the parties' causal role in an event but influenced by spontaneous emotional responses. An event can elicit both positive and negative emotional responses, but the negative responses are particularly relevant to the attribution of blame. Alicke assumes that observers will blame the party most who elicits the most negative reactions or confirms the most negative expectations, even though this may have little to do with that party's causal role in the events. The model has not yet been tested in relation to judgments about rape victims. However, it does suggest that complainants who conform to negative stereotypes about women, such as those encapsulated in rape myths, may be blamed more because they elicit negative evaluative responses from those who accept these views.

Legal Considerations: Objective versus Subjective Standards

The jury's verdict will depend on the relevant law as well as the evidence in the case. One important consideration is whether the law requires the defendant's thoughts or actions to be assessed subjectively, ie from the defendant's point of view, or objectively, ie from the point of view of the hypothetical 'reasonable man'.

Research studies have compared the impact of objective as against subjective standards of reasonableness in self-defence cases involving battered women who killed their abusive partners. These show that when jurors are asked to base their assessment of reasonableness not on the hypothetical 'reasonable person' but on their understanding of the subjective situation of the defendant, they arrive at different verdicts. Verdicts of 'not guilty' were significantly more likely if jurors were instructed to adopt a subjective rather than an objective standard of reasonableness (Follingstad, Shillinglaw, DeHart and Kleinfelter, 1997; Terrance, Matheson and Spanos, 2000). A possible explanation is that the subjective standard instruction enhances empathy with the defendant because it requires jurors to put themselves in her situation. The more jurors empathise with the defendant, the more likely it is that they will consider her assessment of the situation to be valid and accept her claim to self-defence.

In England and Wales, the determination of reasonableness is also now relevant in sexual assault cases in determining the required mental element for rape. Under Section I of the SOA 2003, it must be proved that the defendant did not reasonably believe that the complainant consented. Whether a belief is reasonable is to be determined having regard to all the circumstances including any steps the defendant has taken to ascertain consent. Since reasonableness is to be gauged from all the circumstances, this means that the defendant's own circumstances or personal characteristics may be taken into account. The test of reasonableness is thus subjective/objective rather than purely objective. In a mock jury study, this subjective/objective test 'generated considerable leniency towards the defendant', far more so than had the test been purely objective (Finch and Munro, 2006: 317). This was because the subjective requirement caused jurors to fall back on classic stereotypes about rape on the ground that the defendant's own thinking might have been influenced by them. On the other hand, jurors who applied 'an unmodified objective standard [. . .] generally held the defendant to a higher standard of care and responsibility' (Finch and Munro, 2006: 317). Thus, it appears that introducing an element of subjectivity into the issue of determining a defendant's belief in consent is likely to raise the conviction threshold.

Juror Attitudes

It is clear that jurors do not leave their long-held attitudes behind in the cloakroom when they enter a court of law, and the models discussed previously present different ways in which individuals refer to preconceived attitudes when asked to make decisions about criminal offences. Ellsworth (1993), in the context of research into juries and the death penalty in the United States, has argued that attitudes impinge on verdicts in three ways: by affecting jurors' perceptions of witness credibility, by guiding their construction of a plausible 'story' to account for the evidence and finally by affecting their threshold of what has been established 'beyond reasonable doubt'. Even though this research does not deal with sexual assault, it is relevant to the analysis of the justice gap in sexual assault cases in that it highlights the impact of jurors' preconceived attitudes on their decisions. As shown in chapter two, there is ample evidence that stereotypical views and prejudicial attitudes about rape victims are widespread and that they influence opinions about specific cases. Thus, individuals adhering to rape myths may be less likely to find the complainant credible (particularly if the case does not conform to the real rape stereotype), may be more likely to construct a story in line with the defendant's version of events and be less willing to convict.

The rationale underlying jury trials is 'to allow community standards and values of fairness and equity to be a part of legal decisions through citizen participation' (Vidmar, 2005: 137). But there is a downside to this. If community views about the offence in question are at odds with characteristics of the case they are called on to decide, principles of fairness and equity may be compromised. Jurors come to a trial with particular mental representations or 'prototypes' of the offence in question. A prototype describes the most typical exemplar of a criminal offence, one that best represents the characteristics which are thought to be typical of the offence. The real rape stereotype can be seen as a prototypical representation of the criminal offence of rape shared by a large number of people. Studies have shown that lay prototypes of offences may overlap, but seldom completely match the legal definitions, and that mock jurors are more likely to convict a defendant the closer the case is to the prototype of the offence (Smith, 1991).

The influence of attitudes on decision-making within the criminal justice system is demonstrated by research on racial and ethnic prejudice. Both in Britain and in North America, members of black ethnic communities are disproportionately likely to be stopped by police and charged, tried and convicted for criminal offences compared with members of the white majority (eg Clancy, Hough, Aust and Kershaw, 2001; Sommers and Ellsworth, 2001; US Department of Justice, 2006). Racial prejudice has been cited as a factor explaining this finding and a number of experimental studies support this claim. In a recent meta-analysis, Mitchell, Haw, Pfeifer and Meissner (2005) found a significant tendency by white mock jurors to treat black defendants more harshly than white defendants, especially in the absence of instructions from the judge. However, they also found that black jurors show greater harshness towards white defendants. This points to the operation of a general in-group bias whereby members of one's own group tend to be judged more leniently than out-group members. Stephan (1974) reported a similar in-group bias for gender, with participants judging defendants of the same gender more leniently. The large body of evidence on men's more lenient judgments of rape defendants discussed in chapter two can also be seen as a case in point. Several studies have demonstrated that jurors' in-group biases, be they defined along racial or gender lines, seem to operate primarily when case-based evidence or instructions from the judge are ambiguous (eg Pfeifer and Ogloff, 1991). A racial in-group bias in a rape case was found only when the evidence presented was marginally as opposed to strongly indicative of the defendant's guilt (Ugwuegbu, 1979). When jurors are aware of racial or gender issues involved in the case or when the evidence is clear-cut, jurors appear to be able to control and suppress their prejudiced attitudes. But, so often in rape cases the evidence is less than clear-cut, with the result that prejudiced attitudes are more likely to surface.

The impact of rape-related attitudes on case-based decisions is clearly present in jury decision-making about rape cases, reflected in the finding that jurors' adherence to rape myths correlated more strongly with a verdict than the objective evidence presented about the case (LaFree, 1989). Referring to a 'cycle of blame', Sinclair and Bourne (1998) stressed that jurors' decisions are not only influenced by stereotypic beliefs about rape, they also serve to reinforce these very beliefs. They state: 'What comes from a jury in a rape case is more than just a conviction or acquittal: the jury decision also contributes to a definition of what constitutes "real rape"' (p 577). If cases deviating from the real rape stereotype are more likely to end in an acquittal, this verdict strengthens the widely held view that cases less close to the stereotype are not really rape.

3.6 SUMMARY AND CONCLUSIONS

This chapter has reviewed evidence from a wide-ranging literature applying psychological research to the analysis of jury decision-making. It is clear that many of the problems affecting jury decision-making in general are evident in decision-making about sexual assault to the same, if not to a greater extent. There is overwhelming consensus among psycho-legal scholars that the conceptualisation of jurors as rational decision-makers embarking on a fact-finding mission based on the rules of logic and the principles of law is not a valid representation of what happens in jury trials. Instead, jurors are affected in their decision-making by a host of extra-legal influences, including the attitudes they bring to the trial, their emotional responses to the case and the difficulty they experience in focusing strictly on the evidence that is legally relevant. In combination, these factors are likely to introduce bias into the way jurors process information about a case, particularly when the case-based evidence is incomplete or inconclusive.

In order to address jurors' biases and lead them to a more appropriate assessment of the case, expert testimony has been seen by many as a viable strategy. However, the use of expert evidence in rape cases is not a straightforward matter. The exact form and content which expert evidence should take have been matters of controversy. The legal requirement that expert testimony be scientifically valid and reliable demands careful assessment of the available knowledge base. As a result of this, in American courts the original focus of expert testimony on the Rape Trauma Syndrome (RTS) has been replaced by the more generally defined Post-Traumatic Stress Disorder (PTSD). Studies have shown that expert evidence adduced by the prosecution can be effective in dispelling jurors' misconceptions in sexual assault cases but that this depends very much on the manner of its presentation. Its effect may be seriously diluted by defence cross-examination or the appointment of a defence expert. Moreover, biases affecting the way jurors process the evidence in a case may also affect their reception of expert testimony. Chapters eight and nine will return to these issues and discuss potential strategies for improving jury performance.

Part II

New Evidence

4

A Question of Attitude: Prospective Lawyers

IN CHAPTERS ONE, two and three, past research on the nature and extent of the justice gap in sexual assault trials was examined together with research showing how attitudes and cognitive biases impact on judgments about rape. An impressive body of evidence has been generated demonstrating distortions in information processing about rape and illuminating the cognitive and affective processes underlying these judgments. At the same time, the review of the literature has identified some limitations and open questions. The new studies presented in this part of the book were designed to take forward existing research by looking at the attitudes of prospective lawyers as they affect their decision-making about rape incidents, and by exploring the attitudes and judgments of a large sample of members of the public eligible for jury service. The aim was also to evaluate the effectiveness of a mass media campaign designed to challenge rape stereotypes and emphasise the importance of consent. These studies add to the existing evidence by providing a systematic analysis of the single and joint contributions of case characteristics on the one hand, and the preconceived attitudes of participants on the other. In their focus on markedly under-researched groups with potential involvement in the processing of rape cases within the criminal justice system, the studies provide a new contribution to the research in this area.

In chapters four and five, the influence of rape-related stereotypes on judgments about rape cases is explored in three studies using quantitative data obtained from undergraduate law students (Study 1), graduate students training to be lawyers (Study 2) and members of the general public who are eligible for jury service (Study 3) to test the proposition that the justice gap is due in some measure to the influence of extra-legal factors, particularly attitudes towards rape.[1] The aim of these studies was to obtain a picture of the extent to which judgments about rape cases are influenced by attitudes that lead individuals to be responsive to extra-legal factors and to pay less attention to case-based information. The third study also includes an evaluation of a Home Office poster campaign designed to challenge rape stereotypes and raise awareness about the importance of ensuring consent to sex. In chapters six and seven, this

---

[1] This research was supported by a grant from the German Research Foundation (Kr 972/7–1).

quantitative research is complemented by findings from a qualitative study involving in-depth interviews with a sample of judges and barristers.

The two studies described in this chapter looked at the extent to which prospective legal professionals subscribe to rape myths and stereotypes and the way in which information provided about a rape case interacts with these pre-conceived attitudes. In both studies, participants' general beliefs about rape were measured and then related to the way they judged specific hypothetical rape cases. A series of rape scenarios was developed which enabled systematic variation of the information about the complainant and defendant.[2] As argued in chapter two, this widely-used methodology provides a degree of experimental control that cannot be achieved in a naturalistic context using real-life cases. In Study 1, undergraduate law students were asked to make judgments about defendant and complainant responsibility in a series of different sexual assault scenarios involving the use of physical violence. The scenarios varied with respect to complainant-defendant relationship. Study 2 was conducted with graduate students attending vocational training courses to become lawyers. It broadened the range of case scenarios by additionally including assaults in which the defendant exploited the complainant's inability to resist due to intoxication.

The general hypothesis underlying our quantitative studies was that the more a particular case differed from the features laid down in the real rape stereotype in the shape of a violent rape by a stranger, the less likely it was that the defendant would be regarded as criminally liable and the more likely that the complainant would be blamed. It was further assumed that individuals holding stereotypical views about rape would be more responsive to information that was at odds with the real rape stereotype, such as information about a previous sexual relationship between the parties or the absence of physical resistance, than those not endorsing such views. Support for these hypotheses would strengthen our claim that an important reason why many rape complaints do not end in convictions is because they fail to meet *a priori* assumptions about what amounts to a 'proper' rape case.

4.1 STUDY 1: UNDERGRADUATE LAW STUDENTS AND THE REAL RAPE STEREOTYPE

The purpose of this study was to examine the extent to which a sample of under-graduate law students was guided by the real rape stereotype in their judgments of defendants and complainants in clear-cut cases of rape where the complainant expressed her non-consent and the defendant used force. Participants were presented with five separate rape scenarios, each involving different situations and characters. In one scenario, the complainant and defendant were

---

[2] Rather than 'perpetrator' and 'victim', the neutral terms 'defendant' and 'complainant' will be used throughout this chapter.

complete strangers and it thus conformed to the real rape stereotype. In two scenarios the defendant and complainant were acquaintances, and in a further two they were former sexual partners. Following each scenario, participants were asked to attribute blame to the defendant and to the complainant and to indicate how certain they were that what had occurred met the legal definition of rape. The extent to which each participant accepted rape myths (RMA) was separately measured by using a subscale of Cowan and Quinton's *Perceived Causes of Rape Scale* (see chapter two). This scale focuses on perceived 'female precipitation' as a cause of rape, ie the belief that women bring sexual assault on themselves by the way they behave or dress.

As noted in chapter two, many studies have found that men are more likely than women to blame the complainant and less likely to blame the defendant. However, we suggested there that it is not gender *per se*, but men's greater acceptance of rape myths that accounts for this difference. In Study 1, both the gender and the female precipitation beliefs of the participants were considered. This enabled us to examine whether the relationship between gender and attributions of blame is indeed mediated by female precipitation beliefs.

The study aimed to test out three hypotheses:

Hypothesis 1. It was predicted that the closer the relationship between the defendant and complainant prior to the sexual assault, the less blame would be attributed to the defendant, the more blame would be attributed to the complainant, and the less certain participants would be that the incident was rape in the legal sense of the term.

Hypothesis 2. It was predicted that individuals' beliefs in female precipitation would be more closely related to judgments about a rape case the less the case conformed to the real rape stereotype, as represented by the stranger rape.

Hypothesis 3. It was predicted that men would attribute more blame to the complainant and less blame to the defendant than women and would be less certain that an incident met the legal definition of rape. This was assumed to be due to men's greater acceptance of female precipitation beliefs.

Participants

A sample of 74 third-year undergraduate law students at a university in the south of England (32 men and 42 women, mean age 22.4 years) took part in the study on a voluntary basis. Participants had learnt about the law of rape in their second year criminal law course.

Experimental Materials and Measures

Rape Scenarios

Participants were presented with five different rape scenarios. In one, complainant and defendant were complete strangers; in two there was said to have been a prior sexual relationship which had ended before the assault took place; in a further two they were acquaintances without any prior sexual relationship. All scenarios clearly stated that (a) sexual intercourse had taken place through the use of force by the defendant, (b) the complainant had explicitly communicated her non-consent and (c) the complainant had shown active physical resistance to fight off the defendant's advances. An example of the scenarios is presented in table 4.1.

Following each scenario, participants were asked for their assessment of the extent to which the defendant and the complainant were to blame for what happened and to state how certain they were that a rape in the legal sense had been committed.[3]

Table 4.1

Study 1: Example of the rape scenarios – prior sexual relationship

Early one evening last November, Sue was strolling round a bric-a-brac street market. Most of the sellers were already packing up their stalls when Sue, an amateur painter herself, discovered some paintings she liked. The artist turned out to be Bill with whom she had had a 'one-night stand' ten years ago but had not seen since. Bill was pleased to see her again, and they started talking about painting. It was getting later and later, and they decided to continue their conversation in a nearby café. They talked about all sorts of things. Sue was fascinated by the personality of the young painter and felt strongly attracted to him. He also seemed to find her attractive, and after a while, they started kissing. Sue felt flattered by his attentions. Several hours went by and they suddenly realised they were the last customers. They paid their bill, and he walked her home where she asked him in. Once inside her flat, he started kissing her again, but in a more demanding way. Sue began to feel uneasy. She pushed him back and asked him to leave. He got angry and told her not to make a fuss, since after all she had asked him into her flat which was clearly an offer to have sex. She was shocked by this remark and asked him to leave immediately. As she tried to open the front door, he grabbed her and pushed her against the door. He put his hand over her mouth and, despite her attempts at fighting him off, he had sexual intercourse with her. When questioned by the police, Bill denied rape and said that Sue consented. He told them that Sue compensated for her failure as an artist by having numerous sexual relationships with other artists.

---

[3] To rule out the possibility that the order in which the scenarios were presented had an effect on how participants judged the individual scenarios, the order of presentation was systematically varied. Five versions of the questionnaire were created in which each scenario appeared once in each position from first to fifth. The female precipitation measure was presented after the case scenarios in all versions.

Measuring Defendant Blame

In order to measure how much participants blamed the defendant, they were asked to respond to the following four questions: (a) 'How much do you think D [defendant's name] is to blame for the incident?'; (b) 'How much do you think D had control over the situation?'; (c) 'How strongly do you think that D ought to be held criminally liable for rape?'; (d) 'How likely do you think it is that D thought C [complainant's name] consented to have sex with him?' Participants were asked to respond using a seven-point scale ranging from (1) = not at all to (7) = very much.

Complainant Blame

In order to measure how much participants blamed the complainant, they were asked to respond to the following four questions: (a) 'How much do you think C [complainant's name] is to blame for what happened?'; (b) 'How much do you think C had control over the situation?'; (c) 'How likely do you think it is that C could have avoided the incident?'; (d) 'How sorry do you feel for C?' Participants were asked to respond using the same seven-point scale as above.

Certainty of Rape

In order to measure how certain participants were that a rape in the legal sense had taken place, they were asked the following question: 'How certain are you that the incident is rape in the legal sense of the term?' Again, participants were asked to respond using the same seven-point scale.

Female Precipitation Beliefs

Participants' endorsement of female precipitation as a cause of rape was measured by the Female Precipitation subscale of the 'Perceived Causes of Rape Scale' (PCRS) devised by Cowan and Quinton (1997). Participants were asked to indicate how much they endorsed each of the following six propositions:

> Rape is caused by: (1) women who tease men; (2) women who allow men to intimately touch them; (3) women's use of drugs or alcohol; (4) women who dress sexy; (5) women allowing the situation to get out of control; and (6) women who do unsafe things (such as being out alone, hitch-hiking).

They indicated their agreement with each statement using a seven-point scale ranging from (1) = strongly disagree to (7) = strongly agree.

Results

For each scenario, mean scores were computed across the four items of the defendant blame and complainant blame measures.[4] Acquaintance rape and rape by a former sexual partner were each represented by two scenarios. Ratings of defendant blame, complainant blame and rape certainty did not differ between the scenarios within each of the two categories of acquaintance and ex-partner rapes and were therefore combined. Responses to the six items of the Female Precipitation scale were also averaged into an overall score. The mean endorsement of female precipitation beliefs was 3.12 (on a scale of 1 = completely disagree to 7 = completely agree),[5] and 32.4 per cent of participants had average scores above the midpoint of the scale, ie tended towards the 'agreement' side of the response scale.

The study was based on a two-factorial design. The first factor was participant gender, the second factor was defendant-complainant relationship (stranger, acquaintance, ex-partner). The impact of these factors was studied on three dependent variables: (1) defendant blame, (2) complainant blame and (3) certainty that the incident was rape.

Hypothesis 1 predicted that participants would blame the defendant less, be more uncertain that the incident was rape and blame the complainant more the closer the prior relationship between the two. Statistically significant differences

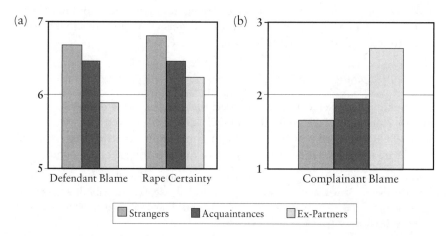

Figure 4.1 *Study 1: Attributions of defendant blame and rape certainty ratings (a) and complainant blame (b) as a function of defendant–complainant relationship*

---

[4] Internal consistencies for the resulting scales were good, with Cronbach's Alphas ranging from .73 to .83.

[5] $SD = 1.46$; $\alpha = .87$; scale range 1–7.

were found that fully support the hypothesis.[6] The means are presented in figure 4.1.

As predicted, less blame was attributed to the defendant and more blame was attributed to the complainant the closer the relationship between the two prior to the alleged attack. Furthermore, participants were less certain that a rape had occurred the closer the relationship between complainant and defendant.

Hypothesis 2 predicted that individuals' beliefs in female precipitation would be more closely related to judgments about a rape case the less the case conformed to the real rape stereotype. Table 4.2 shows the correlations between female precipitation beliefs and perceptions of defendant blame, complainant blame and certainty that the incident was rape in the three complainant-perpetrator relationships.

Table 4.2

Study 1: Correlation of female precipitation beliefs with attributions of defendant blame, complainant blame and rape certainty ratings[7]

	Defendant blame	Complainant blame	Rape certainty
Strangers	.01 [a]	.44*** [a]	−.05 [a]
Acquaintances	−.35** [b]	.59*** [a]	−.37*** [b]
Ex-partners	−.59*** [c]	.74*** [b]	−.45*** [b]

** $p < .01$, *** $p < .001$

In line with our prediction, the lowest correlations between female precipitation beliefs and judgments of defendant blame, complainant blame and rape certainty were found for the stranger rape. Neither defendant blame nor rape certainty ratings correlated with female precipitation beliefs when the defendant was a stranger. However, even in this clear-cut 'classic' case, the complainant was seen as significantly more to blame by individuals endorsing female precipitation beliefs. This demonstrates the pervasive influence of rape myths as found in previous research (see chapter two). For the acquaintance rape scenarios, female precipitation beliefs were significantly correlated with ratings of defendant blame, complainant blame and rape certainty. The more participants believed in female precipitation as a cause of rape, the more they blamed the complainant, the less they blamed the defendant and the less certain they were that the incident was rape. As predicted, the highest correlations were found for

---

[6] A multivariate analysis of variance was computed with repeated measures on the relationship factor. The analysis yielded a significant multivariate effect of defendant-complainant relationship, $F (6,66) = 15.55$, $p < .001$, and all three univariate effects were significant, Fs between 15.00 and 39.61, $p < .001$. For each dependent variable, all three means were significantly different at $p < .01$.

[7] Within columns, coefficients with different superscripts are significantly different at $p < .05$, based on Steiger's Z for overlapping correlated rs.

the ex-partner rape scenarios. Perceptions of defendant blame, complainant blame and rape certainty were significantly more affected by female precipitation beliefs when the defendant was a former partner than when he was an acquaintance or stranger. Altogether, the findings lend conclusive support to Hypothesis 2 by showing that female precipitation beliefs become more influential the more a particular case differs from the real rape stereotype, working against the likelihood of finding the defendant guilty.

In support of Hypothesis 3, men attributed less blame to the defendant and more blame to the complainant, as shown in figure 4.2.[8] However, men were no less certain than women that the incident was rape. Information about defendant-complainant relationship influenced men's and women's perceptions in a parallel fashion.[9] Both gender groups blamed the defendant less, were less certain that the incident was rape, and blamed the complainant more the closer the relationship between the parties.

The final analysis examined the proposition that men's greater readiness to blame the complainant and exonerate the defendant was due to their greater acceptance of rape myths, in particular female precipitation beliefs. This hypothesis regards female precipitation beliefs as a *mediator* between participant gender and attributions of blame as well as rape certainty ratings (Baron and Kenny, 1986). To support the mediation hypothesis, four requirements have to be met:

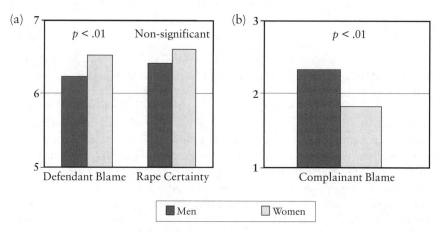

Figure 4.2 *Study 1: Gender differences in attributions of defendant blame and rape certainty ratings (a) and complainant blame (b).*

---

[8] The MANOVA showed a significant multivariate effect of gender $F(3,69) = 3.57$, $p < .05$. The univariate effects for defendant blame and complainant blame were significant, Fs between 7.84 and 8.74, $p < .01$, but the univariate effect for rape certainty was not. The interaction between participant gender and defendant-complainant relationship was non-significant.

[9] The interaction of gender and defendant-complainant relationship was non-significant.

1. Gender must be significantly related to female precipitation beliefs. In a preliminary analysis, this was found to be the case. Men scored higher ($M =$ 3.53) on female precipitation beliefs than women ($M = 2.83$).[10]
2. Female precipitation beliefs must be linked to ratings of blame and rape certainty. This was also found to be the case, as shown in table 4.2 (see p 81).
3. Gender must be related to ratings of blame and rape certainty. Gender was found to be related to defendant and complainant blame, as shown in figure 4.2, but not to rape certainty ratings which were therefore excluded from the mediation analysis.
4. Finally, the critical evidence for the mediation effect is that the direct links between gender and the ratings of defendant and complainant blame disappear or become weaker when female precipitation beliefs are included in the analyses.

Figure 4.3 presents the results pertaining to the mediation hypothesis.[11]

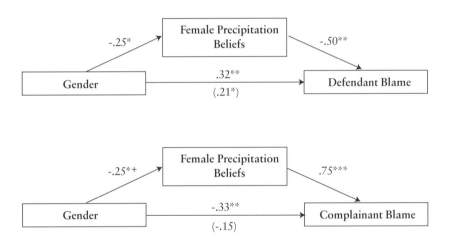

Figure 4.3 *Female precipitation beliefs as a mediator between participant gender and attributions of blame*

Note: Positive paths from gender indicate higher scores for women; negative paths indicate higher scores for men. The figures in parentheses denote the coefficients when female precipitation beliefs were included in the analyses.

---

[10] $t(72) = 2.14, p < .05$.
[11] A series of regression analyses was conducted to test the mediation hypothesis. Participant gender was included in the analyses as a dummy variable coded (-1) for men and (+1) for women, so negative paths indicate that men scored higher than women on the respective measure. Attributions of blame to the defendant and to the complainant were averaged across the three defendant-complainant relationships to create overall scores of defendant and complainant blame for the mediation analyses.

As predicted, the direct path from participant gender to attributions of blame decreased both for defendant and complainant blame when female precipitation beliefs were added to the model, supporting the mediation hypothesis.[12] The findings thus support the proposition that men's greater tendency to blame the complainant and exonerate the defendant can be explained at least in part by the fact that they are more likely to think that women precipitate rape through their appearance or behaviour.

Discussion

This study was designed as the first in a series of empirical investigations into the influence of rape stereotypes on judgments about specific rape cases. It aimed to test whether law students who had undergone two years of under-graduate training were affected in their judgments about rape scenarios by the real rape stereotype, particularly if they subscribed to female precipitation myths. It was found that participants judged the role of the defendant and the complainant differently in the acquaintance and ex-partner cases compared with the stranger rape scenario. In the acquaintance rape scenarios, they saw the defendant as less blameworthy, attributed more blame to the complainant and were less certain that the incident was rape than in the classic stranger rape. In the ex-partner rapes, they were even less inclined to blame the defendant and to regard the incident as rape and were more inclined to blame the complainant. Yet all the scenarios involved the use of force by the defendant as well as active physical resistance and a clear verbal statement of non-consent by the complainant.

The study also found that a substantial proportion of participants expressed some agreement with female precipitation beliefs. This made them more responsive to information about a previous relationship between the complainant and the defendant, reflected in an increase in attributions of blame to the complainant, a decrease in attributions of blame to the defendant and a decreased certainty of rape. While participants' female precipitation beliefs did not play much of a role when they were asked to judge the stranger rape, they affected judgments of the acquaintance rapes and were particularly influential in the ex-partner rapes. Individuals endorsing female precipitation beliefs entertain a stereotypic conception of rape that predisposes them to seize on any information highlighting the woman's potential responsibility for an assault. The information that the complainant had engaged in interactions with the defendant on an acquaintance basis or even in a previous consensual sexual relationship is used by these individuals as a cue that indicates her precipitating role.

---

[12]   Sobel tests indicated that the reduction in the direct link due to including female precipitation as a mediator was significant in both cases, Sobel test scores of 1.91, $p < .05$, for defendant blame and -2.08, $p < .05$, for complainant blame (Sobel, 1982).

The present findings suggest that this cue overrides the impact of other elements of the evidence, such as physical resistance and the use of force by the defendant, that clearly speak against complainant precipitation.

Finally, the findings of Study 1 address the issue of gender differences in judgments of rape cases. In line with many other studies (see chapter two), we found that men were more inclined than women to blame the complainant and saw the defendant as less blameworthy. Our findings traced this gender difference back to an underlying difference in the acceptance of female precipitation beliefs, shown to be greater in men than in women.

The responses of the students in Study 1 were highly similar to those of undergraduate students in a parallel study conducted in Germany (Krahé, Temkin and Bieneck, 2007). The English students had studied law for two years and had received specific instruction about the law of rape and sexual assault. However, they proved to be no less susceptible than the German students, who had received no specific instruction about the law of rape, to the schematic processing of the case material on the basis of rape stereotypes.

4.2 STUDY 2: SCHEMATIC PROCESSING BY VOCATIONAL LAW STUDENTS

Study 1 found evidence of schematic processing on the basis of rape stereotypes among final year undergraduate law students who were asked to judge the defendant and complainant in specific rape scenarios. It might be argued that their reliance on stereotypes at the expense of a more data-driven appraisal of the evidence was due to their limited professional knowledge and that this problem might diminish with their exposure to professional training. If this training could be shown to lead to more data-based scrutiny of the evidence, then the finding that third-year law students were susceptible to schematic processing of rape cases would not be a reason for great concern. To address this possibility, Study 2 was conducted with a sample of graduate students engaged in vocational training to enter the legal profession in England and Wales. In terms of legal knowledge, this group was more heterogeneous than the undergraduate students since many were studying for the Graduate Diploma in Law.[13] However, unlike the undergraduate law students, not all of whom would go on to train to enter the legal profession, these graduate students were enrolled in professional courses intended to lead them into a legal career. Even though only a proportion were likely to practise in the area of criminal law, they came from the general pool from which CPS prosecutors, solicitors, barristers and eventually judges involved in rape trials are drawn. Therefore, exploring their attitudes in relation to sexual assault and the relationship of these attitudes to judgments

---

[13] The Graduate Diploma in Law is a course designed for students with a first degree other than in law who wish to enter the legal profession.

made about specific cases has some relevance in terms of understanding and explaining the justice gap.

The first aim of the study was to examine whether these prospective legal professionals would be influenced to a similar or to a lesser extent by information about a past relationship between the defendant and the complainant and would be equally or less likely to bring their beliefs about female precipitation to bear on judgments about the cases than the third-year undergraduates in Study 1.

The second aim was to extend the range of rape scenarios to include situations where the complainant was affected by alcohol and unable to resist. In Study 1, the case scenarios all involved unambiguous information as to the non-consensual nature of the sexual acts, namely use of force by the defendant and physical resistance by the complainant. Cases where the woman is too affected by alcohol to resist provide even more room for schematic notions to be employed (see also chapter two). Based on this line of reasoning, scenarios in which the defendant used physical force were compared with scenarios in which the defendant exploited the fact that the complainant had expressed her non-consent to his sexual advances but was incapacitated by alcohol and unable to resist. In England and Wales, the legal definition of rape does not only cover the use of force by the defendant, but extends to any situation where the complainant does not consent (see chapter one). Thus, in legal terms, there is no differentiation between the two coercive strategies. However, evidence about the real rape stereotype suggests that 'commonsense' definitions of rape do make such a distinction. Past research has shown that when the complainant is intoxicated at the time of the assault, the case is considered less credible and is less likely to lead to a guilty verdict than where the complainant is sober at the time of the attack (Krahé, Temkin and Bieneck, 2007; see also chapter two). It was therefore predicted that ratings relating to the defendant and complainant would vary as a function of whether the defendant used force or exploited the complainant's alcohol-induced incapacitation.

A third objective of the study was to look more closely at participants' assessments of the criminal liability of the defendant than was the case in Study 1. To achieve this, participants were asked to indicate how certain they were that the incident was rape, to assess the defendant's criminal liability for rape, to give a verdict and to recommend an appropriate sentence if they considered him to be guilty.

Finally, the study sought to address the question of whether female precipitation beliefs are indeed causally related to judgments about defendant liability and complainant blame. It might be argued that both female precipitation beliefs and judgments about defendants and complainants could be driven by a third variable that is the causal factor behind both. This interpretation, which cannot be ruled out by the analyses in Study 1, would undermine our proposition that female precipitation beliefs are causally responsible for the tendency to exonerate the defendant and blame the complainant.

Bohner, Reinhard, Rutz, Sturm, Kerschbaum and Effler (1998) have developed a way of testing the causal influence of rape myths. They reason that if one group of study participants have rape myths brought to the forefront of their minds by asking them to complete a rape myth questionnaire and if they are *then* asked to make judgments about rape, the impact of rape myths on those judgments should be greater than in a comparison group where this process takes place in the reverse order. In their study, they asked men (a) to complete a questionnaire measuring rape myth acceptance, which would bring rape myths to their attention, and (b) to indicate the likelihood that they would sexually assault a woman. One group of participants completed the rape myth acceptance questionnaire *before*, the other group *after* indicating the likelihood of their raping a woman. In the first group, a closer association between rape myth acceptance and likelihood of raping was predicted and found than in the second group (see also Bohner, Jarvis, Eyssel and Siebler, 2005). This indicates that making men think about rape myths lowers the threshold for sexual aggression in those who are inclined to accept the myths as true, pointing to a causal influence of rape myth acceptance on subsequent judgments. In Study 2, this approach was used to test whether female precipitation beliefs are more closely linked to judgments of defendant liability and complainant blame if they are brought to the attention of participants before rather than after they are asked to make judgments about the case scenarios.

Thus, aiming to replicate and extend the findings from Study 1, Study 2 sought to test out five hypotheses:

Hypothesis 1. It was predicted that vocational law students who were asked to assess rape scenarios would be less inclined to hold the defendant liable, recommend shorter sentences and assign more blame to the complainant in scenarios where there was a previous relationship between the two parties. The defendant would be least likely to be considered liable and the shortest sentence would be recommended in the ex-partner rape, followed by the acquaintance and stranger rapes. Most blame would be attributed to the complainant in the ex-partner rape, followed by the acquaintance rape, and least blame would be attributed to her in the stranger rape.

Hypothesis 2. This hypothesis predicted that certainty of defendant liability as well as recommended sentences would be lower and perceptions of complainant blame would be higher when the defendant exploited the complainant's incapacitated state and her resulting inability to resist as compared with cases in which physical force was used. Participants were expected to be more responsive to information about prior defendant-complainant relationship in the alcohol-related rapes than in the force scenarios. The closer the previous relationship, the more participants would be inclined in the alcohol-related rapes to reduce their ratings of defendant liability and the sentences they would recommend for the defendant if he was found guilty and to increase their ratings of complainant blame.

Hypothesis 3. This hypothesis predicted that the more participants subscribed to the belief that women precipitate rape, the less they would be inclined to hold the defendant liable, the shorter the sentence they would recommend and the more they would be inclined to blame the complainant. It was predicted that the impact of female precipitation beliefs would be greater in cases involving the exploitation of the victim's intoxicated state than in cases involving the use of force. Female precipitation beliefs were expected to drive perceptions about the defendant and complainant to a greater extent the closer their previous relationship.

Hypothesis 4. Concerning the role of gender, it was predicted that men would be less inclined than women to hold the defendant legally liable, would recommend shorter sentences and would be more inclined to blame the complainant, and that this difference would be attributable to their greater adherence to female precipitation beliefs. The gender difference was expected to be greater in the alcohol-related cases and in the cases involving a previous relationship between the defendant and the complainant.

Hypothesis 5. The final prediction referred to the causal influence of female precipitation beliefs on judgments about the cases. It predicted that female precipitation beliefs measured *before* the presentation of the rape scenarios would be more closely related to ratings of defendant liability, recommended sentences and complainant blame than these beliefs measured *after* the case scenarios.

Participants

A sample of 121 graduate students who were attending vocational law courses at a London college participated in the study. Forty-seven were men, 72 were women, two failed to indicate their sex. The average age was 26.3 years. Forty-three per cent of participants held a first degree in law, 33.9 per cent had a first degree in the humanities (mostly history and English literature), 9.1 per cent were science graduates and 11.6 per cent had a first degree in business studies or politics. Three participants (2.4 per cent) failed to indicate their first degree. Participants were invited via the college email list to take part in a study on impression formation about sexual assault cases. They completed the questionnaire during a session scheduled at the college and received a payment of £5.00.

Experimental Materials and Measures

Rape scenarios

Six rape scenarios were used in the study, each with different situations and characters. All contained a clear statement of the complainant's non-consent but varied with regard to complainant-defendant relationship prior to the assault (stranger, acquaintance without a sexual relationship, ex-sexual partners). They also differed in terms of the coercive strategy used by the defendant. Three scenarios involved the use of force by the defendant, taken from Study 1. Three new scenarios were added in which the defendant exploited the complainant's incapacitated state. In each of these, the complainant had consumed moderate amounts of alcohol but, because she was not used to drinking, was disproportionately affected by it (feeling sick and dizzy). There was no indication in the scenarios that the assailant had intentionally made the complainant drunk, but it was expressly stated that he took advantage of her alcohol-induced incapacitation. Table 4.3 provides an example of the alcohol-related scenarios.

Table 4.3

Study 2: Example of the rape scenarios involving complainant intoxication – ex-partners

Mary and John had broken up a little while ago after a three-year relationship, but they kept in touch and met up occasionally. For Mary's birthday, her friends planned a surprise party at her house. They invited many people (including John), and the party was a great success. Mary and John enjoyed each other's company. They laughed about memories from the time when they were still together, they danced a lot and also flirted a little bit. Mary's friends had converted a table into a cocktail bar, and one of them mixed Caipirinhas. Mary, who was not used to drinking, soon felt rather tipsy. It was almost morning when the last guests said goodbye, with John being the only one to stay behind. He offered to help Mary with the clearing-up, but Mary was so drunk that she was unable to do any of it, so John cleared the whole place up himself. When he had finished, he carried Mary into her bedroom, lay her down on her bed and took her clothes off. When he saw her lying there naked and sleeping, he took his own clothes off, lay down next to her and had sexual intercourse with her. Mary woke up when she felt his body on top of her and asked him to stop, but he took no notice and she was too drunk to stop him. After agonising about what to do for several weeks, she decided to report the matter to the police.

Following each scenario, participants were asked to indicate their perceptions of defendant criminal liability and complainant blame and to indicate what they thought to be an appropriate sentence for the defendant in the event that he was found guilty.[14]

---

[14] Six versions of the questionnaire were created in which each scenario appeared once in each position from first to sixth. This was to rule out the possibility that the order in which the scenarios were presented had an effect on how participants judged the individual scenarios.

1. Defendant Liability

To relate the judgments about the defendant more closely to the context of legal decision-making, the focus was changed from a general measure of perceived blame in Study 1 to a more specific focus on criminal liability in Study 2. The rape certainty item used in Study 1 was incorporated into this new measure. Four questions were asked: (a) 'How certain are you that the incident meets the legal definition of rape?'; (b) 'How strongly do you think that D [defendant's name] ought to be held criminally liable for rape?'; (c) 'If you were a member of the jury, how certain are you that you would decide to convict D of rape?'; (d) 'How certain are you that D should be given a prison sentence?' All responses were made on a seven-point scale ranging from (1) = not at all to (7) = very much, and ratings across the four items were averaged for each participant to give an overall measure of defendant liability for each scenario.

2. Complainant Blame

The same four questions as in Study 1 were used to measure complainant blame: (a) 'How much do you think C [complainant's name] is to blame for what happened?'; (b) 'How much do you think C had control over the situation?'; (c) 'How likely do you think it is that C could have avoided the incident?'; (d) 'How sorry do you feel for C?' The same seven-point response scale was used, and ratings across the four items were averaged for each participant to give an overall measure of complainant blame for each scenario.

3. Recommended Sentence

An open-ended question about sentencing was asked following each case: 'If D is convicted of rape, what sentence do you think he ought to receive in this case?'

Female Precipitation Beliefs

These were measured, as in Study 1, by six items from the Perceived Causes of Rape Scale developed by Cowan and Quinton (1997; see p 79). Participants responded to each item using a seven-point scale ranging from (1) = strongly disagree to (7) = strongly agree.

Salience of Female Precipitation Beliefs

In order to manipulate the extent to which participants had female precipitation beliefs in mind when responding to the questionnaire, half the sample were given the female precipitation items before the scenarios, the other half were given the scenarios first, followed by the female precipitation scale.

Results

The first hypothesis predicted that vocational law students would be less inclined to hold the defendant liable, recommend a shorter sentence and assign more blame to the complainant if there was a previous relationship between the two parties.[15] It was found that ratings of defendant liability, complainant blame and recommended sentences were indeed significantly affected by information about a prior relationship with the complainant, as shown in figure 4.4.[16]

The defendant was seen as significantly less likely to be liable in the ex-partner cases than in the stranger cases, with the acquaintance scenarios lying in the middle. Recommended sentences in the ex-partner cases were significantly lower than sentences in the stranger and the acquaintance rapes. Finally, the complainant was blamed significantly more in the ex-partner cases than in the stranger cases. Again the acquaintance scenarios fell in between. Thus, Hypothesis 1 was supported by the data.

Hypothesis 2 predicted that coercive strategy, ie whether the defendant used force or exploited the complainant's intoxicated state, would also influence

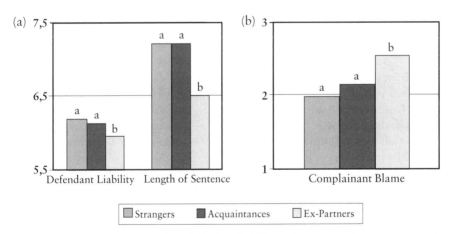

Figure 4.4 *Study 2: Ratings of (a) defendant liability and recommended sentences, and (b) complainant blame as a function of defendant–complainant relationship*

a,b Means with different superscripts differ at p < .05.

---

[15] Analyses of variance were conducted for defendant liability, complainant blame, and recommended sentences, using complainant-defendant relationship and coercive strategy as within subjects factors and belief in female precipitation as between-subjects factor.

[16] $F(2,228) = 4.55, p < .05$ for defendant liability, $F(2,228) = 3.08, p < .05$ for complainant blame and $F(2,164) = 3.82, p < .05$ for length of sentence.

participants' judgments of the cases, leading to lower ratings of defendant liability, shorter sentences, and higher complainant blame where the complainant was intoxicated. However, no significant effects were found for coercive strategy. Neither ratings of defendant liability nor perceptions of complainant blame were affected by whether the defendant used force or exploited the complainant's incapacitated state. Information about coercive strategy also failed to have an impact on sentencing recommendations.[17] Thus, Hypothesis 2 was not supported by the data.

Hypothesis 3 referred to the influence of female precipitation beliefs. The average level of agreement with the items reflecting female precipitation beliefs was 2.68 (on a scale ranging from 1 = complete disagreement to 7 = complete agreement).[18] Under a fifth (17.4 per cent) of participants had scores in the top half of the response scale, ie tended towards agreement with female precipitation beliefs. Men scored higher on the female precipitation measure than women, but the difference failed to reach significance.[19] Participants were divided into four groups on the basis of their female precipitation scores: Group 1 (very low) scored two standard deviations or more below the mean, Group 2 (low) within one standard deviation below the mean, Group 3 (high) within one standard deviation above the mean and Group 4 (very high) two standard deviations or more above the mean.

In line with our prediction, those highly accepting of female precipitation as a cause of rape showed a general tendency to exonerate the defendant, as reflected in the decrease in liability ratings from the very low to the very high group.[20] Moreover, the four groups differed in their susceptibility to information about the relationship between complainant and defendant as shown in figure 4.5.[21] Participants who did not accept female precipitation beliefs thought the defendant was liable regardless of his relationship to the complainant. In contrast, those participants showing the highest acceptance of female precipitation beliefs were not just least inclined to hold the defendant liable overall, they showed a steep drop in liability ratings when the defendant was an ex-partner. In fact, they were the only group whose perceptions of defendant liability were dependent on the defendant's prior relationship with the complainant.

Recommended sentences also differed as a function of participants' female precipitation beliefs. Participants showing very low acceptance of female precipitation beliefs recommended significantly higher sentences (average = 9.24 years) than the other three groups (averages ranging from 5.96 to 6.87 years).

---

[17] None of the interaction effects involving coercive strategy were significant.

[18] The female precipitation measure was again highly reliable with $\alpha = 85$.

[19] $M = 2.98$ for men and $M = 2.53$ for women F $(3, 117) = 3.52, p < .07$.

[20] $F (3,114) = 13.77, p < .001$. Means of 6.63, 6.31, 6.08, and 5.40 for the very low, low, high and very high groups, respectively.

[21] This was evidenced in a significant interaction between female precipitation beliefs and information about complainant-defendant relationship, $F (6,228) = 3.04, p < .05$.

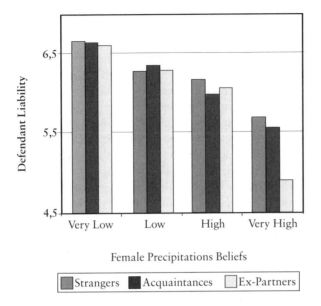

Figure 4.5 *Perceived defendant liability as a function of participants' female precipitation beliefs and prior relationship with the complainant*

Finally, female precipitation beliefs were found to affect ratings of complainant blame. The more participants endorsed the belief that women precipitate rape, the more they blamed the complainants across the six cases. On the seven-point scale, the respective average scores were 1.79 for the very low group, 2.21 for the low group, 2.86 for the high group and 3.61 for the very high group.[22]

However, the tendency, predicted in Hypothesis 3, that female precipitation beliefs would work to the disadvantage of the complainant particularly in the cases furthest removed from the real rape stereotype, such as the ex-partner case where the complainant was too incapacitated by alcohol to resist, was not apparent in the ratings of complainant blame. Complainant blame increased the more participants accepted female precipitation beliefs, regardless of whether the defendant was alleged to have used force or exploited the complainant's incapacitated state.

Hypothesis 4 predicted that men would be less inclined to hold the defendant legally liable compared with women, recommend shorter sentences and attribute more blame to the complainant, and that this difference could be attributed to men's greater adherence to female precipitation beliefs.

[22] The significant main effects of female precipitation beliefs were $F_{(3,82)} = 2.80$, $p < .05$ for recommended sentences and $F_{(3,114)} = 36.62$, $p < .001$ for complainant blame. All four groups differed significantly on the latter measure.

Furthermore, it was predicted that the gender difference would be greater in the alcohol-related cases and in the cases involving a previous relationship between the defendant and the complainant. In contrast to these predictions, male and female participants in this study did not differ in their perceptions of defendant liability, recommended sentences and complainant blame. They also failed to differ significantly in their acceptance of female precipitation beliefs.

The findings about the lack of gender effects in judgments about defendant and complainant are consistent with our proposition that individual attitudes about rape are more important than being male or female as far as judgments about rape are concerned. However, the data also showed that men and women did not differ significantly in their adherence to rape myths. While this finding replicates an earlier study with psychology undergraduates (Study 2 in Krahé, Temkin and Bieneck, 2007), it is at odds with the evidence of the other two studies presented in this chapter and chapter five, and also with the body of literature reviewed in chapter two where men were consistently found to endorse rape myths more than women. We will return to this ambiguity in the general discussion in chapter five.

Finally, Hypothesis 5 referred to the causal link between female precipitation beliefs and judgments about the cases. It was argued that if adherence to female precipitation myths was found to be more closely linked to judgments about defendants and complainants when these myths were brought to the attention of participants *before* as opposed to *after* the case scenarios, this would point to their causal role. To test this hypothesis, overall scores of defendant liability and complainant blame were created by averaging across the six case scenarios.[23] Then, correlations were computed between female precipitation scores and defendant liability and complainant blame, respectively, for each of the two orders of presentation. As predicted, the correlation between female precipitation beliefs and judgments of defendant liability was higher when participants responded to the female precipitation scale prior to judging the case scenarios than when they did so after judging the scenarios.[24] The difference was in the predicted direction, but it failed to reach statistical significance. A similar pattern was found for sentencing recommendations.[25] Again, the difference was in the predicted direction but failed to reach statistical significance. For ratings of complainant blame, the correlation was also higher when the female precipitation scale was presented first.[26] For this measure, the difference between the two correlation coefficients was significant. Thus, Hypothesis 5 received qualified

[23] $M = 6.61$, $SD = .81$, $\alpha = .78$ (defendant liability), $M = 6.74$, $SD = 4.29$, $\alpha = .92$ (recommended sentences) and $M = 2.53$, $SD = .93$, $\alpha = .75$ (complainant blame) for the aggregate scores.

[24] $r(61) = -.60$, $p < .001$ when participants responded to the female precipitation scale first, $r(60) = -.42$, $p < .001$ when they responded to the scenarios first.

[25] $r(60) = -.28$, $p < .05$, when the female precipitation scale was presented first and $r(61) = -.14$, n.s. when the cases were presented first.

[26] $r(61) = .80$, $p < .001$ as opposed to $r(60) = .57$, $p < .001$, significant reduction in r, Fisher's z-transformation, $p < .05$. Here the correlation is positive, indicating that blame ratings *increased* the more participants endorsed female precipitation beliefs.

support from the data. Female precipitation beliefs were more closely associated with judgments about the defendants and complainants in the six rape cases when they were presented before the case descriptions, but the increase was significant only for the ratings of complainant blame.

Discussion

The purpose of this study was to investigate the role of rape-related stereotypes in judgments about rape cases in a group of prospective lawyers who were at a more advanced stage of their legal training than the undergraduate law students in Study 1. We hypothesised that case information that deviates from the real rape stereotype as well as prejudicial attitudes about rape held by the participants would lead to more lenient judgments about the defendant and to more blame being attributed to the complainant, thus reducing the odds of a conviction. In line with this assumption, the graduate vocational students in the present study were less inclined to think the defendant was legally liable, recommended a shorter prison sentence and blamed the complainant more in the scenarios where the defendant and complainant were described as former sexual partners than in the scenarios in which they were presented as strangers. This was true despite the fact that in all the scenarios it was stated that the complainant had clearly expressed her refusal to engage in sexual intercourse with the defendant.

Perceptions of defendant liability, complainant blame and appropriate sentences in case of a conviction were unaffected by the type of coercive strategy used, ie whether the defendant used physical force or whether he exploited the fact that the complainant was too incapacitated by alcohol to show physical resistance. This finding is at odds with the results of an earlier study of psychology students without any legal training, who were less likely to find the defendant liable and more likely to blame the complainant, when he exploited the complainant's inability to resist than when he used physical force (Krahé, Temkin and Bieneck, 2007). It may be the case that the graduate students in Study 2 were more aware of the legal definition of rape and knew that exploiting another person's inability to resist was covered by it and therefore did not differentiate between the force and alcohol scenarios in their judgments. However, since knowledge of the legal definition of rape was not tested in the study, this explanation remains tentative.

As predicted, participants' belief in female precipitation as a cause of rape had a significant impact on their judgments of the scenarios. The more they believed that rape is precipitated by women who engage in risky or provocative behaviour, the less inclined they were to hold the defendant liable, the shorter the sentences they recommended and the more blame they attributed to the complainant. Female precipitation beliefs had the greatest impact on the ex-partner cases. While all participants were given the same scenarios to assess, those who scored high on female precipitation beliefs were more inclined to make use of information provided in the scenarios which was at odds with the real rape stereotype. This is an indication of schematic processing. It demonstrates that if case information meets with personal attitudes that suspect women of provoking sexual assault, a situation arises that is particularly detrimental to the perceived credibility of the complainant and the likelihood of a conviction.

Unlike the findings from Study 1, no gender differences were found in Study 2. Men and women did not differ in their perceptions of defendant liability, sentencing recommendations and attributions of blame to the complainant. Importantly, they also failed to differ in terms of their acceptance of female precipitation as a cause of rape. In chapter two, it was argued that evidence for gender differences in the literature on attributions of blame in rape cases is inconsistent and that in those cases where gender differences were found, they reflected underlying differences in rape-related attitudes. The present findings provide indirect support for this conclusion by showing that the absence of gender differences in ratings of defendant liability and complainant blame is matched by the absence of differences in the acceptance of female precipitation beliefs. There was considerable variation in the extent to which participants adhered to female precipitation beliefs, but the variation did not follow gender lines.

The findings from Study 2 also provide some support for the claim that female precipitation beliefs play a *causal role* in leading to more lenient judgments about defendants and higher attributions of blame to complainants. When participants were reminded of their own female precipitation beliefs by completing the female precipitation measure *before* being presented with the case scenarios, differences in the acceptance of female precipitation beliefs were more closely linked to differences in ratings of complainant blame than when this scale was given to participants *after* being given the rape scenarios. For ratings of defendant blame and recommended sentences, similar patterns were found, but they failed to reach statistical significance. It has to be noted that the sample size in this study was small, which undermined the chances of detecting significant differences in the strength of the association between female precipitation beliefs and case judgments depending on the different orders of presentation. The significant difference with regard to ratings of complainant blame is therefore an important finding.

Overall, the findings from Study 2 provide further support for the suggested attitude problem underlying low conviction rates in sexual assault cases. They show that despite explicit statements of non-consent by the complainant, background information pertinent to the real rape stereotype, such as about a previous relationship between the parties, affected the way prospective lawyers perceived defendant liability and complainant blame. It also influenced sentencing recommendations, with lower sentences recommended for ex-partners than for strangers and acquaintances. However, it also became apparent that not all observers responded to this kind of background information in the same way and that their attitudes towards rape were important moderators. The more participants believed that rape was precipitated by women, the more they blamed the complainants and the less likely they were to hold the defendants liable in the specific rape scenarios they were asked to judge. As a consequence of varying the order in which the female precipitation measure and the rape scenarios were presented, some support was derived for the proposition that female precipitation beliefs are not merely associated with, but causally responsible for differences in judging defendants and complainants in rape cases (see Bohner *et al*, 1998; 2005; for a similar finding).

The present findings are highly consistent with those derived from a similar study conducted in Germany (Krahé, Temkin, Bieneck and Berger, in press). In a sample of 129 graduate students with a first degree in law, it was found that the closer the previous relationship between defendant and complainant in the scenarios, the less participants were inclined to think that the defendant should be held liable, the more inclined they were to blame the complainant and the shorter the sentences they recommended. When judging identical case scenarios, participants believing in female precipitation as a cause of rape were less inclined to hold the defendant liable, recommended shorter sentences and were more ready to blame the complainant than those who accepted these beliefs to a lesser degree or not at all. Whether or not they were reminded of the legal definition of rape under German law prior to reading the scenarios made no difference at all to their judgments about the cases, suggesting that prospective legal professionals in an advanced stage of their training also fall back on their stereotypes when judging individual cases.

In terms of the practical implications of Study 2, participants were drawn from the population from which lawyers in rape cases will be recruited. In England and Wales, no previous studies have looked at this particular group in terms of their attitudes towards rape and propensity for schematic information processing, and there is a similar shortage of evidence for this group in the international literature. The present findings show that graduate students engaged in vocational training to enter the legal profession are susceptible to background information about defendants and complainants in line with rape stereotypes. Their reliance on this information undermines the attention and weight they accord to critical data-based information, such as explicit statements of non-consent by the alleged victim. The more participants believed in female precipitation as a cause of rape, the more they were influenced by background information related to rape stereotypes, showing that differences in general attitudes about rape infiltrate judgments about specific cases. Even though participants in this study were asked to evaluate hypothetical as opposed to real cases, there is reason to suspect that a similar reliance on schematic processing would affect their responses to real-life cases (see chapter three).

5

A Question of Attitude: The General Public

IN CHAPTER FOUR, we presented new evidence that prospective lawyers are susceptible to schematic information processing on the basis of rape myths and stereotypes when judging rape scenarios. In addition to legal professionals, members of the general public in their capacity as jurors or lay judges in different criminal justice systems, are centrally involved in legal decision-making about rape cases. Members of the public, like present and prospective members of the legal profession, have been under-represented in past research in this area. As shown in chapter three, there is clear evidence from the mock jury paradigm that juror attitudes influence the way they approach the evidence and reach a verdict. Therefore, it is critical to gain a better understanding of how members of the public, who meet the eligibility criteria for jury service, judge rape scenarios and how their judgments are affected by their attitudes about rape. We argue that if rape myths are prevalent in society at large, they are likely to be introduced into the courtroom and affect juror decision-making, resulting in a selective dismissal of cases at odds with stereotypic notions. The third in our series of studies was designed to test this proposition.

If potential jurors are shown to judge rape cases on the basis of biased and prejudiced views, there is arguably the need to seek to change these attitudes. The Home Office recently conducted a mass media campaign in England and Wales which was specifically directed at young men and was designed to raise awareness about the need for consent in sexual relationships. Study 3, which is described in this chapter, included an evaluation of the effects of two posters used in the campaign. It explored whether seeing the posters while judging rape scenarios would lead participants to pay more attention to the issue of consent. While the immediate objective of the study was to evaluate the posters used in this particular campaign, the analysis also has broader relevance for addressing the effectiveness of media campaigns as part of rape prevention initiatives (see chapter ten).

5.1 STUDY 3: EXPLORING SCHEMATIC PROCESSING
BY MEMBERS OF THE PUBLIC

Most citizens in the 18–69 age bracket in England and Wales are now potential jurors,[1] so the responses of members of the public to rape cases such as those described in our scenarios are pertinent to understanding the role of schematic processing of rape cases in court. Therefore, the first objective of Study 3 was to examine the responses of members of the public to the case material presented to the prospective lawyers in Study 2. In this respect, Study 3 represents a replication of Study 2 with a different target group whose perceptions of rape cases are also highly relevant. The second objective of the study was to evaluate the effectiveness of two posters from the Home Office Consent Campaign. This section will present the hypotheses, methodology and results of the study in relation to schematic processing, and the next section presents the evaluation of the posters.

Schematic Processing of Information about Rape

The first part of the study was designed to test whether members of the public are affected by information about defendant-complainant relationship, the use of force and the complainant's alcohol-induced inability to resist to the same extent as prospective lawyers, and whether those who hold stereotypic attitudes about rape are particularly susceptible to this information. With respect to rape-supportive attitudes, the two studies described in chapter four focused on one particular aspect, namely female precipitation beliefs which were measured using Cowan and Quinton's Perceived Causes of Rape Scale (1997). In Study 3, we argue that endorsement of a broader spectrum of misconceptions about rape is similarly linked to the minimisation of defendant liability and attribution of complainant blame. In order to demonstrate this, the study used in addition the Acceptance of Modern Myths about Sexual Aggression Scale (AMMSA) by Gerger, Kley, Bohner and Siebler (2007, see chapter two, section 2.2). Their instrument is designed to measure acceptance of 'modern' myths about sexual aggression, defined as 'descriptive or prescriptive beliefs about sexual aggression (ie about its scope, causes, context, and consequences) that serve to deny, downplay or justify sexually aggressive behavior that men commit against women' (Gerger *et al*, 2007: 425).

In order to see whether the findings of Study 2 would be replicated, Study 3 aimed to test the following hypotheses:

---

[1] Under s 1 of the Juries Act 1974, citizens between the ages of 18 and 69 who have lived in the country for at least five years since the age of 13 and are not mentally disordered or otherwise disqualified can be summoned for jury service. The Criminal Justice Act 2003 (see s 321 and sch 33) extended the range of those who are eligible. Jurors are chosen at random from the electoral register.

Hypothesis 1. It was predicted that, like prospective lawyers, members of the public who were asked to assess rape scenarios would be less inclined to hold the defendant liable, more inclined to blame the complainant and to recommend shorter sentences if there was a previous relationship between the two parties. Most blame would be attributed to the complainant in the ex-partner rape, followed by the acquaintance rape, and least blame would be attributed to her in the stranger rape. By the same token, participants would be least inclined to hold the defendant liable and would recommend the shortest sentences in the ex-partner rape, followed by the acquaintance and stranger rapes.

Hypothesis 2. It was predicted that ratings of defendant liability as well as recommended sentences would be lower and perceptions of complainant blame would be higher when the defendant exploited the complainant's incapacitated state and her resulting inability to resist as compared with cases in which the defendant used physical force.

Hypothesis 3. It was predicted that when asked to apply their minds to rape scenarios, the more participants subscribed to rape myths, (a) the less they would be inclined to hold the defendant liable, (b) the shorter the sentence they would recommend and (c) the more they would be inclined to blame the complainant. The impact of rape myth acceptance was expected to be greater in cases involving the complainant's alcohol-induced incapacitation than in cases involving the use of force. Ratings would also be affected more by rape myth acceptance the closer the previous relationship had been between the defendant and the complainant. We expected that the broader scale measuring acceptance of modern rape myths would yield parallel findings to those obtained for female precipitation beliefs, with higher acceptance of rape myths linked to lower assessments of defendant liability, lower recommended sentences and increased attributions of blame to the complainant.

Hypothesis 4. It was predicted that men would be less inclined to hold the defendant legally liable than women, would recommend shorter sentences and would be more inclined to blame the victim, and that this difference could be attributed to men's greater adherence to rape myths.

Methodology: Schematic Information Processing

Participants and Procedure

A total of 2176 members of the general public in the UK participated in the study which was run as a web-based, online survey. Of these, 893 were men and 1283 were women. They ranged in age from 18 to 69, the same age bracket as for jury service, with a mean age of 29.3 years ($SD = 10.23$). Two strategies were used to recruit participants. The first was to distribute the link to the questionnaire via email to institutions as well as individuals, asking them to forward the link to other people whom they thought might be interested in participating in the study. This yielded data from 793 participants who completed the questionnaire on an unpaid voluntary basis. The second strategy was to recruit participants through a commercial agency that sent out emails to registered members of their panel with an invitation to participate in the study. A total of 1385 participants was recruited through this channel. The company gave them a small payment for their participation. The majority of participants (1755 or 80.7 per cent) had British citizenship, the second largest group (4.6 per cent) were US citizens, followed by Indians (1.1 per cent), Australians (0.9 per cent) and Canadians (0.6 per cent).

In terms of educational background, 75.6 per cent of participants had more than five GCSEs, 55.7 per cent had three or more A Levels, 44.7 per cent had a bachelor's degree, and 15.7 per cent had a master's degree. In comparison with figures for the population of working age in 2003, the sample was somewhat better educated than the national average.[2] A minority of 314 participants (14.4 per cent) had been called to jury service, and 147 of those (6.8 per cent of the total sample) had actually served as jurors. Participants recruited via the two different routes did not differ in any of the demographic background variables.

Rape Scenarios

The same rape scenarios and measures were used as in Study 2 (see chapter four). Participants were asked, following each scenario, to rate the legal liability of the defendant, provide ratings of complainant blame and recommend an appropriate sentence if the defendant was found guilty.[3]

Rape Myth Acceptance

Female precipitation beliefs as a specific aspect of rape myths were measured by the same scale used in the previous studies, taken from the Perceived Causes of Rape Scale developed by Cowan and Quinton (1997). In addition, a 16-item short form of the *Acceptance of Modern Myths about Sexual Aggression* scale (AMMSA; Gerger *et al*, 2007) was used, based on research by Eyssel, Bohner and Siebler (2006). It includes items such as 'Women often accuse their husbands of marital rape just to retaliate for a failed relationship', 'Women like to play coy. This does not mean that they do not want sex', 'Many women tend to

---

[2] National figures for the population of working age show that in 2003 16.3% had a first or higher university degree, 24.1% had A levels or equivalent vocational training and 21.7% had GCSEs at Grades A+ to C as their highest qualification. 13.7% reported other qualifications, and 15% had no qualifications; see: http://www.statistics.gov.uk/STATBASE/ssdataset.asp?vlnk=7743

[3] As in the previous studies, different versions of the questionnaire were created in which each scenario appeared once in each position from first to sixth. This was to rule out the possibility that the order in which the scenarios were presented had an effect on how participants judged the individual scenarios. The rape myth acceptance measures were always presented after the scenarios.

misinterpret a well-meant gesture as a "sexual assault" ', or 'The discussion about sexual harassment on the job has mainly resulted in many a harmless behaviour being misinterpreted as harassment'. Responses were made on a scale ranging from (1) = completely disagree to (7) = completely agree.

Results: Schematic Information Processing

To examine the first three hypotheses, three factors were included in the analysis, ie defendant-complainant relationship, coercive strategy and participants' rape myth acceptance, to study their separate and joint effects on perceptions of defendant liability, attributions of complainant blame and recommended sentences.[4]

In support of Hypothesis 1, it was found that ratings of defendant liability were influenced by information about complainant-defendant relationship. The defendant was seen as most liable in the stranger rape scenario, followed by the acquaintance and ex-partner rapes. As predicted in Hypothesis 2, defendants were held more liable when they used force than when they exploited the complainants' intoxicated state.[5] However, when both variables were considered in combination, it emerged that it was only in the force scenarios that perceptions of defendant liability decreased the closer the relationship between defendant and complainant.[6] Defendant liability ratings in the alcohol-related scenarios did not vary between the stranger, acquaintance and ex-partner cases. Comparing defendant liability ratings in the three alcohol-related cases, they were found to be significantly lower than in the force-related stranger and acquaintance rapes, but significantly above those in the force-related rape of an ex-partner. The mean defendant liability ratings for the different case scenarios are shown in the top panel of figure 5.1.

Sentencing recommendations closely matched the liability judgments. Recommended sentences in the force scenarios decreased the closer the relationship between defendant and complainant, as shown in the bottom panel of

---

[4] Thus, the design was a 3 (defendant-complainant relationship: stranger, acquaintance, ex-partner) by 2 (coercive strategy: force, exploitation of victim's intoxication) by 4 (rape myth acceptance: very low, low, high, very high) design with repeated measures on the first two factors. It was tested in a series of analyses of variance using defendant liability, recommended sentences and complainant blame as dependent variables. Due to the large sample size, small effects can reach statistical significance without necessarily reflecting a substantial difference. To address this problem, only those effects that accounted for at least 4% of the variance, as indicated by eta^2 were considered meaningful and will be interpreted.

[5] Because the sentencing recommendations given by the participants varied widely, they were classified into six categories: 0 = no prison sentence; 1 = less than 1 year; 2 = 1–3 years; 3 = 4–6 years; 4 = 7–10 years; and 6 = more than 10 years.

[5] $F_{(2,1995)} = 271.50$, $p < .001$, $eta^2 = .21$, for the main effect of complainant-defendant relationship and $F_{(1,1996)} = 162.21$, $p < .001$, $eta^2 = .08$ for the main effect of coercive strategy on defendant liability.

[6] $F_{(2,1995)} = 237.21$, $p < .001$, $eta^2 = .19$, for the interaction effect. The three means in the force condition were significantly different at $p < .05$.

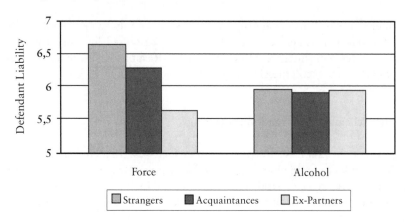

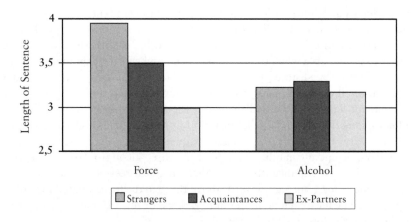

Figure 5.1 *Study 3: Interaction of Relationship and Coercive Strategy (Force vs. Alchol) on Ratings of Defendant Liability (Top Panel) and Recommended Length of Sentence (Bottom Panel).*

Note: The scale points on the length of sentence measure were 0 = no prison sentence, 1 = less than 12 months, 2 = 1 to 3 years, 3 = 4 to 6 years, 4 = 7 to 10 years, 5 = more than 10 years.

Figure 5.1.[7] Sentencing recommendations for the alcohol scenarios did not differ significantly in relation to defendant-complainant relationship. All three sentencing recommendations for the alcohol-related cases were significantly lower than the recommended sentences for the stranger and acquaintance rapes involving force, while being significantly above those for the ex-partner rape involving force.[8]

[7] Main effects for defendant-complainant relationship and coercive strategy were found, but they were qualified by a significant interaction between the two variables, $F (2,1127) = 244.30$, $p < .001$, eta$^2 = .30$. All means of the force scenarios were significantly different.

[8] All ts significant at $p < .001$.

In terms of perceptions of the complainant, she was blamed significantly less in the stranger rapes than in the acquaintance and ex-partner rapes. She was also blamed less in the force-related than in the alcohol-related cases.[9] But when the two variables were considered in combination, it emerged that in the force scenarios, complainant blame was particularly high when the defendant was an ex-partner, as shown in figure 5.2. By contrast, in the alcohol-related cases the complainant was blamed *less* where the defendant was an ex-partner than when he was a stranger or acquaintance.[10]

Hypothesis 3 predicted that perceptions of defendant liability, complainant blame and recommended sentences would differ in relation to participants' acceptance of female precipitation beliefs as well as their acceptance of a wider range of modern rape myths. Average agreement with the female precipitation items was 2.99 on a scale ranging from 1 = complete disagreement to 7 = complete agreement, average agreement with the modern rape myths items was 3.90. On both measures, participants were divided into four groups. Group 1 (very low) scored two standard deviations or more below the mean, Group 2 (low) within one standard deviation below the mean, Group 3 (high) within one

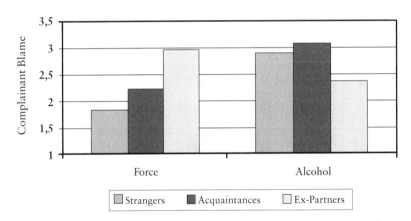

Figure 5.2 *Study 3: Interaction of relationship and coercive strategy (force vs alcohol) on ratings of defendant liability (top panel) and recommended length of sentence (bottom panel)*

[9] F (2,1996) = 149.01, p < .001, eta^2 = .13, for the defendant-complainant relationship main effect and F (1,1997) = 546.91, p < .001, eta^2 = .22, for the coercive strategy main effect.

[10] Follow-up t-test indicated that the incapacitated complainant raped by an ex-partner was blamed less than the complainant raped by the ex-partner using force. Complainant blame in the three alcohol-related cases was significantly higher than in the stranger and acquaintance rapes using force (all t-values significant at p < .01).

standard deviation above the mean and Group 4 (very high) two standard deviations or more above the mean.[11]

As predicted, the more participants believed in female precipitation myths, the less liable they assessed the defendant to be, particularly in the ex-partner rapes.[12] The top half of figure 5.3 shows the findings.

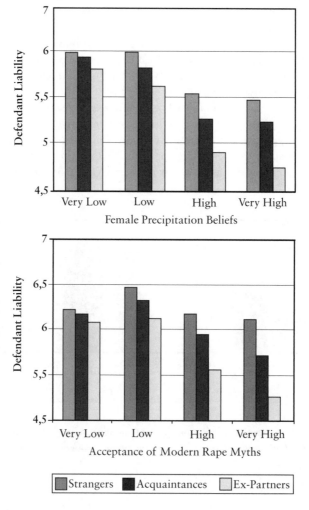

Figure 5.3 *Study 3: Perceived defendant liability as a function of participants' female precipitation beliefs, acceptance of modern rape myths and prior relationship with the complainant*

[11] The internal consistency was α = .90 for the female precipitation scale and α = .85 for the modern rape myth acceptance scale.

[12] F (3,1996) = 76.87, p < .001, eta^2 = .10, for the main effect of female precipitation beliefs and F (6,3992) = 17.62, p < .001, eta^2 = .04, for the interaction between female precipitation beliefs and defendant-complainant relationship.

While all four groups reduced their ratings of defendant liability the closer the relationship between defendant and complainant, those with higher acceptance of female precipitation beliefs showed even more leniency towards a defendant who assaulted an ex-partner. Highly similar effects were found for the second measure of rape myth acceptance, the AMMSA scale, as shown in the bottom half of figure 5.3.[13]

Sentencing recommendations also differed depending on female precipitation beliefs and modern rape myth acceptance.[14] The more participants endorsed these rape-supportive attitudes, the shorter the sentences they recommended in the event that the defendant was found guilty. Participants who scored 'very low' on female precipitation beliefs recommended significantly longer sentences (average rating of 3.75 on the sentencing scale from 0 to 5) than those in the 'low' group (average rating of 3.37), and both groups were significantly harsher than those who scored 'high' and 'very high' on female precipitation beliefs (average ratings of 3.18 and 3.12 respectively on the sentencing scale). The pattern was very similar across the three defendant-complainant relationships and the alcohol and the force scenarios.[15]

As predicted, just as defendant liability ratings decreased, ratings of complainant blame increased the more participants believed in female precipitation and modern rape myths.[16] As shown in figure 5.4, average complainant blame ratings were up from 1.54 in the group 'very low' on female precipitation belief to 3.37 in the 'very high' group. Similarly, complainant blame ratings were up from 1.75 in the group which was 'very low' on acceptance of modern rape myths to 3.38 in the 'very high' group.[17]

Thus, the findings show that differences in rape-supportive attitudes are reflected in the participants' approach to the rape scenarios. They also show the extent to which these attitudes are accepted in this sample of members of the public. As reported above, the average ratings on both measures of rape-supportive attitudes were below the midpoint of (4) on the response scale ranging from (1) to (7), suggesting that the group of participants as a whole tended more towards disagreeing than towards agreeing with the statements in these measures. However, on the female precipitation measure, 25.3 per cent of participants scored on the 'agreement' side of the scale, ie had scores above the

---

[13] $F_{(6,3992)} = 20.26$, $p < .001$, eta^2 = .04. No interactions were found between coercive strategy and the two measures of rape myth acceptance on defendant blame.

[14] $F_{(3,1128)} = 15.09$, $p < .001$, eta^2 = .04, for the main effect of female precipitation beliefs, $F_{(3,1128)} = 5.65$, $p < .001$, eta^2 = .03, for modern rape myth acceptance. For the AMMSA measure, the means were 3.51 for the very low, 3.45 for the low, 3.21 for the high and 3.19 for the very high groups. The range was 0 = no prison sentence; 1 = less than 1 year; 2 = 1–3 years; 3 = 4–6 years; 4 = 7–10 years; and 5 = more than 10 years.

[15] No interactions were found between the two rape myth acceptance measures and complainant-defendant relationship or coercive strategy on recommended sentences.

[16] $F_{(3,1996)} = 320.42$, $p < .001$, eta^2 = .33, for the main effect of female precipitation beliefs, $F_{(3,2000)} = 224.65$, $p < .001$, eta^2 = .25, for modern rape myth acceptance.

[17] No interactions were found between the two rape myth acceptance measures and complainant-defendant relationship or coercive strategy on perceived complainant blame.

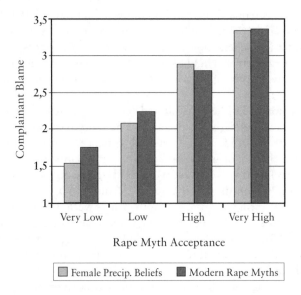

Figure 5.4 *Study 3: Effects of rape myth acceptance on ratings of complainant blame across all scenarios*

Note: On both measures, all four group means differ at p < .05.

midpoint of the scale. More men (37.1 per cent) than women (17.2 per cent) fell into this group. On the modern rape myth measure, 44.4 per cent of the participants had scores above the midpoint of the scale (59 per cent of the male and 34.2 per cent of the female participants). The higher percentage on the modern rape myth acceptance scale supports the claim that this instrument captures more subtle and less obvious stereotypical beliefs about rape (Gerger *et al*, 2007). Thus, a substantial minority of participants showed support for female precipitation beliefs and modern rape myths.

Hypothesis 4 predicted that (a) men would be less inclined to hold the defendant legally liable, would recommend shorter sentences and would be more inclined to blame the complainant than women, and that (b) this difference could be attributed to men's greater adherence to rape myths. Contrary to the first prediction, men and women did not differ substantially in their perceptions of defendant liability, sentencing recommendations and complainant blame.[18] However, as predicted, men showed greater acceptance than women of female precipitation beliefs (average ratings of 3.49 for men and 2.64 for women) and modern myths about sexual aggression (average ratings of 4.27 for men and 3.64 for women).[19]

[18] ie, did not explain 4% or more of the variance; $F (1,1996) = 49.75$, $p < .001$, $eta^2 = .02$, for defendant liability, $F (1,1128) = 2.22$, $p = .13$, for sentencing recommendations, and $F (1,1997) = 9.49$, $p < .001$, $eta^2 = .01$ for complainant blame.

[19] $F (1, 2173) = 187.85$, $p < .001$, $eta^2 = .08$, for female precipitation beliefs, $F (1, 2173) = 250.26$, $p < .001$, $eta^2 = .10$, for modern rape myth acceptance.

Given that higher rape myth acceptance and endorsement of female precipitation beliefs were linked to lower defendant liability, shorter sentences and higher complainant blame ratings, these findings suggest an indirect effect of gender on perceptions of defendants and complainants via rape-supportive attitudes. Rape myth acceptance was linked to judgments about defendants and complainants in the same way in men and women.[20]

5.2 STUDY 3: EVALUATING A RAPE-AWARENESS POSTER CAMPAIGN

In 2006, the Home Office launched a media campaign in England and Wales designed to raise awareness about the importance of consent in sexual interactions. The campaign used a combination of posters, advertisements in magazines, stickers on condom vending machines and radio broadcasts specifically to target men between 18 and 24 (Home Office, 2006c). The aims of the campaign are set out in table 5.1.

Table 5.1

Study 3: Aims of the Home Office Consent Campaign launched in March 2006
(Taken from: http://www.homeoffice.gov.uk/documents/consent-campaign/)

> This campaign aims to reduce incidents of rape by ensuring that men know they need to gain consent before they have sex. We also hope to reduce the number of offences committed and increase reporting rates.
>
> We are determined to close the gap between the increasing number of rape cases reported and the low number of convictions. We have changed the law on consent and changed court procedures to make giving evidence easier for victims of rape and other sexual crimes, but we also need to change public attitudes to rape if we are really to make a difference.
>
> We hope that this campaign will lead to greater awareness and understanding of what consent means, as well as dispelling myths about the type of people who commit rape.

In our study, we used the two posters which featured in the campaign (referred to henceforth as the 'prison' poster and the 'no-entry' poster) for an experimental evaluation of their effectiveness in influencing perceptions about sexual assault. The posters, which were displayed for a month in cloakrooms in eight cities in England and Wales, also received extensive press coverage. They are shown in figure 5.5.

The effects of media campaigns designed to influence individual attitudes and behaviour are notoriously difficult to evaluate in a systematic fashion. It is often

---

[20] As indicated by a non-significant gender by rape myth acceptance interaction on both measures.

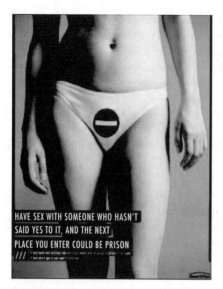 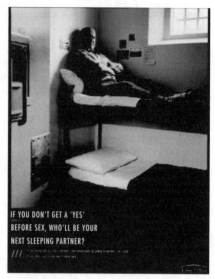

Figure 5.5 *Posters from the Consent Campaign by the Home Office (2006c) used in Study 3*

not feasible to run true experiments in which participants are randomly assigned to seeing or not seeing the poster, or even to measure who saw the material and who did not (Perloff, 1993). Therefore, if such campaigns are evaluated at all, success is often measured simply by the amount of interest they generate and how much they are liked by the public, which may have little to do with the effects intended by the campaign designers (Derzon and Lipsey, 2002; see also chapter ten).

In the case of the Home Office campaign, an evaluation was commissioned by the Home Office which focused on the extent to which members of the target group had noticed the posters and advertisements. It also tested recall of the central message of individual advertisements (Home Office, 2006d).[21] Street interviews were conducted with men aged between 16 and 34 which revealed that 54 per cent of respondents said they had seen at least one of the adverts from the campaign. When asked about the message in the prison poster, 45 per cent thought that it was saying that if you commit rape you could go to prison. Thus, it can be concluded that the campaign has been successful in that it has been widely noticed and a substantial number of people have understood the intended message.

It is certainly true that the campaign's success in achieving its aims can be measured in part by the extent to which the target group recalled and understood its message. However, this alone is not sufficient. What needs to be shown

[21] The authors are grateful to the Home Office for a copy of the evaluation report.

is that exposure to this message affects people's attitudes and behaviour. The favoured method for assessing such effects is an experimental randomised control design in which participants are assigned to either an experimental condition (in the present case: the posters) or a control condition (Sidani, 2006). Differences between the two conditions are indicative of the effects of the experimental condition. In one of the few studies conducted in a field setting, Etter and Laszlo (2005) evaluated the effects of a poster campaign designed to raise awareness about the dangers of passive smoking. Participants who saw the posters did not show any greater decline in their smoking behaviour or an increased intention to quit from pre- to post-campaign than those who had not done so. In another study, Pechmann and Reibling (2006) similarly demonstrated that even though teenagers remembered the anti-smoking advertisements shown to them in a school setting, this did not affect their smoking intentions, which were no different from that of a control group who had not seen the advertisements.

Thus, it is clear that the evaluation of the poster campaign conducted on behalf of the Home Office was incomplete. It should have included a systematic assessment of whether it had brought about the intended changes in attitudes to consent. This issue was addressed in the present study, where the focus was placed on the immediate effects of the posters on judgments about rape cases. Participants were either shown or not shown one of the two posters while assessing different rape scenarios so that differences in ratings of defendant liability, complainant blame and recommended sentences could be attributed to the presence or absence of the posters.

Participants in our study had the posters brought to their attention. When the posters were displayed during the campaign, the attention of members of the public could not be similarly guaranteed. In Study 3, the posters were in sight as participants made their judgments about the rape scenarios, whereas the posters would need to have been recalled from memory if they were to be effective in real-life interactions. Thus, if the posters failed to have an impact on study participants, they would be unlikely to achieve the effect intended by the campaign where their impact was bound to have been far less immediate. If on the other hand the posters succeeded in influencing participants, this would not necessarily indicate their effectiveness in the real world, but would at least show that it is possible to use such visual material to strengthen adherence to a consent standard.

The theoretical basis for assuming that showing the posters before and during the presentation of the case scenarios would influence responses to the case scenarios derived from the concept of 'cognitive priming' widely supported by social cognition research (Kunda, 1999). According to this concept, by presenting a stimulus (the 'prime') prior to a judgment task, the associations attached to the stimulus will be activated and will influence subsequent responses. Supporting this assumption, it has been demonstrated, for example, that participants who were first shown an aggression-related stimulus as a prime (such as a picture of a weapon) were subsequently faster at recognising aggression-related words than those who were shown non-aggressive primes, such as pictures of plants (Anderson, Benjamin and Bartholow, 1998). Similarly, in research on mass media and political persuasion, it has been shown that the more prominently a particular issue featured in the media, the more recipients' opinions on that issue influenced their voting behaviour (Iyengar and McGrady, 2005).

Applied to the present study, this line of research suggests that the posters could function as cognitive primes, enabling participants more easily to access positive cognitions supporting the importance of consent. This should make them more sensitive to the fact that in the scenarios the defendants ignored the complainants' explicit statements of non-consent and should make them less likely to blame the complainant, more likely to see the defendant as criminally liable and more inclined to recommend a harsher sentence.

A second line of research relevant to analysing the potential effectiveness of poster campaigns comes from the literature on persuasive communication, in particular dual-process models of attitude change (Chen and Chaiken, 1999; Petty, Cacioppo, Strathman and Priester, 2005). These models, reviewed briefly in chapter three (section 3.5), posit that people are persuaded by messages via two different routes: a central or *systematic* route in which the message is carefully considered and evaluated, and a peripheral or *heuristic* route in which they evaluate the message on the basis of superficial cues, such as the status or credibility of its source. When people lack the ability and/or motivation to engage in systematic message processing, they rely on peripheral cues in deciding whether to accept a message. However, compared with the central route, persuasion via the peripheral route is short-lived. Studies have shown that when their motivation is low or their ability impaired, eg because they are distracted, people are influenced equally by poor and good quality arguments, whereas they reject the poor arguments when motivated and able to examine them properly (Petty *et al*, 2005). Posters displayed in public places have to compete for the recipient's attention with a host of other stimuli and are likely to elicit peripheral rather than central message processing. Their effectiveness is therefore more dependent on superficial cues, such as the potential to catch the recipient's attention by unusual or graphic images, than on a careful scrutiny of its stated message.

From this line of reasoning, it follows that the posters are at best likely to elicit transient and superficial attitude change. To enhance the effectiveness of the posters, a possible strategy would be to combine them with information which addresses the central route of message processing by providing explicit information about consent. To explore this possibility we included a written paragraph explaining the meaning and importance of consent in the legal definition of rape, broadly based on the Sexual Offences Act 2003. This enabled us to test whether a combination of visual material and written information would be superior in terms of changing perceptions of the importance of consent than the posters on their own or, indeed, the written information on its own. The text of the consent paragraph is set out in table 5.2.

Table 5.2

Study 3: Text of the paragraph explaining consent

In English law a man commits rape if he has sexual intercourse with a woman without her consent and if he has no reasonable grounds for believing she is consenting. In order to consent she must choose and freely agree to have sexual intercourse with him. That agreement does not necessarily have to be a spoken agreement.

Where she is drunk at the time intercourse takes place, it is necessary to consider whether she had the capacity to consent or was too drunk to give consent. If she was too drunk to choose or freely agree to have sexual intercourse, then she has not consented in law. If he has no reasonable grounds for thinking that she has the capacity to choose and freely agree, then he is guilty of rape.

In order to examine the separate and combined effects of posters and text, some participants received only the poster or the written paragraph, whereas others received a combination of both. A control group was also included that received neither the poster nor the paragraph (see Methodology section below for more detail).

We expected the combination of text and poster to be more effective in influencing perceptions of defendant liability and recommended sentences than either medium alone. This prediction was derived from the heuristic-systematic model of attitude change (Chen and Chaiken, 1999), which assumes that the two routes to persuasion can operate concurrently and reinforce each other.

Based on this line of reasoning, three hypotheses were examined about the effects of the Home Office posters, in combination with the effects of written information about the importance of consent.

Hypothesis 5. It was predicted that participants who were presented with one of the Consent Campaign posters prior to and while responding to the rape scenarios would be more inclined to hold the defendant liable and recommend a longer sentence than participants in a control condition who were not exposed to the poster.

Hypothesis 6. It was predicted that the poster would be more successful in influencing judgments in the direction predicted in the previous hypothesis when combined with a written paragraph emphasising the importance of consent in the legal definition of rape than when the poster was presented on its own.

Hypothesis 7. It was predicted that if Hypotheses 5 and 6 were correct, then the effects of the poster and consent paragraph would be most pronounced on participants at intermediate levels of rape myth acceptance. They would have a minimal effect on those who were very low on rape myth acceptance, who would be well aware of the importance of consent already, and on entrenched believers in rape myths, who were likely to be resistant to change.

No specific prediction was made as to whether the poster on its own would be more successful than the written paragraph on its own, but the design of the study enabled this question to be addressed.

The analysis of the posters was based on the same sample of members of the public who provided the data reported in the first part of this chapter. A full description of the sample is given in the methodology section above (see pp 101–2).

Methodology: Poster Evaluation

Posters and Consent Paragraph

The two posters from the Home Office Consent Campaign shown in figure 5.5 were used in the study, either alone or in combination with the consent paragraph in table 5.2. Six different versions of the questionnaire were created, two with one of the two posters, two with one of the posters combined with the consent paragraph, one with the consent paragraph alone, and one with neither poster nor consent paragraph. Participants were randomly allocated to one of the six conditions. In the poster versions, one of the two posters appeared on the screen after participants had read the introductory text and moved on to the second page. There was no text accompanying the poster, and participants were free to look at it as long as they liked before moving on to the next page. All subsequent pages displayed the poster on the right hand side of the screen. This ensured that the poster was constantly in view as participants completed the questionnaire. In the version with the consent paragraph, this replaced the poster on the right hand side of the questionnaire. In the combined poster and paragraph condition, the written paragraph was placed under the poster on every page. Finally, in the control condition, the space on the right side of the screen remained blank.

Results: Poster Evaluation

In line with the objectives of the campaign, Hypothesis 5 predicted that participants exposed to the posters would be more inclined to hold the defendant liable and recommend harsher sentences than participants in a control condition who were not exposed to the posters. Hypothesis 6 predicted that the effect of the posters would be enhanced by combining them with a written paragraph on consent.

The results showed that there was no support for either hypothesis as far as sentencing recommendations were concerned. Recommended sentences were not affected by the posters with or without the consent paragraph.[22] On ratings

---

[22] These hypotheses were examined through, ANOVAs with poster condition, defendant-complainant relationship and coercive strategy as independent variables (with repeated measures on the last two factors) and ratings of defendant liability and sentencing recommendations as dependent variables.

of defendant liability, an overall effect of the poster manipulation was found to be too small to be interpretable.[23] The average ratings of defendant liability for the six conditions are shown in figure 5.6.

Of the average scores shown in figure 5.6, only the one for the prison poster was significantly different from the remaining conditions, but the difference was in the opposite direction from that predicted in Hypothesis 5. Seeing this poster while judging the scenarios led to *lower* ratings of defendant liability than the other five conditions (ie the no-entry poster, both posters in combination with the consent paragraph, the consent paragraph only and the control condition). Neither of the two conditions presenting the poster in combination with the consent paragraph differed in a statistically significant way from the control condition in their impact on perceived defendant liability. Thus, the data failed to support Hypothesis 5 and Hypothesis 6. The posters did not alert participants to the lack of consent in the scenarios, and neither did the consent paragraph or a combination of the two.

Hypothesis 7 postulated that the posters and consent paragraph would have a greater impact on participants with intermediate levels of rape myth acceptance because they would be most easily influenced. We argued that those very

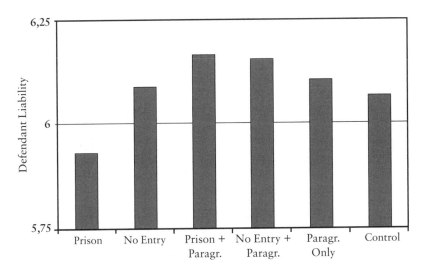

Figure 5.6 **Study 3: Effects of campaign posters and consent paragraph on ratings of defendant liability**

Note: The rating for the prison poster condition was significantly lower than all other means. None of the remaining differences between the conditions was significant. Liability ratings were made on a scale from 1 (not at all) to 7 (very much).

---

[23] $F (5,1998) = 2.54$, $p < .05$, eta^2 = .01, for the poster condition main effect, $F (10,3996) = 2.30$, $p < .05$, eta^2 < .01, for the interaction with defendant-complainant relationship, $F (5,1998) = 2.84$, $p < .05$, eta^2 < .01, for the interaction with coercive strategy.

low on rape myth acceptance would not require a reminder, while those with entrenched rape myth beliefs would be resistant to change. However, the posters and the consent paragraph were ineffective in increasing perceived defendant liability or recommended sentences regardless of how strongly participants believed in rape myths. This was true for both the 'modern rape myths' scale and the more specific scale measuring female precipitation beliefs.[24]

It could be argued that the apparent ineffectiveness of the posters in the sample as a whole which included different age groups, is not a fair reflection of their potential since they were specifically directed at young men between the ages of 18 and 24. To address this claim, the analyses were repeated for the sub-sample of younger men. To ensure a sufficient sample size, all men up to the age of 30 were included in the analysis, yielding 703 eligible participants. The pattern of results was similar to the one obtained for the total sample. Recommended sentences were unaffected by whether or not participants saw the posters and/or consent paragraph. On ratings of defendant liability, findings differed from those obtained for the total sample in that the prison poster on its own did not produce a worse result than the other conditions.[25] The means for the different conditions are shown in figure 5.7.

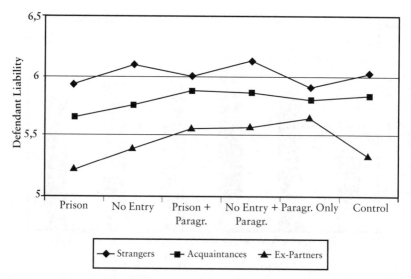

Figure 5.7 *Study 3: Effects of campaign posters and consent paragraph on ratings of defendant liability on men up to the age of 30*

---

[24] The interaction between rape myth acceptance and poster condition were non-significant for both the female precipitation and the modern rape myths measures.

[25] A significant, but small interaction was found between poster condition and defendant-complainant relationship, $F (10,1340) = 2.49$, $p < .01$, $eta^2 < .02$. Post-hoc tests indicated that neither the stranger nor the acquaintance rape cases were affected by the experimental conditions. For the acquaintance rape cases, the prison poster mean was significantly lower than the paragraph only mean but did not differ from the remaining conditions (see Figure 5.7 for means).

None of the five conditions involving the posters and/or the consent paragraph produced defendant liability ratings that were above the control group. The slight differences in means apparent in the figure between the control condition and the three conditions presenting the paragraph were not significant. Thus, looking specifically at the young male target group, it must be concluded that compared to the control condition, the posters and the consent paragraph had no effect, neither alone nor in combination.

Discussion: Schematic Information Processing and Poster Evaluation

With respect to stereotypic perceptions of rape cases, the findings from over 2000 citizens living in the UK largely support the results of the two previous studies with prospective legal professionals. They show that judgments about defendants and complainants in rape scenarios were affected both by participants' acceptance of rape myths and by information activating stereotypes about rape. All case scenarios contained an explicit verbal statement of non-consent from the alleged victim. Nevertheless, defendants were seen as less likely to be liable when the complainant was an acquaintance or former partner rather than a stranger, and when he had exploited her intoxicated state rather than using force. In line with the real rape stereotype, liability ratings and recommended sentences were highest when the defendant was a stranger and when force was used. Perceptions of defendant liability and sentencing recommendations in the alcohol-related rapes were generally lower than in the force-related cases and were unaffected by information about whether he had known the complainant before.

A complementary pattern was found for perceptions of complainant blame. Participants thought the woman was more to blame when the defendant was an acquaintance or ex-partner. They also blamed her more when she was too affected by alcohol to resist rather than being overcome by force. However, looking at the combination of defendant-perpetrator relationship and coercive strategy, a noteworthy finding emerged for the cases in which the woman was too incapacitated to resist. When the defendant was a stranger, the woman was blamed *more* when she was too affected by alcohol to resist than when she was overpowered by force. By contrast, in the ex-partner rapes, she was blamed *less* when she had drunk too much to resist than when force was used. Furthermore, in that situation she was also blamed less than where she was raped, when incapacitated, by a stranger or an acquaintance. A possible interpretation of this finding is that drinking despite not being used to alcohol was regarded as more careless in the company of a stranger or acquaintance than in the company of a former partner. Participants may have felt the complainant should not have needed to be on her guard and aware of the risk of a sexual assault when interacting with a former partner in the same way as she should have been when interacting with a person she knew less well.

It is noteworthy that assessing the complainant as less culpable in this case did not lead participants to hold the defendant more liable. One could argue that the man should have been aware of his former partner's susceptibility to the effects of alcohol and that he had exploited his former partner's trust, which would make his actions particularly blameworthy and deserving of a harsher sentence. However, there was no evidence of elevated ratings of defendant liability or recommendation of longer sentences in the present data.

While participants were generally swayed in their judgments by information pertaining to rape stereotypes, individual attitudes also made a difference. Support for stereotypical beliefs about rape was substantial, with a quarter of the participants tending to agree rather than disagree with the views expressed in the female precipitation scale and 44 per cent with those expressed in the modern rape myth acceptance scale. Men had higher mean scores, and their mean score on the modern rape myth measure was above the midpoint, ie on the 'agreement' side of the response scale. Finally, despite overall means being below or only just above the scale midpoint, individual differences in rape-supportive attitudes, even at a relatively low level of endorsement, were linked to differences in judgments about defendants and complainants in the case scenarios. The more participants believed in female precipitation as a cause of rape and accepted modern myths about sexual aggression, the more they were inclined to blame the complainant, the lower they rated the defendant's legal liability and the shorter the sentences they recommended. When judging defendant liability, rape-supportive attitudes particularly affected judgments in the ex-partner and alcohol-related rapes, ie those cases that differed most from the real rape stereotype.

With regard to gender differences, Study 3 showed that gender as such made no difference to perceptions of defendant liability, complainant blame and recommended sentences. What did make a difference in this regard was the extent to which participants subscribed to rape myths. More men than women were at the high end of the rape myth acceptance range. Thus, gender exerted an indirect effect on judgments about rape cases. The present findings closely match those found in a study with German law graduates using a similar methodology (Krahé, Temkin, Bieneck and Berger, in press), showing that although gender *per se* may be unrelated to judgments about defendant and complainants, differences between men and women with regard to rape myth acceptance indicate that gender is a relevant variable in understanding judgments about rape cases.

The second aim of this study was to evaluate the effectiveness of two posters from the Home Office Consent Campaign which was designed to raise young men's awareness of the importance of consent, a campaign that cost £400,000 (Home Office, 2006d). The short-term effects of the posters were tested, both on their own and combined with a written paragraph explaining the meaning of consent in the legal definition of rape. It was argued that if the posters when brought to the attention of participants did not have an immediate effect on them while responding to information about a woman's non-consent, it would be unlikely that the posters would be effective under the more elusive conditions which prevail when they are publicly displayed. Unfortunately, the present study was unable to demonstrate the effectiveness of the posters. Whether or not participants were shown the posters while judging the rape scenarios made practically no difference to the way they perceived the liability of a defendant who blatantly ignored the woman's expression of non-consent, and it had no effect on the sentences they recommended if he was found guilty. The consent paragraph also failed to have an impact, either on its own or in combination with the posters. The only effect that did emerge was contrary to the campaign's objectives. The prison poster actually reduced ratings of defendant liability.

Follow-up analyses with the subgroup of young men, at whom the campaign was specifically directed, showed that the prison poster was particularly counterproductive in the context of the ex-partner rape scenarios, the very cases in which raising awareness about consent might be thought to be most critical. A possible explanation for this finding is that rather than emphasising the importance of consent, the poster highlights the undesirability of the consequences a defendant would face if found guilty of rape. Participants may have asked themselves whether they would want the defendant in the scenario to end up as shown on the poster and may have tuned down their liability ratings in order to protect him from such a fate. The caption on the poster 'If you don't get a "yes" before sex, who'll be your next sleeping partner?' might even be read as suggesting that the man might himself be subjected to sexual aggression once in prison, thus shifting the focus from consent to punishment and revenge. In fact, 5 per cent of those interviewed in the Home Office's own evaluation of the campaign thought the poster message was that if you rape you will get raped in prison (Home Office, 2006d).[26] Overall, there is little evidence in the present data that the posters were effective in achieving the stated goal of promoting awareness about consent and dispelling myths about rape (see table 5.1), and there are indications that the prison poster might even have been counterproductive.

5.3 GENERAL DISCUSSION AND CONCLUSIONS FROM THE THREE STUDIES

The three studies presented in chapters four and five examined the role of stereotypical beliefs about rape in reaching judgments about specific rape cases. They were designed to support our claim that schematic information processing infiltrates the normatively prescribed data-driven appraisal of the evidence to the disadvantage of the complainant. Across all studies, including undergraduate law students, graduate students in vocational legal training and a large sample of members of the public, the findings show a high degree of consistency. The

---

[26] The poster's message is also somewhat misleading. If the majority of rapes are unreported and of those reported only 5% end in conviction, there is in fact a very low probability that men who rape will end up in prison.

final study also included an evaluation of a recent poster campaign designed to highlight the need for consent in sexual interactions. This section will integrate the findings from the three studies and highlight their implications for the attitude problem we see as underlying the justice gap in sexual assault.

Defendant-Complainant Relationship and Coercive Strategy

In every rape scenario used in the three studies, the complainant's non-consent was made explicit by her stating as much in so many words. Yet, despite the presence of this key element of the legal definition of rape, participants were influenced in their perceptions of defendant liability and complainant blame by information tapping into the real rape stereotype. They were more convinced that the defendant should be held liable and blamed the complainant less in stranger rapes than in rapes by acquaintances and, in particular, rapes by ex-partners. In Study 3, they were also more convinced that the defendant should be held liable and that the complainant was less to blame when force was used to obtain sexual intercourse against the complainant's will than when the defendant exploited the complainant's incapacitated state. There was, however, one exception to this pattern, which applied to the rape of an intoxicated complainant by her ex-partner. Participants attributed less blame to the complainant in this situation than where she was too affected by alcohol to resist a stranger or an acquaintance. This finding hints at the underlying considerations leading to complainant blame. It seems that women are blamed for alcohol-related rape because they are seen as having put themselves at risk. In the case of rape by an ex-partner, however, a woman may be forgiven for being caught off guard because she had less reason to distrust him than a stranger or acquaintance. Complainants were judged more leniently in these cases, but defendants were judged no more harshly for this abuse of trust than those who raped an incapacitated stranger or acquaintance. This is another indication of the double standard applied to the actions of men and women.

Rape-Supportive Attitudes

Across the three studies, a highly consistent pattern also emerged with respect to the impact of generalised attitudes about rape. Although the extent to which participants agreed with female precipitation beliefs differed somewhat between the three studies (being lowest in the vocational law students and highest in the undergraduate law students), differences in rape-supportive attitudes were consistently related to differences in judgments about the cases. Participants' belief that women precipitate rape through their appearance and behaviour was a strong predictor of assessments of defendant liability and complainant blame in the given situations throughout the three studies. The more participants subscribed to this belief, the more they blamed the complainant, the less convinced they were that the defendant was liable, and – in studies 2 and 3 – the shorter the sentence they recommended. Parallel effects were found for the more general measure of acceptance of modern myths about sexual aggression included in the last study. Perceptions of complainant blame differed as a function of participants' support for female precipitation beliefs and rape myths, regardless of the relationship between defendant and complainant or the coercive strategy used by the defendant. For defendant liability, it was shown that the tendency of those believing in rape myths to exonerate the defendant was particularly strong in the ex-partner cases, ie those scenarios that were most different from the real rape stereotype. Even though all participants tended to be less convinced that the defendant was liable in these cases compared with the classic forcible rape by a stranger, those accepting rape myths showed a more pronounced downward adjustment of perceived defendant liability.

It is important to note that all participants based their judgments on the same 'data', ie the same case descriptions, so it cannot be argued that the differences found in ratings of liability, complainant blame and appropriate sentences were the result of differences in the cases to be judged. Instead, it is clear that identical case material was interpreted in different ways, resulting in different conclusions, depending on the attitudes brought to the study by the participants. This is clear evidence of schematic information processing in a task that is normatively defined as data-driven. While attitudes had a comparatively small effect on cases matching the real rape stereotype, ie the forcible stranger rape, they became more influential as the cases deviated from the stereotype. Our findings based on simulated cases thus fit in with evidence from other sources, such as analysis of police files, that the non-stereotypical cases – which represent a large part of those reported – are disproportionately affected by the justice gap (see chapter two).

The Role of Gender

While there are certain differences in the results of each study, one finding that comes over loud and clear is that the crucial determinant of judgments about rape cases is the extent to which people subscribe to rape myths. Thus it tends to be attitudes rather than an unbiased evaluation of the facts which determine judgments in these cases. It is also clear from a large body of previous research as well as our studies 1 and 3 that men subscribe to rape myths to a greater extent than women. The one exception to this highly consistent pattern is the lack of gender differences in rape myth acceptance found in Study 2. On the basis of a single study, it is difficult to explain this finding. One possibility is that gender differences were eroded by participants' emerging identity as professional lawyers, but this would need to be explored in future research.

Given the indirect effect of gender on perceptions of rape cases via rape-supportive attitudes, gender may be seen as a 'marker' of differences in attitudes which influence perceivers' judgments of rape cases. Men outnumbered women by a substantial margin among participants showing agreement with female precipitation beliefs (studies 1 and 3) and modern rape myths (Study 3). Therefore, on the basis of statistical probability, the odds of including individuals with prejudicial attitudes about women's role in sexual assault will be lower the more female members there are on a jury. However, this is too crude a measure to warrant the conclusion that women are likely to give rape complainants a fairer deal. Differences between men and women at the group level do not mean that an individual female will be less prone to rape stereotypes than an individual male. A substantial proportion of women endorsed rape myths to a greater extent than many men in our samples. Just like men, women scoring higher on female precipitation beliefs were less inclined to hold the defendant liable, recommended a shorter sentence and blamed the complainant more than women who were less accepting of these beliefs. In terms of policy implications for rape trials, these findings suggest that intervention efforts should be directed first and foremost at altering attitudes towards rape by challenging rape stereotypes which attribute blame to women and exonerate men. Strategies for doing this will be considered in chapter ten.

Evaluating the Rape Awareness Posters

A particular aim of Study 3 was to evaluate two posters designed to raise awareness about the importance of consent as part of a wider Home Office media campaign on rape prevention. The posters used in the campaign were subjected to an experimental evaluation in which their potential for increasing recipients' responsiveness to the issue of consent was examined in a large sample of the general public. The posters did not enhance participants' perceptions of defendant liability, nor did they affect sentencing recommendations in any way. Indeed, one of the posters led to reduced ratings of defendant liability compared with a control condition. This indicates that they failed to raise awareness of the fact that complainants expressed their non-consent in all the scenarios. When the posters were combined with a written paragraph explaining the meaning and importance of consent in the legal definition of rape, this made no difference.

The findings from the evaluation underline the need for careful design and pre-testing of the material used in media campaigns. We have no information about how precisely the posters were developed, but independent research was carried out before the advertising launch. On the basis of the present findings, it seems that their potential for producing the intended changes in attitudes and judgments, including the risk of backfiring, was not sufficiently tested in the developmental stage of the campaign. We are not claiming that our data entirely rule out the possibility that the posters would be more effective in their natural habitat, although it is hard to see how they could be subjected to a stringent evaluation in those circumstances. However, the absence of any effects in the present data in the direction intended by the campaign designers is not an encouraging sign. It is true that the posters were only one element of a broader media campaign, but whether the combined effects of the different elements would be more effective is an open question. Clearly, future interventions, such as a broader campaign to tackle myths about rape envisaged by the Home Office (Home Office, 2006d), should be based on thorough preliminary research, grounded in theories of attitude change, to select effective media messages. In chapter ten, we will discuss other media campaigns designed to raise rape awareness and make a case for exploring their potential in combination with rape education programmes based on face to face instruction.

6

Rape, Rape Trials and the Justice Gap: Some Views from the Bench and Bar

SO FAR IT has been suggested that rape stereotypes, while by no means universally ascribed to, remain deeply embedded in the culture. Rape myths and stereotypes involve derogatory beliefs about rape victims. They focus on false allegations, the lack of credibility and sexually permissive conduct of those who allege rape and their own precipitating role in the events which occurred. These myths and stereotypes serve to cast doubt on complainants' allegations and the significance of their experience, frequently reducing rape to an attack, out of the blue, by a stranger on a faultless victim. In the preceding chapters it has been shown that aspirant lawyers and members of the public often subscribe to such stereotypical views. The present chapter seeks to explore this matter further by looking at the results of a qualitative interview study with a group of barristers and judges. It will consider first their views of the problems involved in obtaining convictions in rape cases including those caused by police, barristers and juries. This provides further support for the conclusions derived from the quantitative data already discussed. It will then go on to look at some of the attitudes of the interviewees themselves towards the issues surrounding rape which may also play a role in the justice gap.

6.1 METHODOLOGY OF THE INTERVIEW STUDY

Semi-structured, in-depth interviews on the basis of anonymity were conducted, coded and analysed by the first author in the context of a Home Office study looking into the impact of the sexual history provisions contained in sections 41–43 of the Youth Justice and Criminal Evidence Act 1999 (Kelly, Temkin and Griffiths, 2006). The interviews ranged beyond these provisions into the general area of the crime of rape itself, rape trials and the treatment of rape in the criminal justice system as well as into other aspects of the evidential law surrounding rape. This unpublished data is presented here and in chapter seven.

Sample

A total of 17 judges (15 men and 2 women) and 7 barristers (3 of them women) were interviewed in London and Manchester across 5 courts in 2003, resulting in 24 interviews altogether. The sample is not representative in a statistical sense of the total population of judges and barristers involved in rape trials, but it brings together a broad range of professional experience in dealing with rape cases. All judges were 'rape-ticketed', ie specifically licensed to try rape cases, but represented a spectrum in terms of their experience in doing so. At one end was a judge nearing retirement who had tried hundreds of rape cases during his time on the bench. At the other were those who had not been 'ticketed' for long and had tried fewer than 10 rape cases. In the middle were those who had tried 30–40 cases. All had considerable experience of trying other sexual cases, and some had experience of dealing with these cases as barristers or in one case as a solicitor. The sample, therefore, whilst small, comprised judges with substantial experience of presiding over sexual cases. The judges also varied in terms of the proportion of their caseload that was currently devoted to trying rape cases, ranging from 80 per cent to five per cent in one case.

The barristers were at different points in their careers: two were Queen's Counsel[1] and the rest had been practising for between 10 and 21 years. All were experienced in dealing with sex cases, and six out of seven were highly experienced, having both defended and prosecuted, although most specialised in one or the other.

Interview Schedule and Procedure

Interviews were conducted individually in a semi-structured format, providing a set of pre-defined questions but encouraging interviewees to go beyond those questions to address issues they considered important in the way rape was dealt with by the courts. A summary of the interview schedule is set out in Appendix 2. To ensure anonymity, interviewees were assigned numbers randomly rather than in the order in which they were interviewed. They are denoted as Judge 1 to Judge 17 and B1 to B7, respectively, throughout this chapter. Full notes were taken of all the interviews, and most were tape-recorded and then transcribed. The judges and barristers gave generously of their time, with interviews lasting a minimum of one and a half hours.

---

[1] Senior barristers appointed by the Lord Chancellor.

6.2 THE PERCEIVED PROBLEMS

Interviewees were asked whether they had any concerns about how the criminal justice system is currently dealing with rape cases. Most were willing to concede that despite real improvements to the way the criminal justice system works in rape and related cases, there was a range of problems which had a bearing on low conviction rates. They identified, *inter alia*, problems arising from the conduct of police, barristers, juries and judges.[2] Their observations shed further light on the quantitative research findings set out in previous chapters.

Poor Policing

In chapter two several studies were cited which showed that rape myths were accepted to a significant extent by police officers, and that the attrition of rape cases within the criminal justice system is primarily occurring at the police investigation stage. A sceptical attitude towards rape complaints born of an adherence to rape stereotypes appears to be a factor in the manner in which rape complaints are classified, investigated and pursued. The qualitative data in the present study further suggests that police slackness, possibly resulting partially from this scepticism, hinders the prosecution of rape and provides opportunities for defence counsel to roll out the stereotypes and myths of rape to good effect as far as their clients are concerned.

Evidence-gathering

Five interviewees were highly critical of evidence gathering by the police which led to gaps in the prosecution case. Judge 13 criticised the police for failing to collect evidence in the 'golden hour'. She said that very often there were witnesses, 'people in the next-door room who've heard something. Somebody who took the complainant along to the police station or somebody who called the police'. Often the police waited until they had tracked down and interviewed the suspect before attempting to get statements from such witnesses, by which time they had often disappeared or were unable to give as clear a statement as they might have done had they been interviewed immediately. Judge 17 spoke of one case where the police had taken the complainant's statement two months after she reported rape. After the case had been listed for trial, it was also realised that no statements had been taken from two crucial witnesses. By this time there was a hopeless muddle as to what happened when. He finally ended up reporting the investigating officer to the area superintendent. Judge 10 referred to a recent

---

[2] Interviewees also expressed concerns about special measures. With three exceptions, all the interviewees were of the opinion that TV link was detrimental to the prosecution.

case in which the complainant had reported rape immediately to the police but this had never been mentioned to the CPS. Evidence that she had done so was subsequently discovered in the police officer's notebook.

Judge 17 referred to police reluctance to do necessary forensic examinations for reasons of cost:

> I think that there is a reluctance, because of cost, to carry out all necessary forensic examinations. They'll say 'Oh we sent her knickers away, but we didn't send the bra away', or something like that, and it may be significant.

Police failure to marshal the available evidence leaves complainants vulnerable in a situation in which their credibility, the central issue, already faces a major challenge from stereotypical assumptions.

Statement-taking

B3, a QC who had specialised for many years in defending rape cases, explained that police statement-taking was invariably a gift to defence lawyers (see generally on this Heaton-Armstrong, Shepherd, Gudjonsson and Wolchover, 2006). Police officers always failed to write down enough of what the complainant had said. This gave the defence lawyer the chance to make her out to be a liar for failing to say to the police what she was now saying in court or for saying that she had told things to the police which were not contained in her statement. He explained exactly what he did to exploit this situation:

> If you're alleging you've been raped, and [the police] take a very short statement from you, you come to the Crown Court to give evidence, and an experienced, skilful prosecution counsel examines you in chief, and gets all the detail, and all the dimensions of the whole experience. Of course I'm going to stand up and say, 'Well you never said any of this in your witness statement'.[. . .] Sometimes then a complainant [. . .] is so thrown by it, that she'll say, 'Oh well I told the officer but he/she didn't put it in there'. And then you just hit them again, even harder, because you say 'Well the statement was read back to you afterwards. You were told you could add, alter or correct anything you wanted to'. They can't deny that, because if they do, the officers will say, well yes they did, so there's another potential lie.

Thus, poor statement-taking leading to apparent inconsistencies and contradictions in the complainant's story allows defence lawyers to cash in on general suspicions about the credibility of rape victims. B3 considered that police officers needed far more training in statement-taking and that complainants would be helped if they were videoed when making their complaint because 'in the case of a genuine complainant, it will leap off the screen'.[3]

---

[3] The Government has now decided to allow such videoed statements in court: see Office for Criminal Justice Reform (2007).

Failure to Probe the Evidence

B3 expressed the view that some police officers, in seeking to empathise with rather than to judge rape complainants, were failing to probe their accounts of what happened and were thereby doing them a disservice since probing might reveal the need for further evidence gathering:

> So I don't think there's enough probing, which might lead to evidence that might tend to corroborate what the complainant is saying, and/or which might at an early stage demonstrate areas of weakness where other areas might be helped or at least it gives her then a chance to explain something which at first blush might appear to be a little inexplicable.

Defence Counsel Behaving Badly

The tactics used by defence counsel in rape cases, which involve exploiting the stereotypes of rape, maligning the complainant's behaviour and attempting to discredit and even harass her, were identified in a previous study based on interviews conducted in 1996 (Temkin, 2000: 229–36). In the present study B1, a QC, commented on the continuing bad behaviour of some defence counsel:

> But there are barristers still who defend who simply want to destroy a complainant. And I mean that. They know that if they can turn her into a snivelling wreck, or make her look like a complete tart, they will win their case, and it's wrong. And section 41 has gone a long way to stopping that, but people will still try and do it, because that's the way.[4]

Barristers would also commonly ask complainants if they were after the compensation money from the Criminal Injuries Compensation Scheme, and some would search for a single lie told by the complainant and use that to argue strongly that the complainant was not someone to be believed about anything, including her claim of rape.

Defence strategies combined with the fact that complainants are already unnerved by the court setting ensure that often they are no match for skilled and experienced counsel. Indeed, B3 confessed that it was simply too easy to defend in rape cases and that the imbalance between an experienced defence counsel and a complainant was so great that he had finally decided that he could no longer carry on with this work:

> On a personal level, it wasn't very satisfactory, because I became conscious [. . .] there's an imbalance [. . .] between cross-examining a rape complainant who, whether she's telling the truth or not, is in a highly emotional state, potentially if not actually very nervous, is in an alien environment, and, of course, once you've been jury advocate for five, seven, eight, ten years, you're in your natural habitat, and it's a very unfair contest.

---

[4] See Burton, Evans and Sanders (2007) confirming the persistence of defence bad practice.

One judge also voiced some mild criticism about defence barristers who remind the jury time and again of the need to be sure:

> You'd be forgiven for raising your eyebrows when you hear defence counsel mention the burden and standard of proof for the fifth or sixth or seventh time! (Judge 11)

Incompetent Prosecuting Counsel

Defence narratives based on stereotypical assumptions about rape need to be challenged if prosecutions are to be successful. Prosecuting counsel have to be up to the job of doing so. However, there was considerable consensus among judges and barristers about low standards in prosecuting. Identical views had been expressed in an earlier study of barristers who had been interviewed mostly in 1996. Clearly, not much had changed in the seven-year period since then (Temkin, 2000: 227). Both judges and barristers in the present study expressed concerns about the inexperience and incompetence of prosecuting counsel, and that the CPS did not do enough to monitor performance. It was suggested that all too often prosecuting counsel failed to make the points which could or should be made. B1 emphasised the need for highly experienced counsel to prosecute in rape cases, particularly where children or people with disabilities were involved:

> It is a specialist area. You need to know what you're doing in these cases. You need to know what to look for, you need to know how to get the people to give the evidence, you need to know the law without having to look it up. Inappropriate questions, you have to be very hot, and stop things being done to the complainant. It takes quite a lot for a judge to say to a defence counsel 'That's an inappropriate question', whereas if you're acute on the uptake as a prosecutor – I mean you don't even stand up and say 'I object', – you just say 'No', or 'You can't ask that', and defence counsel will normally back down.

B3 commented that very often in date rape cases the attitude was, 'Well, you know, Buggins can prosecute that, it's a dead easy case. But rape is rape is rape'. He said that by contrast 'you have a lot of rapes going to defenders who are very good at what they do'.

There was concern that rape cases were no longer regarded as serious cases requiring highly expert counsel. Judge 5 expressed great concern that there had been a serious downgrading of prosecution counsel and considered that this was a major factor in poor conviction rates:

> In my view, and this is another reason why [. . .] the conviction rate in rape is low, is because the Crown Prosecution Service do not brief counsel adequately experienced both in conduct of sexual cases and in terms of call. [. . .] It is my perception that over the years [. . .] that there has been a serious downgrading of the counsel who represent the prosecution. You know, when I started only a silk[5] would do it. Then you would

---

[5] Queen's Counsel, a senior barrister.

get a silk usually defending, but not prosecuting. Then it didn't matter whether it was a leading junior. Now it seems to me it doesn't really matter whether it's Uncle Tom Cobley or all. And that is something I feel very, very strongly about. The Crown Prosecution Service certainly here are not keeping a proper eye on the advocates they brief, and they are not briefing adequately for cases of this kind, which do call for skills. They don't have staff in every court all the time as you used to have, they don't have staff who are experienced in knowing whether an advocate is good or not, they haven't got a clue.

Judge 5 did not consider that upgrading the payment for prosecuting in these cases had made any difference: 'It doesn't matter if you're being equally paid if the Crown Prosecution Service is still briefing somebody who's not competent to do the particular trial'. In her view, close monitoring of prosecution counsel and an improvement in the standards of prosecuting in sexual cases 'would make a very big difference to your conviction rates'.

In its 2004 policy document, the CPS states its commitment 'to instructing advocates who have the right skills to prosecute rape cases including their ability to deal sensitively with victims and witnesses'. It promises also to ensure that prosecuting counsel is proactive in objecting to inappropriate questioning about complainants' sexual history and that they object to allegations about her character or demeanour (Crown Prosecution Service, 2004: 17).[6] These undertakings are to be warmly welcomed and will need to be effectively monitored.

Judges' Attitudes towards Complainants

Stereotypical attitudes towards rape may translate into a lack of sympathy for and impatience with its alleged victims. It was the opinion of B1, a QC who had specialised in sexual cases, that some older judges have a less than empathetic approach to complainants:

Some of the older judges are very dismissive. [. . .] A woman that's having difficulty giving evidence, and is sort of struggling to say things or crying, and judges are sort of, 'Come on, come, come', you know, 'Come on', do you know what I mean? I've had women who've literally walked out of court three or four times during giving their evidence because it's too much, and the judge is sort of irritated. And, you know, 'If she does that again, we'll just have to stop the case'.

On the other hand B5 commented:

The sort of remarks that you hear and occasionally still make it into the national press are largely gone. Judges who have their tickets to conduct rape trials are generally very good, particularly with young witnesses. I think the judges are very good.

Thus, the interviews suggest that there is very good practice to be found among some trial judges, but with others old attitudes and approaches persist.

[6] See also ch 9 for further steps which the CPS is now taking.

Juries

Interviewees had a considerable amount to say about juries in rape cases. Their observations dovetail significantly with the findings from the quantitative studies set out in the previous chapters of this book. Ten interviewees (seven judges and three barristers) regarded juries as a barrier to convictions in rape cases. Of these, three pointed out that juries were simply a microcosm of society. B1 considered that if anyone was to blame for poor conviction rates, it was society itself: 'People should realise that juries acquit, it's not the system, the system doesn't fail women: we as a society fail them'. (B1) The jury barrier was thought to operate in different ways and for a variety of reasons.

The Influence of Rape Stereotypes and Schematic Reasoning

Some interviewees showed a keen awareness of the stereotypes and myths about rape that influence jury decision-making. For example, Judge 18 commented:

> I think one of the problems is that in the public perception, rape is Jack the Ripper. And I think they find it very difficult to go from Jack the Ripper to Don Giovanni. The Jack the Ripper type of rapes don't, I think, create any great problem for juries. They convict. But there aren't, actually, when you go through the figures, very many of them.

In his view, in cases which did not match the Jack the Ripper stereotype, juries brought their own experience to bear and were inclined to believe that rape allegations were brought by women who consented at the time but afterwards regretted it.

Judge 16 also spoke of the difficulty of getting juries to convict in relationship rapes where a judge would have no doubt that a rape had taken place:

> I have seen complainants, for example in cases where there has been a relationship with the defendant, and I, with what I hope with some experience of gauging the veracity of evidence, have been quite convinced that the complainant has been telling the truth, but a jury take, if you like, the rough-and-ready first-time approach of there's been this relationship and therefore we cannot be sure of guilt.[7]

B5 considered that juries had totally unrealistic expectations of how genuine victims should behave:

> People expect victims of rape to behave in an unrealistic fashion, because that's what society imagines or people imagine they would do – to complain straightaway, to be distraught, to fight [. . .] not to give in. I think any woman in that situation would [give in] – you're not physically capable of struggling. [They] look for injuries on a victim when, you know, in the vast majority of cases there are no injuries. I think all of those are people's perceptions of what a rape is and those are unrealistic expectations.

---

[7] Compare findings in studies described in chs 4 and 5 where defendants charged with the rape of an ex-partner were consistently judged more leniently.

Three interviewees considered that juries do not decide cases on the facts but would decide them in the face of the evidence. Judge 1 said:

> The problem, which I do not understand, is that even with women on the jury, juries are sometimes loath to convict when they should. Now no amount of legislation will alter [that] factor. [. . .] I could give you examples of cases of acquittals, not many, in the teeth of the evidence.

Judge 1 provided two examples of cases where the complainant had in his view undoubtedly been raped, but where the jury acquitted. In the first, the defendant was the complainant's former partner who claimed a desire on her part for rough sex in order to 'explain the horrible bruises and tears on her chest [. . .] which is the usual answer to this sort of case'. It was, he thought, this previous relationship which explained the acquittal. The second case, which the judge described as 'the worst case ever', involved the targeting and gang rape of a 15-year-old girl who had not at first been frank with her mother about what had happened. Judge 1 said that he had been so shocked by the acquittals in these two cases that he had thereafter changed his approach to summing up:

> Now I'm bound to say, [. . .] those two cases changed my attitude to summing up. Because I believe in summing up down the line, and letting the jury come to their conclusion. But I've come to the conclusion that in these cases it is necessary for the judge to make the points that ought to be made.

Judge 15 considered that juries do not decide cases on their facts but in the light of their own experience, which results in wrongful acquittals:

> There are very few other areas of law where people, I suspect, will not necessarily concentrate on the facts but draw on their own experience [. . .] they're asked to decide the case on the facts. I'm not convinced that they do.

Judge 18 mentioned a case in which the evidence against the defendant had been beyond doubt but the jury had nonetheless acquitted:

> Their evidence was cast iron, in my view they were extremely good, sensible teenagers who gave their evidence, slightly embarrassed, obviously, but very, very well. The jury knew that this man had served ten years for sexual offences, and they acquitted him. I'm bound to say there were gasps all round the court.[8]

The judge commented that even if juries were told of the accused's previous convictions, this would be no guarantee that they would come to the right result.

Attributing Blame to the Victim

B1, a QC, considered that juries were moralistic in their judgments about female behaviour and were prone to acquit in the face of the evidence:

---

[8] In this case, the accused had been released on licence from his 10-year sentence for sexual offences. After the jury had delivered its verdict, the judge deliberately dealt with a separate and revealing breach of this licence. The jury then exited shamefaced from court.

> Juries seem to judge rape cases differently. They become desperately moralistic, and there's a lot of 'Well, I wouldn't have dressed like that, and I wouldn't have done this' and [. . .] it doesn't appear to come out in any other sort of case.

Similarly B5 commented:

> I don't think any amount of change in the law will change certain jurors' attitudes to saying 'Well, she went back to his flat, she deserves it', or 'oh it's six of one half a dozen of the other, we can't decide'.

B1, along with other interviewees, considered that there were certain cases which were sure-fire losers, no matter how great the skill or experience of prosecuting counsel. These were cases involving estranged couples, date rapes where some consensual intimacy had taken place or cases where the girl was drunk and found a man having sex with her (see chapter two).[9]

B3 explained how, when defending, he would concentrate on the complainant's behaviour. The obvious effect of this strategy would be to invoke female precipitation myths in the minds of the jury. By way of example he mentioned a woman he knew who went up to a man's room in a hotel for a brandy after having a meal with this man in a hotel:

> You can imagine, can't you, an articulate skilful defence advocate in his speech to the jury saying, 'Well, look at the circumstances. How long had she known him? She's an intelligent woman, she's a very educated woman [. . .] why do you think she went to his room for a brandy when she could so easily have had a brandy at the bar?' And that of itself might just be sufficient for the jury to conclude she's probably telling the truth, but we just can't be sure.

He added:

> I would think 50–60 per cent of the acquittals I've been involved in when defending have resulted from circumstances where I'm able to address the jury on the basis that if you looked at the behaviour of the complainant and the circumstances, they just could not be sure that she's telling the truth, the whole truth and nothing but the truth.

Judge 12 said that juries do not like cases involving two adults where the complainant agrees to go up to D's flat for coffee. He commented: 'People get themselves into situations'. He took the view that judges were more likely to convict in those situations but thought that it was a good thing that juries dealt with such cases.

Disbelieving Attitudes and Lack of Experience

Judge 15 thought that there was a real problem in gaining convictions in cases involving the sexual abuse of children because juries were loath to believe what

---

[9] The particular difficulty of gaining convictions where the complainant was drunk highlighted by B1 and other interviewees sheds further light on other research findings that some men target women who are drunk or whom they could get drunk. See ch 2 and, eg Kelly (2002: 12); Koss and Cleveland (1997); Regan and Kelly (2001).

could happen to children. They were gullible and could be taken in by implausible defences or led astray by tangential matters:

> I had an acquittal in a rape the other week, where I'm bound to say, I put my head in my hands – this was systematic sexual abuse. And I mean the evidence was very compelling, except for one problem, that the child initially had not been entirely straight in the early stages, which was entirely understandable, and because there was therefore the fact that she had lied once, the jury acquitted. I was in disbelief, frankly. I mean that was a very strong case.

Judge 18 similarly stated that in the more horrific cases, juries were unable to 'get their mind round' the fact that the things which were described could actually have happened:

> Juries find it difficult, almost as though they don't want to believe that somebody has been treated in the way which is alleged, or that the defendant has acted in that particular way.

Judge 1 pointed out that juries had difficulty drawing inferences from the facts and the evidence. This is clearly a particular difficulty in rape cases where there will almost never be witnesses to the event:

> But I always say this about juries: juries like to see blood on the knife. They don't like inferring. And there are plenty of times when a judge will infer and a jury will not. Now, many times they're wrong, but sometimes they're right.

Judge 15 spoke of the reluctance of an inexperienced jury to convict once defence counsel has rammed home the standard of proof required:

> If it is a question of the word of the man against the woman alone, they've been reminded of the burden and standard of proof three times at least, and they can't hack it. The defence may draw upon the golden thread more often if there's not much else. And then you're asking them to be sure, and most of them – they're in here for a fortnight-if they're a first week jury, until they've drawn blood, they tend to shy away from conviction. That's I think our perception.

Thus, the judges and barristers drew on their own experience of situations where acquittals were likely to occur. Their impressions formed on the basis of first-hand observations of real trials concur markedly with the findings in Study 3 (see chapter five). They provide vivid confirmation that stereotypical conceptions of rape shared by members of society play an important role in the attrition process.

Penalties for Rape

Six interviewees considered that juries were deterred from convicting by the severe penalties for rape or by their inaccurate perceptions of these penalties. This was because juries did not consider non-stranger rape to be that serious and believed complainants were at least partly to blame. Judge 5 commented:

> And principally because I think there is still a perception amongst the general public who form juries, that if you've been in a relationship with the man, or if you go out with him and you go to a pub and have loads and loads and loads of drinks with him, and then on a particular occasion he has sex with you, well, I mean, OK, maybe you didn't want it, but it's not so terrible is it, after all, and it isn't worth him going to prison for six years [. . .] And therefore, as they have no alternative, they acquit. And I think that that is one of the most important considerations.

Judge 15 also commented:

> I think jurors have a perception as to the sentence that inevitably follows from rape. I think that the juries perhaps feel that if we convict this man of rape – and they're always well dressed at the trial, aren't they, they come across in their best – then this man's going to get ten years.

Two interviewees indicated that they themselves considered that sentences for "date rape" had indeed become too high.

The impressions of the judges as far as rape penalties are concerned accord with research findings. Kerr's (1978) mock jury research, for example, found evidence that the more severe a prescribed penalty for a given crime the more evidence of guilt is necessary for conviction by a jury. Similarly, Kaplan and Simon (1972) found that when penalties are increased, conviction rates by mock juries may decrease. A more recent mock jury study found that participants were significantly more likely to convict of rape where they were allowed to render a verdict *and* recommend a sentence (Allison, 1996). By having the power to control the sentence, it appears they felt less reluctant to convict. This pattern was especially prominent for women.

Female Members of the Jury

Six interviewees blamed women members of the jury for undeserved acquittals or hinted that they might be to blame, but all lacked any proper evidence to support their claims. Judge 18 based his views in part on discussions he had with his usher who picked up snippets of conversation from jury members as he escorted them to and fro. B1 said that a lot could be gleaned from the manifest reactions of members of the jury to certain evidence. Judge 18 said that his usher and his clerk were keeping a tally on the make-up of the sexes in juries in rape trials in his court. On this basis he concluded, along, he said, with some fellow judges that 'in those cases where there are acquittals that you find it difficult to accept, the jury consists of a majority of women'. He went on to state:

> Now I can think of two particular cases that I've had in the last eight or nine months, excellent complainants, very well-given evidence, and if I'd been sitting alone or sitting, as I say, with my clerk and usher in a three-man court, they would undoubtedly have been convicted. And yet, to our utter astonishment, there were acquittals, and in one jury I think there were eight women, and in the other I think there were seven.

Judge 18 averred that if anybody thought that more female judges would improve conviction rates, they were likely to be sorely disappointed. However, it is not entirely clear that this spot of empirical research is convincing. If the seven or eight women all voted to convict and the remaining males to acquit, the result would have been an acquittal in each case.

B5 also said: 'I think actually often women are harder on female victims than men on the jury'. When asked to explain how she could tell she said: 'You can see how receptive they are to certain points'.

Judge 6 commented:

> You know, professional opinion has moved on, but I don't think that the views of – I don't like the word 'ordinary members of the public', but if I can say [. . .] middle-aged ladies, if you like [have moved on].

Judge 5 on the other hand thought that it was young men on juries who might baulk at convicting another man of non-stranger rape since they could visualise themselves in the defendant's situation. B1 echoed this view that the problem lay on 'both sides of the sex divide':

> 'There but for the grace of God' go so many people, I think comes into people's perception: 'I remember when I was a youngster I didn't get myself into those situations', or 'I remember when I was a youngster and I did get myself into those situations, and how would I have felt'.

The hunches of interviewees about women on juries in rape trials do not accord with psychological research which suggests that the truth is more complex. As shown in chapter two, many studies demonstrate that women are *more* inclined to hold defendants liable, less inclined to attribute blame to victims and more likely to demand longer prison sentences for the assailant than men are. However, as shown in the literature and the studies described in chapters four and five, the crucial determinant of judgments about rape cases is whether a person of either sex has negative attitudes about rape victims and endorses rape myths. Studies mostly show that women are less inclined to have such attitudes. However, women who do endorse rape myths do not differ in their judgments about rape cases from men with similar attitudes.

Overall, the judges and barristers interviewed in this study identified between them a number of problems in the prosecution of sexual assault that, in their view, had some bearing on the low conviction rate for this type of offence. These included poor evidence-gathering, low standards of prosecuting, the behaviour of defence counsel and judges and the attitudes of juries. The stereotypic views about rape that interviewees perceived in some juries are in striking accordance with the findings of systematic quantitative studies described in the earlier chapters. This convergence of observations from real trials and mock jury research strengthens the basis for claiming that the justice gap is indeed, in some measure at least, a problem of attitude.

6.3 ATTITUDES TOWARDS RAPE AND THE JUSTICE GAP

This chapter has looked at some of the problems perceived by interviewees in the processing of rape cases. It now goes on to consider the attitudes of the interviewees themselves towards rape and the justice gap since these too may have some bearing on the attrition process.

Serious, Less Serious and Non-Serious Rape

The susceptibility of mock juries and members of the public to stereotypical thinking about rape has been demonstrated in this and previous chapters. The interviews with judges and barristers show that juries are not alone in this respect. One aspect of the real rape stereotype is that stranger rape is perceived as invariably infinitely more serious in terms of its impact on the victim than other forms of rape, even though numerous research studies reveal this not to be the case (see Koss, Goodman, Browne, Fitzgerald, Keita and Russo, 1994, for a summary). Asked whether he thought that stranger rape was more serious than date rape, Judge 7 replied:

> Without a shadow of a doubt. And in my view, on the victim, when you see the victims, it is far more serious.

Judge 11 also considered that stranger rape was more frightening and traumatic, commenting, 'When it's the boyfriend, you're probably not in fear of your life'. This fails to acknowledge the number of women in the UK who are murdered each year by their partners (Crown Prosecution Service, 2005).

Interviewees commonly distinguished between 'serious' rapes and others:

> I think in the most serious of rape trials you will always get your conviction. I mean that's not to say that in the ones where there are acquittals they're less serious, but in the ones where society really deserves protection – serial rapists or a stalker – you do generally get your conviction. (B4)

B4 conveyed his view that non-stranger rape was not necessarily that serious and that if the public thought it was, there would be more of an uproar about the poor conviction rate.

False Allegations

There is no evidence that false allegations are made more frequently in rape than in other cases (for discussion see Rumney, 2006; Temkin, 2002a), but three judges and one barrister referred to false allegations as a particular issue in rape cases. Judge 17 commented:

I think it's very easy to make a false allegation. It's increasingly easy. Particularly as now you no longer have the corroboration rule. I think the very nature of the cases tends to be one word against another. [. . .] I think there are many more cases now in which there are false allegations. The difficulty is to weed those out and not weed out weak allegations which are true but in which the evidence is weak.

In a recent radio programme,[10] a lately retired judge similarly expressed his belief in the frequency of false allegations:

It is very emotive to tell us that 14,000 allegations were made in 2004 and only 2500 were prosecuted. [. . .] Perhaps Ken McDonald [the Director of Public Prosecutions] will tell us why these were not prosecuted. Is it not that there are unfortunately thousands of false allegations?

Stereotypical views about rape held by judges and barristers may affect the conduct of trials and communicate themselves to juries with obvious consequences for the justice gap.

The Justice Gap

Only three interviewees were entirely happy with the way that the criminal justice system currently deals with rape. As shown above, all the rest voiced concerns, offered a variety of thoughtful explanations for what they were prepared to concede might be low conviction rates in rape cases and also referred to a number of problems which the criminal justice system was facing in processing rape complaints. However, when interviewees were asked for their views about the justice gap in rape cases,[11] only Judge 1 was prepared to concede that there was in fact a justice gap. Other interviewees denied or showed resistance to this idea, and some were plainly annoyed at the suggestion. B6 described it as 'a nonsense'. Denial came in several distinct forms. Most respondents simply blamed the Crown Prosecution Service (CPS) for fielding cases which were hopeless from the start and which gave the appearance of a justice gap when in fact there was none. Judge 5 said: 'I think that the CPS doesn't have a rigorous enough approach'. Judge 2, a senior judge, commented:

Well, I have a theory, and it's my personal one, it's unsupported by any cast-iron evidence, and that is that the CPS give a less critical evaluation of the prospects of success where there is a complaint of rape than they do in other classes of serious criminal allegations.

Judge 4 blamed what he described as the 'abolition of corroboration' (see chapters one and seven) for leading to a situation in which the CPS did not control the flow of rape cases to the courts. Criticism of the CPS for prosecuting too

---

[10] *Unreliable Evidence*, 'Convicting Sex Offenders', BBC Radio 4 (25 April 2006).
[11] Question 1.4 of the Interview Schedule, see Appendix 2.

many rape cases has been a continuing theme over the past decade. It was expressed by most of the five barristers and five judges interviewed in an earlier Home Office study (Harris and Grace 1999: 35).[12] In the present study, those who criticised the CPS were unaware of the statistics of rape, the fact that the vast majority of cases are not prosecuted and that the CPS is exercising a strong filter. Judge 17's reaction was typical:

> There is no longer a weeding out of those cases which are likely to result in acquittals. The attitude seems to be prosecute-allegation made, prosecute. Irrespective of the merits.

Similarly, Judge 4 believed that the CPS would prosecute whenever a complaint of rape was made to the police. When told by the interviewer that the vast majority of reported rapes never land up in court, he was not prepared to accept this. There was considerable scepticism about the official Home Office statistics. However, not all interviewees blamed the CPS in this way. Three barristers considered that its prosecution policy in rape cases was justifiable. Judge 6 even criticised it for being too conservative.

Five interviewees considered that the justice gap was a concoction of 'pressure groups', ie women's groups, or as B4 put it, 'outside influences'. When Judge 2 was asked why he thought the CPS were prosecuting in 'inappropriate' cases, the following exchange took place:

Judge 2:   *Well, I think they feel vulnerable.*

Interviewer: Why should they feel vulnerable, do you think?

Judge 2:   *Well, I think they feel under pressure.*

Interviewer: From whom?

Judge 2:   *From – well I think there are pressure groups. Do you not agree?*

Interviewer: Like who? Who are you thinking of?

Judge 2:   *Well, I can't think of anyone.*

Judge 8 was prepared to be more specific:

> You see, once you get into the area of rape or of possible future legislation, you start to get into the lobbying parts of the world. And it seems to me that one of the lobbies which is vociferous is the feminist lobby, which is fair enough, they're entitled – but the other side of the coin is you don't hear the same lobbying in relation to males.

Thus, in the course of the 24 interviews, women were blamed on the one hand for complaining through pressure groups about the way rape is dealt with by the criminal justice system and, on the other, for acquitting rapists. The media were also blamed for putting pressure on the police and the CPS to prosecute in cases where they would not readily be inclined to do so:

---

[12] But see Temkin (2000: 226–27) in which a minority of those interviewed took this view.

But now nobody will take the decision to drop a case, and you can quite see why, because they're all petrified they'll be pilloried in the media, that there'll be an outcry or whatever. And so nobody will make a robust decision. (Judge 5)

Politicians and the government were blamed for stirring the pot and creating the perception of a problem which did not really exist:

There is a great deal of rubbish talked about conviction rates in rape cases, and much of it is talked by people who ought to know better, like politicians. And one often wonders if they've ever seen a rape case, the way they talk about them. [. . .] The statistics are meaningless, in my view. (Judge 11)

Many interviewees considered that the idea of a justice gap was based on fundamental misunderstandings about the nature of rape cases in which so frequently it was one person's word against another so that the burden of proof would necessarily be very difficult for the prosecution to discharge. Yet they themselves had pointed to the problems in processing rape caused by failures in evidence-gathering, weak prosecuting and reliance on stereotypical thinking, all of which have a bearing on whether the burden of proof is regarded by juries as having been satisfied.

It is not at all surprising that interviewees demonstrated firm resistance to the idea of a 'justice gap' since this could easily be interpreted as an attack on the legal profession as well as the criminal justice system as a whole. They were understandably nervous at being at the sharp end of the debate on rape convictions in a blame-orientated society. Judge 4, who was vociferous in his rejection of the very idea of a 'justice gap', subsequently declared that he had no doubt that rapists were walking free. In his view, wrongful acquittals were the price we paid for the unrivalled system we had – better that guilty men go free than innocent men be convicted. But this refusal on the part of almost all the interviewees to countenance the idea of a justice gap is problematic. If the justice gap is to be reduced, it does require an acceptance among all key players of its reality.

6.4 SUMMARY AND CONCLUSIONS

The interviews with judges and barristers provide a rich tapestry of opinions about rape and the way it is processed by the criminal justice system. While interviewees almost without exception baulked at the idea of a justice gap and some doubted the statistics, most were willing to concede that despite real improvements to the way that the criminal justice system works in rape and related cases, there was a range of problems which had a bearing on low conviction rates. Some of these had been identified by barristers almost a decade previously (Temkin, 2000). Those mentioned included poor policing, incompetent prosecuting counsel and bad behaviour by defence counsel. The jury was regarded by many interviewees as a further serious obstacle. The stereotypic views about rape that interviewees perceived in some juries are in striking accordance with the findings of systematic, quantitative studies described in the earlier chapters. By contrast, the view expressed by some interviewees that female jurors were particularly to blame for wrongful acquittals is unsupported by research evidence. The judges failed to mention that they too, as a group, might be implicated in the problems surrounding rape trials through their own attitudes which affect the way they apply the law. It is to this issue which we turn in the following chapter.

Judges, Barristers and the Evidential Law in Action in Rape Cases

IN CHAPTER ONE, reform of the evidential law of rape in the shape of the abolition of the requirement for a corroboration warning and control of the use of sexual history evidence was discussed (see also Appendix 1). The purpose of this reforming legislation was to go some way towards countering the adverse effects of stereotypical thinking about rape. Control of the use of third party disclosure provisions is a vital adjunct to these reforms in order to prevent counsel from digging the dirt about complainants and pandering to negative stereotypes about them. In chapter six it was shown that judges and barristers may not themselves be immune from the myths of rape. This chapter will examine the approach of the same interviewees to the law on corroboration, sexual history and third party disclosure which together critically affect the position of the complainant in sexual assault cases. It will focus on interviewees' understanding of and attitudes towards the law and the way they chose to interpret it in order to shed light on the law in action. It will be suggested that judicial unwillingness fully to disengage from the stereotypes of rape as illustrated by the failure to apply the law robustly in these three areas may in its own way contribute to the justice gap.

7.1 CORROBORATION

Knowledge of the Law

Before the enactment of section 32 of the Criminal Justice Act 1994, it was necessary for judges in rape and indecent assault trials to administer a corroboration *warning* to the jury. This was based on the view that the word of rape complainants was not to be trusted in the same way as that of other witnesses. The jury had therefore to be warned that it was dangerous to convict on the word of the complainant alone. However, it was not the case that corroboration itself was a *requirement* before the jury could convict of rape, and the jury was free to convict without it. Today, there is no longer a need for even a warning to be administered (see chapter one; Lewis, 2006). The difference between a corroboration *requirement*, which used to exist for certain sexual offences other than rape,[1] and the obligation to issue a corroboration *warning* is one that seems to have eluded two of the interviewees who appeared to think that Parliament had in 1994 abolished a corroboration *requirement* in rape cases. Judge 6, for example, commented: 'We had this rule that in sexual cases there had to be corroboration'.

Judge 4 appeared to think that the abolition of the corroboration 'requirement' was the reason why so many rape cases were prosecuted. Both judges took a dim view of this supposed change in the law. These judges were not the only ones to make a mistake about the previous law on corroboration. In *R v B*[2] the Court of Appeal appears to have been similarly under the wrong impression with regard to the offence of indecent assault: 'Furthermore, in relation to sexual offences, Parliament has removed the common law protection which was provided by *the requirement of corroboration* in the case of allegations of sexual offences'.[3]

Law in Action

After the 1994 Act abolished the requirement for a corroboration warning, Lord Taylor said in the leading case of *R v Makanjuola*[4] that while *in some cases* it *might* still be appropriate for the judge to warn the jury to exercise caution before acting on the unsupported evidence of the complainant, there would need to be specific evidence in the case suggesting that she was an unreliable witness. However, the present study indicates that judges are not necessarily limiting themselves in the way that Lord Taylor intended. Judge 3, for example, said that where all you have is one person's word against another, you direct the jury to look for supporting evidence. This assertion certainly goes beyond Lord Taylor's judgment. B1 confirmed that, despite the change in the law, judges were still directing juries to look for 'independent support', which would not be done in other, non-sexual cases:

> Judges will still tell juries to look for what they now call 'independent support', [. . .] now the judges will say, 'Oh well, it's always safer to look for independent support' in a case where you have one person's word against another. I mean if you'd said, 'Miss X stole my wallet', and I'd said, 'No I didn't' the judge wouldn't be inviting anyone to look for independent support of that!

Directions such as this go some way towards the institution of a corroboration *requirement*. Moreover, if the judge decides to ask the jury to look for independent support, complicated legal issues arise as to the evidence which is capable

---

[1] For example, procuring a woman for the purposes of prostitution.
[2] [2003] 2 Cr App R 13.
[3] At para.1. Emphasis added. See also paras 22–24.
[4] [1995] 2 Cr App R 469.

of providing such support. For example, where the woman complained to a third party that she had been raped shortly after the event, this is now treated as evidence that the rape took place but, as a result of decisions by the Court of Appeal in cases such as *R v Islam*,[5] it does not apparently count as supporting evidence. Thus, Judge 9 said that, as a consequence of cases such as *R v Islam*,[6] he would usually say to the jury:

> If you find yourself in that position, that you're inclined to believe her but you don't feel that you can say you're sure if there isn't any independent support, please don't fall into the trap of treating recent complaint as independent support because it isn't.

This is likely to confuse a jury and make it harder for the prosecution to bring home a conviction.[7]

B5 said that the abolition of the requirement for a corroboration warning did not prevent defence counsel from emphasising routinely what one would expect to find if the complainant was telling the truth. The expectations mentioned would be based on stereotypical assumptions, such as the need for injuries (see chapter two).

It is clear that the corroboration issue has not disappeared as a result of the Criminal Justice Act 1994 but has simply reappeared in a slightly different guise. This state of affairs, which illustrates the continuity of stereotypical thinking about rape complaints, is hardly conducive to obtaining convictions.

7.2 SEXUAL HISTORY

Under the regime of the old common law, the complainant's sexual history was routinely dragged into court in order to undermine and discredit her. Section 2 of the Sexual Offences (Amendment) Act 1976 was enacted to prevent this harmful stereotyping. The law regulating sexual history evidence is now contained in sections 41–43 of the Youth Justice and Criminal Evidence Act 1999 (henceforth referred to as section 41). Section 41 provides a rule forbidding evidence to be given or questions to be asked in cross-examination about any sexual behaviour of the complainant but it provides four exceptions to this rule. Thus, unless the sexual behaviour evidence comes within one of the four exceptions it is not admissible (see Appendix 1). Section 41 therefore sets far tighter restrictions on the use of sexual history evidence than the previous law contained in section 2 which gave much greater scope to the judges to exercise their discretion. The old and new provisions on sexual history are set out and discussed in more detail in Appendix 1. This section of the chapter highlights

---

[5] [1999] 1 Cr App R 22. See Appendix 1.

[6] *Ibid.*

[7] Hence the proposal, which has now been accepted by the Government, to broaden the concept of recent complaint (Office for Criminal Justice Reform 2006: ch 5; 2007) is unlikely to affect conviction rates where the judge emphasises the desirability of looking for supporting evidence.

and expands on some of the findings published in the Home Office sexual history study which looked at the operation of section 41 in practice (Kelly, Temkin and Griffiths, 2006). The purpose of so doing is to demonstrate that the law in action differs from that on the statute book as a result of the attitudes of the judges and barristers who are charged with the task of implementing it.

Familiarity with Section 41 and its Procedural Requirements

The sexual history study looked at how much knowledge interviewees had about the sexual history provisions set out in section 41 which are quite complex. It was found that some judges' knowledge of the section 41 regime was vague. The lack of applications was a reason given by several judges for their confessed lack of familiarity with the detail of section 41. A case tracking exercise conducted as part of the Home Office study over a three-month period in 2003 in all Crown Courts[8] in England and Wales found that in fact section 41 applications were made in almost a quarter of trials (Kelly *et al*, 2006: 23) but that sexual history was also introduced without the necessary application being made (Kelly *et al*, 2006: ch 6). Clearly, judges unfamiliar with the section 41 requirements would not be in a position to prevent this from happening. B1, a highly experienced QC, claimed that many defence barristers were quite unaware of section 41 or else had little understanding of its implications.

The procedural rules governing section 41 applications are contained in the Criminal Procedure Rules 2005 (see Appendix 1). Their purpose is to ensure that defence applications to bring in evidence of the complainant's sexual history are made in writing before the trial. This is in order that only properly considered applications are made and that the prosecution has time to challenge them. Two barristers were unaware of the existence of the procedural rules. Similarly, almost half, ie seven of the judges interviewed, were entirely unaware of their existence, while an eighth judge had heard about them but had no idea of their content (Kelly *et al*, 2006: vi). It is not entirely surprising, therefore, that the case tracking exercise found that only 5 per cent of applications took place pre-trial (Kelly *et al*, 2006: 23).

Attitudes towards Section 41

Many judges and some barristers were critical of the general approach taken in section 41. The main objection was that the legislation was too limiting and that the circumstances in which sexual behaviour could be relevant could not be predicted in advance by an Act of Parliament:

---

[8] Responses were received from 102 out of 125 courts, corresponding to a response rate of over 70% (see Kelly *et al*, 2006: 22).

I think it's wrong [the section 41 approach], because I don't think you can legislate for every single circumstance [. . .] I don't know what circumstance is going to make it relevant; I certainly know that Parliament isn't the right body of persons to decide it. I think it has to be decided as you go along. (Judge 1)

Several judges regretted what they regarded as the lack of confidence in the judiciary manifested by the enactment of section 41:

It slightly disconcerts me that in so many other areas, in fact in almost every sentence[ing decision], we are trusted to exercise our discretion, but for some reason or other we are not trusted to exercise our discretion on the question of the cross-examination that can be levelled at a complainant in a rape case. (Judge 10)

Several judges felt that section 41 was part of a wider government strategy to control the judges, seen also in legislation on sentencing:

It's what's happening typically these days. We're not going to give the judges discretion, we're going to seek to limit it. (Judge 7)

But three judges had more positive things to say about the new legislation, welcoming it for providing a structure for decision-making and for demanding a rigorous scrutiny of the relevance of sexual history:

I think Section 41 gives you a jolly good starting point and you don't need to go further than that, and it helps to ensure that you do exclude things that can't possibly be relevant. (Judge 6)

Comparing Section 41 and Section 2

Given the discretion it afforded to judges, some interviewees, not surprisingly, were strongly in favour of the previous regime for controlling sexual history evidence which existed under section 2 of the Sexual Offences (Amendment) Act 1976[9]:

In my experience, hardly ever did judges let it [sexual behaviour evidence] in. And if they did, it was for a very good reason, and it ought not to have been kept out [. . .] My experience was it [section 2] worked very well. (Judge 11)

Amongst the barristers, there were mixed views. Several provided reasons for preferring the old law, expressing concern that the new law might exclude relevant evidence. It was also contended that the old law worked perfectly well and that judges had in fact been reluctant to admit sexual history evidence and had had to be persuaded to do so. B4 considered that those appointed as judges should be trusted to use their knowledge and experience to arrive at the right decision.

---

[9] See ch 1 under the heading 'Sexual Offences (Amendment) Act 1976, Section 2' and Appendix 1.

That the section 41 regime is totally different from its predecessor is self-evident. The very aim and purpose of the legislature in passing section 41 was to remove discretion from the judges because of their perceived failure to exercise sufficient control over the admission of sexual history evidence under section 2's discretionary regime. However, six out of the 17 judges in this study were plainly undeterred and, regardless of the new legislation, were not prepared to forego their discretion in these matters (Kelly *et al*, 2006: 53). For several judges it was, more or less, business as usual:

> I don't think really that very much has changed, as far as the law is concerned. What it probably has done, I think, is that it has put people on the alert that previous sexual history is not automatically fair game, and that you're going to need the judge's leave to ask about it, and you're going to have to have decent reasons before you get leave. (Judge 14)

If section 41 has done no more than alert counsel to the need to justify sexual behaviour evidence, a goal which could equally well have been ascribed to section 2, its enactment would seem to have been pointless:

> You see, at the end of the day, I just wonder whether in practical terms there's a great deal of difference [between the old and new regimes], and I suspect that there isn't [. . .] I think that judges tend to take a reasonably generous view when the question of past sexual history is considered. Maybe I'm talking personally, I don't know. But I get the impression, talking amongst colleagues, certainly here, and on occasions at sex courses and so on, that that's the general approach. (Judge 12)

In the interviews, the six judges deployed one or more out of the following four techniques to neutralise section 41.

1. Denial of the Legislative Purpose of Section 41

Judge 6 provided a rationale for section 41 which involved a denial of its true purpose. Thus, he opined that the purpose of section 41 was simply to provide a structure in which to encase the exercise of discretion. In this way he was able to maintain a positive stance towards it: 'A structured approach to the exercise of discretion helps everyone'.

2. Misconstruction of Section 41

Judge 2 insisted that section 41 did leave the judges with a discretion to admit evidence where it would be fair to do so:

> The retention of discretion is very important, because you can't lay down guidelines for every situation, particularly in this class of offence. [. . .] I think ultimately the interests of justice remains [in the statute], does it not?

When asked where this overall discretion to admit sexual behaviour evidence otherwise than in the listed situations was to be found in the legislation, he admitted that he had 'no idea'. He then looked at the Act and suggested that it might come from section 41(2)(b), a subsection which has an entirely different purpose.

3. Invocation of Fair Trial Considerations

Several judges considered that section 41 had to be subordinated to the defendant's right to a fair trial which overreached all other considerations:

> You can always find a way around any statutory obstacles. [. . .] I do not believe that any defendant whose trial demanded the admission of such evidence in the interests of justice, post section 2, will be any worse off in my court post the 1999 Act. If the principles of getting a fair trial haven't changed, how can the 1999 Act impose any greater restraints than section 2 did? (Judge 3)

> If I thought it was germane to the issues that the jury were going to have to decide and that really they were being deprived of evidence that they were entitled to hear, in order to help them make their decision, if you like, it might be that one would consider a test of, well, would the jury say afterwards, 'That was unfair, that we weren't allowed to hear that evidence'. (Judge 14)

When pressed to justify this stance in view of the wording of section 41, Judge 14 backtracked and said that he would apply the statute in clear-cut cases 'however strong my misgivings' but that it might be different in borderline cases:

> Sometimes there are borderline situations where it may be that you would have that discretion, because you could say, 'Well, this is on the cusp of being within this category, I can decide one way or the other'.

4. Interpretation of the Judicial Role in Criminal Trials

Several judges considered themselves to be the ultimate arbiters of relevance and custodians of justice. Neither of these roles could or would be taken from them. 'The interests of justice' represented a higher authority than Parliament. It was something which would reveal itself to them in the course of a trial. That there might be different understandings of what was just for all parties was not acknowledged:

> I'm not one for being unduly fettered. I've been appointed to do a job on the basis that I have a certain amount of judgment, and to be fettered or shackled by statutory constraints, I don't think helps anybody. (Judge 3)

Judge 3 was clear that whether there was a discretion contained in section 41 or not made no difference to him. He would treat the statute as if there was one and the decision of the House of Lords in *R v A*[10] simply eased his path in doing so. Similarly, Judge 16 said that irrespective of the decision in *A* he would have allowed in evidence of a previous sexual relationship with the accused:

[10] See Appendix 1 under the heading '*R v A* and the Human Rights Act 1998'.

> I think it [section 41] is pretty pathetic because it's get-roundable. It only applies to certain things, and I think that realistically, most judges are going to grant it [leave to admit sexual behaviour evidence] if they think that the interests of justice need it. (Judge 11)

Judge 12, who stated that judges would allow in sexual behaviour evidence as and when they considered that there was a 'proper basis for doing so' irrespective of the legislation, was asked what he meant by 'a proper basis'. He replied:

> Well, if it's relevant to the case, and if it's material which in the interests of justice the jury really ought to hear about, so that they can make a proper decision on the allegation, and a decision which is fair to the defendant in all the circumstances.

The cavalier attitude of some judges in the study to the will of Parliament may be contrasted with that of Judge 5, for example, who saw it as his duty as far as possible to seek to follow Parliament's intentions:

> Obviously the law's intended to do justice to people, so you hope you're doing the same thing at the same time, and, you know, I don't have any trouble with the concept that in the criminal courts justice is justice to both sides, the defendant and the prosecution, so, if that's what the law leads you to, that's what it leads you to. (Judge 5)

The Impact of *R v A*

Decided by the House of Lords, *R v A* is the leading case on sexual history evidence, dealing specifically with the situation where the accused claims that he had a previous sexual relationship with the complainant and that this is relevant to the issue of consent (see Appendix 1). Although section 41 does not specifically address this situation, the House of Lords held that such evidence was admissible where it would endanger the fairness of the trial to exclude it.

Only one judge and none of the barristers considered that the decision applied only to situations where there had been a previous relationship with the accused. With one exception, all the judges interpreted it to mean that the judge now had a very broad residual discretion in order to ensure a fair trial under Article 6 (Kelly *et al*, 2006: vi). For some judges it was clear that *R v A* had provided them with a lever to do what they would have done anyway. Thus, Judge 12, who did not consider himself hampered by section 41, was then asked whether he thought that the letter of section 41 was unimportant. He replied: 'Well, isn't that what the House of Lords said to us, that [. . .] one's got to be careful about applying the strict letter of the law, hasn't one?'

Since the decision in *R v A* related only to a narrow issue, this sweeping interpretation, albeit based on certain judicial statements in the case, is hard to justify. Indeed, in the later case of *R v Andre Barrington White*,[11] decided after the study interviews took place, the Court of Appeal made it plain that *R v A*

---

[11] [2004] EWCA Crim 946.

was of limited significance where sexual relationships with third parties were concerned and that judges should adhere to the statutory scheme save in exceptional cases.[12]

Although two judges would have liked to see section 41 scrapped altogether, most felt that the law had now settled down and that as a result of the intervention of the House of Lords, together with a sensible attitude on the part of prosecuting counsel, a *modus vivendi* had been reached. There was no demand for new legislation:

> I'm not sure that we're going to benefit by trying to create another piece of legislation. It seems to me that legislation [. . .] there's a certain amount of research done into it and then it goes off to the Home Office, and legislation comes out, and then we have to go back round to the House of Lords to knock some sense into it. (Judge 8)

Among the barristers, all those who were aware of the decision in *R v A* considered that it gave the judges greater discretion to admit sexual history material but there were differences of opinion as to its reach. B2, who said that the decision had assisted him considerably in defending in a recent case, considered that it gave the judges greater latitude in interpreting the provisions of section 41 to enable evidence to be admitted and that it had provided encouragement to the judges to treat the section more flexibly. However, it fell short of his preference for an open-ended discretion to admit evidence whenever they thought it was just to do so.

In conclusion, with section 41 Parliament attempted to prevent in rape trials the triggering of harmful stereotypes which cast doubt on the credibility and deservingness of complainants because of their sexual history. However, the interviews with judges and barristers disclosed a degree of ignorance of both law and procedure, some judicial interpretations of section 41 which were manifestly wrong and in conflict with its intentions, and a general willingness to give the widest possible interpretation to *R v A*. The findings suggest that in this area the operation of the rule of law is sometimes shaky and malleable. Negative attitudes towards this important legislation have served seriously to undermine it. On the other hand, the sexual history study (Kelly *et al*, 2006) also demonstrates that the new law has begun to shape and change what is considered acceptable in the courtroom.

7.3 THIRD PARTY DISCLOSURE

Chapter one mentioned the procedure by which the defence may seek to find out from third parties information about the complainant for use in undermining her credibility at trial.[13] Third party disclosure (TPD) applications shed further light on the way that counsel seek out information which feeds into negative

---

[12] See Appendix 1 under the heading '*R v A* and the Human Rights Act 1998'.

[13] For the law on third party disclosure, see Appendix 1.

attitudes and stereotypes about complainants in rape cases, in this instance mainly children. This section considers the frequency and nature of such disclosure applications as revealed in the Home Office sexual history study (see Kelly *et al*, 2006) and then goes on to analyse the approach and attitude of the judges and barristers towards the issue of third party disclosure. It will suggest that judicial failure to apply the law properly in this area contributes once again to the justice gap.

Frequency and Purpose of Applications

The Home Office sexual history study was the first study in England and Wales to investigate the extent to which applications for disclosure of confidential records are made in sexual assault cases. The case tracking exercise referred to above[14] which covered three months in 2003 revealed that during this period alone a total of 71 individual TPD applications were made, either before or during trial, across 54 separate cases (23 per cent of the case tracking sample; Kelly *et al*, 2006: 25). This in itself is not a complete picture as there was no response from 23 courts. The most common type of application was for social services records and the combination of social service and medical records accounted for 83 per cent of all TPD applications. Other records included six applications for school or college records, one for NSPCC records, one for employer records and one for Probation Service records. There were 17 cases in the study in which the defence made a TPD application and also applied to have sexual history admitted under section 41.

Interviewees were agreed that applications were overwhelmingly made in the case of child complainants or complainants who were children at the time of the alleged abuse:

> Where you've got children who are school age, then you often get applications for disclosure of school records and reports. Where you've got children who've been taken into local authority care, there are often applications to see the social services files or health files, hospital records. (Judge 11)

The same judge observed: 'They're actually far more frequent than I think they are merited'. Applications in relation to adult complainants were rare but might occur where there was some psychiatric or medical history.

According to the interviewees, records were sought both for what they contained and for what they did not contain. The defence would be looking for evidence of behavioural problems, counselling, previous sexual abuse, previous allegations of abuse, indications that the child had told lies in the past or had a history of telling lies at school. Social service records were frequently sought to see if they could show that there was no record of any complaint of sexual abuse

---

[14] See para 7.2 under the heading 'Familiarity with Section 41 and its Procedural Requirements'.

at the time it was supposed to have happened. Thus, evidence of failure to complain as well as of the making of a previous complaint would both be sought as useful material for undermining the child's credibility. Educational records were requested to see if they could demonstrate that at the time of the alleged abuse the child was making good progress at school. The argument could then be made, relying on stereotypical ideas of how abused children behave, that this was unlikely to have been the case if the child was being abused.

Dealing with TPD Applications

Generally speaking, the trial judge will deal with any disclosure application and very often will take on the task of reading through the files in question. It was clear from the interviews that judges differed in their approach to these applications,[15] as did local authorities.

1. Applying the Law[16]

In order to obtain disclosure of material from a third party, an application has to be made for a witness summons under section 2 of the Criminal Procedure (Attendance of Witnesses) Act 1965 which the court may grant where the document is 'likely to be material evidence'. The decisions in *R v Reading Justices*[17] and *Derby Magistrates Court ex parte B*[18] establish that documents which are not admissible in evidence and are desired merely for the purpose of a possible cross-examination are not material evidence and should not be disclosed for that purpose. The Criminal Procedure Rule Committee has recently drawn attention to reports it has received that 'applications for the production of confidential documents held, for example, by health and local authorities, often were made late and without adequate consideration being given to the relevance and admissibility of the documents concerned' (Department for Constitutional Affairs 2007; see also Auld, 2001).

Several judges interviewed in the study stated that the courts were willing to accede to disclosure requests on a much broader basis than the case law permits and that the term 'material evidence' was being interpreted far more widely than the decisions in *R v Reading Justices* and *Derby Magistrates Court ex parte B* would allow. Judge 16, a senior judge, made it clear that not only did he personally ignore the authorities, but that this was common practice:

> As I understand the authorities, you've got to consider whether or not the document in its present form is admissible in evidence, presumably as some sort of record. You

---

[15] For an unfortunate example, see *R. (TB) v Stafford Combined Court* [2006] EWHC 1645 (Admin); [2007]1 All ER 102 discussed in Appendix 1.

[16] See Appendix 1 for the law on third party disclosure.

[17] [1996] 1 Cr App R 239.

[18] [1996] 1 Cr App R 385.

are not allowed to order the disclosure of a document simply on the basis that, for example, it could form the basis for cross-examination. At the refresher courses that we have to go on every three or four years or so in relation to serious sex cases, this problem is regularly raised. And at the last one I went on, with judges from all over the country, we were all asked, 'How do you approach disclosure in these cases?' and nobody stuck by the strict letter of the law at all.

Judge 10, who also said that he did not follow the authorities, stated: 'If one were to apply the law strictly, very little if anything would be disclosed from those files'.

Instead of following the authorities, the judges employed a different test. Some judges were particularly looking for, and would then order disclosure of, evidence broadly relevant in their view to the complainant's credibility as a witness:

> But the practice tends to be that if there's material in there which indicates the complainant may be unreliable, may be prone to telling lies, and so on, then the tendency is to disclose it. And indeed the prosecution are anxious that it is disclosed [. . .] it may be a history of telling lies at school, for instance, or something of that type. [. . .] I would be uncomfortable if I thought that there was material in a social services file relevant to the credibility of a complainant which I had refused to disclose. It may well be that that material wouldn't see the light of day in a trial, but at least the defendant and his advisors would know about it. It might open up another line of enquiry, I don't know. (Judge 10)[19]

B4 commented:

> You're looking for, I suppose, previous complaints, areas in terms of the truthfulness or otherwise of the complainant, matters generally which might touch upon the motivation for a complaint, [. . .] and I think there's probably a degree of latitude on the part of all concerned, because it is such a serious matter, sex cases.

Other judges were looking for material which, in their view, it would be in the interests of the defendant to have and, if they found it, they would order its disclosure. Judge 5 stated: 'If the file comes to me, I look through it very carefully, and my view of it is if it is or could be of assistance to the defence, I disclose it'.

Again, Judge 17 applied a simple relevance test rather than the prescribed materiality test: 'And then you apply your tests of what issue is it, what relevance is it to that issue. I want to see that there's some real relevance to the case'.

2. Fishing Expeditions

Judge 11 considered that most applications were 'fishing expeditions', in other words the defence was on the look out for material which might assist it in cross-examination without having any evidential basis for making an application. Some solicitors applied automatically. He explained:

---

[19] For a similar approach by the judge hearing a TPD application, see *R (TB) v Stafford Combined Court*, above n 15.

Sometimes there's a perfectly good and valid reason for looking into someone else's records, and sometimes they reveal material that is highly relevant. But that is a minority of cases, probably a small minority. And usually, as I say, it's a fishing expedition to see if you can find some dirt to throw at the complainant.

B7, a barrister who mostly defended in sex cases, confirmed that fishing expeditions were regularly made by defence counsel and also stated that there was frequently no problem in getting them through. B5, who mainly prosecuted, said that it was her practice when prosecuting to seek voluntary disclosure herself in order to review the files. If the local authority would not disclose voluntarily and she felt that they did have some relevant material, then she would make the TPD application herself with the defence on notice so that the judge could review whether disclosure should take place. Thus, she was as concerned as the defence to make sure that the defence had access to material which it might find helpful.

The judges did not have a uniform response to what they could tell were simply fishing expeditions. When the application for the witness summons to produce the file is drawn up, it should identify the documents in question and the grounds on which it is believed that they are likely to constitute material evidence.[20] Judge 16 noted that it would be clear that some of these applications and accompanying affidavits were thinly disguised fishing expeditions. However, Judge 8 thought that it was difficult to know whether an application was a fishing expedition or not and therefore he did not pay much attention to this: 'All I can do is take it at face value'.

Judge 16 said that even though a judge would be perfectly entitled to dismiss an application which was plainly a fishing expedition, he did not do so. This was because by the time the matter reached him, it was often the case that counsel had already been instructed by the local authority to look through the file and might have turned up some evidence which could be helpful to the defence:

> To begin with you know that it is a fishing expedition, but secondly you know that there are in fact documents that really could assist the defence, and in that situation my own instinctive approach to it is that without wishing to encourage vast numbers of fishing expeditions, even if it had been arrived at by an improper route, that if there was a document there which could assist the defence materially, I would order its disclosure.

Judge 17 even commented: 'I think sometimes it's legitimate to make a fishing expedition'. However, Judge 14 took a tougher approach:

> I do not encourage fishing expeditions [. . .] There are a lot of fishing expeditions in that regard. I want an evidential basis for the application in the first place before I grant it. [. . .] Otherwise in every case, with a teenage girl, 'I want to see the school record, there might be something in here'.

---

[20] Rule 28 of the Criminal Procedure Rules 2005 (S1 2005 No 384) sets out the procedure for applying for a witness summons. A new rule 28 was introduced by the Criminal Procedure (Amendment) Rules 2007 (SI 2007 No 699); see Appendix 1.

Similarly, Judge 11 said that when he detected that it was a fishing expedition he would say: 'That's no good, if you can't quote me chapter and verse as to why you need to look for a specific thing in the file, then I'm not going to look at it'.

But Judge 15 adopted an entirely different approach which was to embark on his own fishing expedition. If he saw that there was any reference to social service contact, he would instruct the prosecution to get hold of the files and would then comb them himself for any material which might be of assistance to either side:

> If there's any reference to social work or anything of that sort, I would always say to the prosecution, 'You must get the files from social services and I think you should get them', and then, more often than not, I will look at them myself to see whether there is anything, prosecution or defence, which may be relevant to it, because quite often there is. Sometimes there isn't, but at least I feel comfortable that I've checked.

This initiative would often lead to arguments as to who should bear the local authority's costs, but he nonetheless considered that it was worthwhile. Although the judge was at pains to point out that he was on the look out for prosecution as well as defence points, it was clear that his main concern was to search for defence points in order to ensure that no miscarriage of justice took place.

> I'm looking to see whether there's been a complaint obviously earlier on in time – is there any evidence, for example, which may be a defence point, that notwithstanding the fact that the child has been abused and has gone away, they've wanted to go back to Dad, let's say [. . .] I suppose inevitably you're looking to see if there's been an element of counselling [. . .] if there's been counselling, you want to see whether the same story has been told. If there's no independent evidence as it were. The trouble is that for all the horror stories of the people who get acquitted who shouldn't be, there are the odd nightmare cases [of wrongful conviction].

However, the sort of defence points Judge 15 was searching for rest on dubious foundations, such as ideas about how sexually abused children ought to react to an abusive parent and the expectation that there should be no inconsistency in the different accounts a child has given in counselling and elsewhere of what has happened to her.

3. *Public Interest Immunity*

Where information about the complainant is sought from a third party, such as a local authority, it may seek to resist disclosure of confidential information by claiming public interest immunity (PII). Where PII is claimed, the court must perform a balancing exercise 'balancing on the one hand the desirability of preserving the public interest in the absence of disclosure (ie in protecting the right to confidentiality) against, on the other, the interests of justice'[21] in the sense of fairness to the defendant (see Appendix 1).

---

[21] *R v Governor of Brixton Prison ex parte Osman* [1992] 1 All ER 108 at 116.

The study revealed that different local authorities had different practices with regard to PII and that, despite the decision in *Higgins*,[22] in which the Court of Appeal held that the local authority had a positive duty to apply for PII,[23] some never bothered to claim it. Judge 5 mentioned that the one local authority with which her court mostly had dealings never claimed PII but would always state that it was happy to release the documents to the defence if the judge, having looked at them, 'gives the OK'. B4 spoke of another local authority whose practice was automatically to hand over any material requested by the defence to the judge without the need for any application to be made. Other local authorities would not voluntarily hand over documents but would insist on the section 2 procedures being undertaken. They would appoint counsel to go through the documents requested on their behalf and to claim PII where necessary. However, this practice involved incurring costs which deterred some authorities from dealing with the matter in this way. Where counsel was appointed, counsel would go through the documents and point out what might be relevant to the questions asked in the affidavit in order for the judge to consider whether to disclose or to uphold the PII claim and to perform the balancing exercise mentioned above.

In conclusion, the study found that TPD applications were frequent. They were mainly made in the case of children, particularly those who had been in local authority care or had come to the attention of social services or the educational authorities. Thus, such children were in an unfavourable position in relation to making complaints of sexual abuse and ran the distinct risk of having access granted to private and confidential records.

The assiduity with which some judges scrutinised the files for material which in their view could be useful for the defence in undermining the child's credibility must give rise to some concern. There are issues here of fairness and balance not merely between complainants and defendants, but between child and adult complainants and disadvantaged as against relatively advantaged children. The study suggests that the case law in this area which was designed to restrain this practice is being widely ignored. Stereotypical beliefs about children, how sexually abused children can be expected to behave and about victim precipitation and blameworthiness appear to play a role in the assessments of some judges as to what ought properly to be disclosed to the defence. Only the construct of the fishing expedition was found to act as a constraint, but its effect was limited. While information about the past sexual history of children and young persons revealed through disclosure applications ought to go through the hoops of section 41, where consent is not an issue because the complainant is a child, such applications may be granted under section 41(3)(a).[24] Thus, the practice of some judges with regard to disclosure, combined with the section 41(3)(a) gateway,

[22] (1996) 1 FLR 137.
[23] At 140.
[24] See Appendix 1 under the heading 'Youth Justice and Criminal Evidence Act 1999, Exceptions to the Rule of Exclusion'.

ensure that some children, especially those who are most disadvantaged, are particularly vulnerable to having their sexual history exposed. Recently, in *R (TB) v Stafford Combined Court*,[25] it was accepted by the Divisional Court that 'it would be wrong to have the mindset which supposes that applications for disclosure of medical records of a prosecution witness will usually succeed even in the face of Article 8 objections'. The interviews described in this chapter provide evidence of such a mindset in relation to a range of records. Article 8 of the European Convention on Human Rights protects the right to private life. Lord Justice May took the view in this case that courts should not be so ready to grant disclosure applications in breach of confidentiality and that complainants should be able to contest such applications. It remains to be seen how far present practice will be displaced by Lord Justice May's eloquent judgment and the recent change to the Criminal Procedure Rules which goes some way towards allowing those whose records are sought to have their wishes expressed to the court and taken into account.[26]

7.4 SUMMARY AND CONCLUSIONS

This chapter considered the law in action with respect to three key evidential issues in rape trials, namely corroboration, sexual history and third party disclosure. The interviews conducted in the course of the Home Office sexual history study suggest that the crucial evidential rules on corroboration and sexual history which were designed to counter stereotypical views about rape were not always being applied as intended. Despite the abolition of the requirement for a corroboration warning and the decision in *Makanjuola*, some judges were continuing to tell juries to look for 'independent support' of the complainant's claim which is not generally asked for in other criminal cases. As far as sexual history was concerned, there was a degree of ignorance about section 41 and its procedural requirements. Some judges had a negative attitude towards it and had no compunction about ignoring it. The decision in *R v A* was being widely interpreted as restoring judicial discretion. The law on third party disclosure as set out in the leading cases was also being ignored in order to facilitate defence access to confidential material about complainants mainly in cases involving children.

Thus, the interviews with judges and barristers raise issues about the extent to which the law laid down by Parliament and the higher courts for rape and sexual assault cases is being judicially observed. It is the gap between the law and the law in action which is an essential component of the justice chasm in sex cases. It seems that law itself, which must ultimately be interpreted and applied by the judges, cannot entirely withstand an attitude problem which, in some cases, is too entrenched to budge.

---

[25] [2006] EWHC 1645 (Admin); [2007] 1 All ER 102; see Appendix 1.
[26] See Appendix 1.

Part III

Some Possible Solutions

8

Law Reform

ATTRITION IN RAPE cases is descending from bad to worse in England and Wales. In other countries too attrition has been identified as a problem (Kelly, Lovett and Regan, 2005). This book has attempted to demonstrate that bias and stereotyping are partly to blame for this. Indeed, while lack of evidence is often cited as the reason why many alleged rapes fall out of the system, research suggests that at every stage in the process, rapes which fail to bear the hallmarks of the classic rape or which are committed against complainants who, for extraneous reasons, do not pass muster are weeded out and consigned to the scrap heap.

There is no escaping the fact that tackling this problem is not a simple matter. Chapters eight to ten will explore possible ways in which improvements could be brought about.[1] This chapter will focus on law reform. In the light of the findings set out in this book, it will discuss possible alterations to the law of evidence as well as clarification of the law relating to alcohol and consent. Chapter nine goes on to consider juries and legal education, while chapter ten looks at public education as an avenue for change.

8.1 EVIDENTIAL ISSUES

There are a number of issues relating to the evidential law as it affects rape cases, which have been highlighted in this book. This section will make suggestions for improving jury decision-making by permitting expert evidence and evidence of the good character of the complainant and by tightening up the existing provisions on sexual history, corroboration and third party disclosure.

Expert Evidence

As demonstrated in chapter three, there has been considerable debate in the legal and psychological literature about the uses and possible abuses of expert evidence in rape trials. Much of this debate has been specifically concerned with

---

[1] See also Home Office (2002), Her Majesty's Crown Prosecution Service Inspectorate (2007), Office for Criminal Justice Reform (2007).

the use of evidence of Rape Trauma Syndrome (RTS) and, subsequently, Post-Traumatic Stress Disorder (PTSD). Chapter three discussed the problems involved in referring to either symptomatology as diagnostic tools for establishing whether or not a woman was raped.

A different purpose is the use of such evidence as an educational tool. This book has demonstrated the widespread adherence to stereotypes and myths of both professionals involved in the criminal justice system and the lay public who may sit on juries. In particular, there are specific misunderstandings about the behaviour of 'genuine' rape victims which may prevent complaints of rape from being accorded the weight they deserve. The question is whether providing juries with expert evidence to dispel some of the myths should be allowed and, if so, whether it would work. Many commentators are convinced that such a use of expert evidence is both legitimate and necessary (eg Ellison, 2005; Feild, 1978; Rumney and Morgan-Taylor, 2002; Tetreault, 1989). Many American states have approved the use of expert evidence for this purpose (Garrison, 2000: Appendix).[2] Certainly, there is a wealth of research material concerning the impact of rape on its victims from the social sciences, forensic medicine, psychology and psychiatry which could be harnessed to demonstrate, for example, that victims of rape often suffer no physical injury, do not report immediately and are not always outwardly emotional when reporting rape. In the course of the interviews with judges described in chapters six and seven, three mentioned that there might be something to be said for allowing expert evidence on some aspects of victim behaviour, particularly late complaining. Judge 16 emphasised the impact of a late complaint on the jury: 'The point [the late complaint], of course, is rammed home by defence counsel, and it doesn't surprise me that the juries buy it'.

The 2006 Consultation Paper

The consultation paper issued by the Office for Criminal Justice Reform has proposed that 'general expert evidence' should be admissible in order to help to dispel some of the myths and stereotypes concerning the behaviour of rape victims and to enhance the understanding of judge and jury about the normal and varied reactions of such victims (Office for Criminal Justice Reform, 2006: 16). This measured proposal thus envisages the use of expert evidence purely as an educational tool.[3] The paper proposes that expert evidence should be admitted specifically to address a number of common misconceptions including:

• That if rape occurred against a domestic abusive background, then the victim would leave.

---

[2] See also the Ontario decision in *Queen v . (JE)* (1994) Ont.C.J.Lexis 4017, discussed by Rumney and Morgan-Taylor (2002: 503).

[3] It has nevertheless been opposed by the Council of Circuit Judges; see *The Guardian* (23 January 2007) and the Criminal Bar Association (Criminal Bar Association, 2006).

- That a victim would willingly come to court to give evidence against an abuser.
- Why victims delay reporting.
- Why victims blame themselves.
- Why victims minimise the events and their injuries.
- Why victims have incomplete, discrepant or inconsistent memories of the incident.
- Why victims do not always physically resist or escape.

This list is not intended to be exhaustive. Rightly so, for general expert evidence could also potentially be useful to explain why, for example, victims exhibit apparently inconsistent behaviour and the frequency of multiple abuse in cases where there is evidence of previous allegations. In almost all American courts, expert testimony is admitted to explain counterintuitive aspects of the victim's post-rape behaviour, such as the victim's omission of specific acts from her description of the rape, the victim's inability immediately to tell police the name of her attacker or to identify him two weeks after the rape, her emotional flatness immediately after the assault, her denial of the rape to friends and her loss of memory regarding the events preceding the rape (Fischer, 1989: 8).

The consultation paper proposes that any person who has an expertise in the reactions of victims to rape should be able to give evidence on the matter,[4] not just psychologists or psychiatrists. Moreover, whereas in some American states which favour the use of expert evidence for educative purposes, its use is permitted only in specific rebuttal of defence claims where the defence has 'opened the door' (Fischer, 1989: 9),[5] the proposal in the consultation paper does not envisage imposing such a restriction (Office for Criminal Justice Reform, 2006: 20). However, the prosecution would, as usual, have to disclose the expert's evidence in advance of the trial and the defence would be allowed to bring forward its own expert. The consultation paper also proposes that the evidence allowed would be confined to general background evidence. 'Oath helping' or evidence as to the specific credibility of the complainant in the case would not be admitted; neither would opinions as to the complainant's veracity. Such a use, it is stated, would not be permitted in English law.[6] The proposal, moreover, appears to be confined to rape cases alone:

> We propose that such general expert evidence should only be called in rape cases. This is because rape is a unique offence. The majority of rapes occur between acquaintances. Often, there is little outside evidence that supports the victim's account given

---

[4] There is no suggestion that research findings on the characteristics or behaviour patterns of rapists and paedophiles should be admissible even to challenge some of the rape myths that may be utilised by the defence. Presumably the view taken was that such expert evidence would be more prejudicial than probative. In the unusual case of *Key v The State of Texas* (1989) 765 S.W.2d 848 evidence that it was not uncommon for rapists to establish a brief relationship with their victims was held to have been correctly admitted (see Fischer, 1989: 8).

[5] *People v Beckley* 161 Mich.App. 120, 128 409 NW.2d759, 763 (1987).

[6] Cf *Robinson* (1994) 98 Cr App R 370.

that such offences usually occur in private. In the majority of non-stranger rape cases the identity of the attacker is not disputed and there will be no conclusive forensic or medical evidence. At the moment, the only evidence as to what allegedly occurred is being considered against a background of misperceptions and myths as to how proper victims should behave which is going unchallenged. (Office for Criminal Justice Reform, 2006: 17)

All the reasons which are given for confining the proposal to rape apply equally to other sexual assaults and it would be hard to justify excluding them from it.

Arguments in Favour of the Consultation Paper's Proposal

It is often said that expert evidence in rape trials to educate juries is unnecessary because jurors are people of the world and have common sense knowledge about how the victims of rape behave (Office for Criminal Justice Reform, 2006: 19). However, given the proven and widespread biases against complainants in rape cases, such education would appear, on the contrary, to be highly necessary. In a study by Frazier and Borgida (1988), for example, the knowledge about rape and rape victims' behaviour of a group of experts was compared with that of non-experts. It was found that the non-experts did not appear to be aware of the frequency of multiple victimisation experiences or the behavioural changes often apparent following a rape. While most realised that victims might delay in reporting the matter, they were nevertheless suspicious of late complaints.

It has also been claimed that if juries need to be informed, this task is best performed by the existing players at the trial – judges, counsel and forensic medical examiners (FMEs) (Office for Criminal Justice Reform, 2006: 19). It is certainly true that where, for example, the defence has drawn attention to the complainant's failure to report immediately, some judges will comment on this. One judge explained that he would say to the jury:

> Defence counsel has said that if this had really happened she would have run off immediately to the police, but ask yourselves if, given that it was her uncle, that's what she would have done.[7]

Prosecuting counsel can also comment in similar terms where the issue is delay. However, it would not be appropriate for either judge or counsel to dwell on the matter or draw on the literature which shows conclusively that delay in reporting rape is normal and why this is so. Compulsory warnings to juries, imposed by statute, that there may be good reasons for a late complaint and that a late complaint is not necessarily a false complaint, have proved to be notably unsuccessful in Australia. This is because judges have undermined the warnings by relying on the common law and instructing juries that delay is a factor to be considered in assessing the complainant's credibility (Lewis, 2006; Temkin,

---

[7] Judge at JSB seminar, November 2004.

2002a: 193–94). Judges cannot be relied on to refrain from issuing counter-warnings of this sort.

Where other stereotypes are concerned, challenge by judge or counsel may be far more difficult. It would, for example, generally take an expert to explain how and why victims might appear to have inconsistent memories of the incident. There is also limited scope for judges to address the issue of stereotyping in their final direction to the jury because this might be construed as favouring the prosecution. Moreover, reliance on judges and barristers effectively to challenge stereotypes seems rather like pie in the sky, since some subscribe to them themselves or lack the knowledge about rape which might cause them to reflect on widespread and erroneous assumptions about it. The same is true of FMEs. There is a certain amount that FMEs do or could do to dispel rape myths. FMEs often emphasise that in the vast majority of cases victims of rape do not experience manifest injuries. In the interview study, B5 expressed the view that FMEs could do more than this, by pointing out that victims were commonly not hysterical or highly emotional in the immediate aftermath of rape. But FMEs may lack the knowledge effectively to address stereotypes in this way or, again, may subscribe to them themselves. Moreover, there may have been no medical examination after the rape so that an FME will not then be called as a witness. Thus, the opportunities for jury education within the adversarial system are strictly limited. The use of expert evidence is one of the few avenues available.

The consultation paper envisages legislation to implement its proposal. Although Ellison (2005: 261–66) has argued persuasively that it would be perfectly possible for the prosecution to adduce expert evidence under existing law, since there is clearly doubt about this in professional circles, legislation would be the swiftest way forward.

Difficulties and Drawbacks

While there is much to be said for the proposal put forward in the consultation paper, it carries with it some unavoidable drawbacks. It is, of course, only fair that defence counsel should be able to produce its own experts. But the consultation paper states: 'As the evidence is general, it would be difficult for another expert to dispute any findings' (Office for Criminal Justice Reform, 2006: 19). However, it would be naïve to imagine that defence experts would not be used in such cases. The three judges mentioned above who discussed this matter were certainly of this opinion. Two of them said that, in the case of a late complaint, the defence expert was likely to suggest that in the particular circumstances of the case in hand the complainant could have complained earlier:

> If you're allowing the prosecution to adduce such evidence, then the defence bring in their expert to say, 'Well, you know, in the circumstances of this case, of course she could've complained'. (Judge 16)

Judge 15 made a similar point, referring to a particular case:

> But in that case there is a psychiatrist from [named hospital], a woman psychiatrist, who was coming to give evidence to say that it was singularly unusual for the period of delay, for the woman only to disclose at a certain point in her psychiatric treatment. So that highlights the difficulty – you're going to get a counterbalance.

Where no defence expert is called, the prosecution expert will almost certainly be cross-examined with a view to discrediting his/her evidence. Attention will typically be drawn to the exceptions which inevitably exist to any generalisation about victims and to the fact that the expert is paid by and has discussed the facts of the case with the prosecution beforehand. Spanos, Dubreuil and Gwynn found that the effects of expert evidence evaporated almost entirely with such cross-examination (1991–92: 38, 43). The judge might even feel obliged, although this hardly seems necessary, to point out to the jury in the case of a late complaint that just because rape victims commonly delay in complaining, that does not mean that this complainant who did delay is necessarily a rape victim.

The consultation paper accepts without question the constraints of the so-called 'oath-helping rule', but this 'rule' merits further scrutiny. In *Robinson*, it was accepted that the prosecution could call an expert to rebut the evidence of a defence expert or even a suggestion in cross-examination that a prosecution witness was unreliable due to some mental abnormality or personality disorder outwith the jury's experience. However, the prosecution expert's evidence should go no further than was necessary to meet the challenge of the defence's evidence and should not extend to oath-helping. In practice, in sexual abuse cases, it is not uncommon for the defence to call an expert to give evidence, for example, about false memory syndrome, and the prosecution will then call its own expert to challenge this. But the suggested distinction between evidence which does no more than meet the challenge of the defence expert's evidence on the one hand, and oath-helping evidence on the other, is likely to be one that is difficult to sustain. Inevitably, the one merges into the other. It is unfortunate that the consultation paper shied away from interrogating the oath-helping rule.

It has also to be recognised that while it is relatively simple to contest some of the most egregious misunderstandings about rape through use of the research evidence, victim-blaming attitudes are a very different matter. People who make moralistic assumptions about what is correct behaviour for women and consider that women bring rape on themselves are unlikely to be deflected from their beliefs by research studies about the impact of rape on its victims. Research about the behaviour patterns of some sexual offenders could do so, but is most unlikely to find its way into a courtroom.

Research suggests that expert evidence may well be effective in dispelling certain rape myths but this may depend on how it is presented (see chapter three). The consultation paper is adamant that the expert evidence must be general and not specific to the victim or witness in order to comply with the current law on oath-helping. Mock jury research conducted by Brekke and Borgida (1988) shows that jurors may find it difficult to grasp the connection between abstract data about groups and judgments about specific individuals unless the link with the case is made fairly explicit (see also Gabora, Spanos and Joab, 1993, discussed in chapter three). Their research demonstrates that expert evidence works best where the expert is asked to comment on hypothetical situations which closely resemble the case in hand: 'When expert testimony was more abstract, jurors seemed less able or less willing to apply it to the case and juror judgements seemed to be relatively unaffected by its presence' (Brekke and Borgida, 1988: 379). While less effective, general evidence which is supplemented by specific concrete examples was found to work better than general evidence on its own. Thus, this research suggests that the efficacy of any change in the law to permit the use of expert evidence will depend on the extent to which it permits experts to move from broad generalisation to the use of hypotheticals and examples.

Brekke and Borgida (1988: 376) also found that the point at which the expert evidence was introduced was crucial. Expert testimony had the greatest impact when it was presented as the first piece of prosecution evidence. By introducing such evidence early on in the trial, it is able to have its effect before stereotypical beliefs and causal theories have time to set in and hold sway. The prosecution may choose the order in which it calls witnesses, and this research suggests the earlier the better.

To conclude, the sheer prevalence of rape myths indicates that non-experts are not knowledgeable about the facts of rape or about certain key factors which have a bearing on the critical issue of the credibility of complainants. However, current research, albeit limited, suggests that the impact of expert evidence, far from swamping the case as some might fear, is likely often to be modest. In domestic violence cases where myths also abound, expert evidence is currently being used where appropriate to assist the prosecution (Crown Prosecution Service, 2005). The view taken here is that, despite the difficulties, there is good reason to implement the consultation paper's moderate proposal and to allow the prosecution to import expert evidence into rape trials on those occasions when it considers that this would be useful. This strategy would be assisted by further research into how expert evidence is best deployed and the circumstances in which it is likely to be most effective.[8]

Evidence of Good Character

In sexual assault trials, the credibility of complainant and defendant assumes a higher level of importance than in most other criminal cases. Defendants may

---

[8] In its response to the Consultation Paper, the Government has expressed firm reservations about permitting expert evidence in rape trials and has said that it will continue to explore alternative ways of introducing general expert material into the courtroom 'in a controlled and consistent way with a view to dispelling myths as to how victims behave after incidents of rape' (Office for Criminal Justice Reform, 2007: 21).

well be men without any previous convictions, persons of standing in the community – teachers, doctors, dentists and clergymen. Defendants are allowed to call witnesses to support their assertions of good character and are also entitled to a good character direction from the judge. Indeed, even those with a criminal record for old, different or trivial offences may also benefit from such a direction (Munday 2005: 254–63).[9] In a recent paper advising defence counsel on strategy in rape trials, a leading QC recommended: 'Make the very best of character evidence. Call some individuals if you can. It goes a long way to improving the "feel" of the defence case after your client has fouled up in evidence'.[10]

There is no equivalent right to use character evidence so far as the complainant is concerned, and she will have to contend with the additional baggage of the rape myths which will surround her complaint. Yet the complainant may herself be a person of good character. It should be possible for her to be able to bring forward character witnesses in the same way as it is for the accused. Without this, the proceedings risk becoming severely skewed. There is authority for allowing the complainant to adduce evidence in support of her complaint in highly specific circumstances.[11] But the view taken here is that a more generous approach should be taken so that it should be possible to call character witnesses for the complainant whenever this is necessary to obtain some parity with the accused.

Sexual History, Corroboration and Disclosure

One form of potentially inadmissible evidence that may unduly influence jurors' decision-making is information about the complainant's sexual history. The importance of controlling the use of sexual history evidence in the courtroom has long been recognised in the common law world, but legislative attempts to do so have met with mixed success (see chapter seven and Appendix 1). An evaluation of the current legislation in England and Wales revealed the extent to which it was being evaded and undermined. Its recommendations included tightening both the law itself and the procedural provisions surrounding it, as well as improved training about the law for judges and barristers (Kelly, Temkin and Griffiths, 2006: 76–77). In response to these recommendations, the 2006 consultation paper envisaged changes to the Criminal Procedure Rules, but no mention was made of any further plans to implement the rest of the recommendations (Office for Criminal Justice Reform, 2006: 11). A new Rule 36 of the Criminal Procedure Rules 2005 accordingly came into effect in November 2006. This makes it clear that applications to introduce sexual history evidence must be made pre-trial. However, under rule 36.7, it remains possible for a judge to

---

[9] See also *R v Payton* EWCA Crim 1226; [2006] All ER (D) 385 (May).

[10] *Prosecution and Defence Advocacy in Rape Cases*, paper presented to Western Circuit Rape and Serious Sexual Offences Seminar, 2007.

[11] See *R v Riley* [1991] Crim LR 460; *R v Amado-Taylor* [2001] EWCA Crim 1898.

allow such an application at trial. All applications have now to be made in writing and, where an application is allowed, the prosecution can apply for a special measures direction to assist the complainant in giving her evidence.[12]

While rule 36 is an improvement on its predecessor, it remains likely that applications will continue to be made at trial. The best way of defeating this defence bad habit is for judges to voice their clear displeasure and at the same time to give careful consideration to such applications, insisting that all the requirements for making them are complied with and that the complainant's needs are fully met.[13] In this way, the advantages of applying at trial may diminish. It is suggested here that further consideration should now be given to implementing the rest of the recommendations contained in the evaluation study. In particular, provision needs to be made to allow prosecution appeals against erroneous decisions to admit such evidence. This would strengthen the need for decisions about sexual history to be made pre-trial.[14] There should also be continuing monitoring of the operation of the legislation (Kelly *et al*, 2006: 76–77).

Chapter seven also demonstrated that despite the abolition in 1994 of the requirement for a corroboration warning, there is evidence that the Court of Appeal's ruling in *Makanjuola* is being effectively ignored and that juries are frequently being told to look for 'independent support'. Chapter seven further noted the frequency of third party disclosure applications, that many were thought to be fishing expeditions and that judges were largely ignoring the case law on the subject. It is doubtful whether either matter can be dealt with purely by judicial education, and it is suggested that further legislation is necessary to tighten the law in both areas.[15] However, so long as prosecution rights of appeal are limited, enforcement of the law is likely to be problematic.

8.2 CONSENT AND INTOXICATION

It is clear that drink features prominently in cases of rape (Her Majesty's Inspectorate of Constabulary, 2007: 77). A large body of evidence reviewed in chapter two shows that if the complainant is portrayed as drunk, she is perceived as less credible and the perpetrator is seen as less likely to be culpable. A complainant who is drunk at the time she is raped is very far removed from the real rape stereotype. Her claim is thus more likely to be regarded as false by the

---

[12] This might allow her, for example, to give evidence by television link from a different room in the court building: see Youth Justice and Criminal Evidence Act 1999.

[13] It is most unlikely that such applications will be turned down because they are out of time: cf *R v Sutton Coldfield Magistrates' Court* [2006] EWHC 307, [2006] 4 All ER 1029.

[14] Where the defence fails to apply pre-trial, an appeal by the prosecution against the judge's decision to allow sexual history evidence should follow the procedure set out in s 64 of the Criminal Justice Act 2003.

[15] A working party under the aegis of the Office for Criminal Justice Reform is currently considering the law relating to third party disclosure.

police, and her complaint is less likely to result in conviction (see chapter two). Our own study with members of the public (see chapter five) also showed that cases in which the complainant was raped while she was under the influence of alcohol were judged differently and mostly less favourably than cases where the defendant used force. The findings suggest that the issue of victim intoxication is closely related to the perception of victim culpability.

In a mock jury study which explored the impact of social attitudes towards intoxication on the outcome of rape trials, Finch and Munro (2005b) found that participants were strongly influenced by myths which were not grounded in fact. For example, some tended to believe that so long as a person was conscious they were capable of expressing resistance to unwanted sexual contact and that a non-consenting person would struggle even when intoxicated. Some appeared to assume that consent was always present unless the complainant by her words or actions made it clear that it was not. The authors concluded that, 'in the absence of clear judicial or statutory guidance, jury decision-making in rape cases involving intoxicants will rely on extra-legal concerns' (Finch and Munro, 2005b: 69).

In combination, these findings highlight the problems involved in dealing with the issue of consent in cases where the complainant was intoxicated at the time of the alleged assault, and they raise the question whether the law on drunkenness and rape is in need of further clarification. The next section will briefly review the existing law and then discuss recent suggestions for law reform in this area.

Existing Law[16]

A variety of situations can apply where sexual intercourse takes place with the complainant (C) who is intoxicated at the time. The problem is how to distinguish them both factually and legally. They include the following:

(a) C was drunk and decided to have sexual intercourse with the defendant (D) which she would not have done had she been sober.
(b) C is so drunk that she is unaware of what is going on or that D is proposing to have sex with her. Although she expresses consent, it is not consent to sexual activity.
(c) C is paralytically drunk but is aware of what D is proposing and consents to it.
(d) C is paralytically drunk and does not express her non-consent either verbally or by physical resistance.
(e) C is paralytically drunk but does express her non-consent.

---

[16] See now *R v Bree* [2007] 2 All ER 676 in which it was held that the issue of consent where the complainant was intoxicated is sufficiently addressed by the definition of consent in s 74 of the SOA 2003 and that capacity to consent could be lost before the complainant became unconscious.

(f) C is unconscious through drink or drifts in and out of consciousness.

(g) Without C's knowledge or consent, D has spiked C's drink with the result that any of the above situations might apply.

It is clear that in situation (a) there is no liability for rape. In situation (d), it was held in *Malone* that there is no requirement that the absence of consent be demonstrated or communicated to the defendant for the *actus reus* of rape to exist.[17] In situation (f), C was not deemed to consent at common law if unconscious at the time of intercourse.[18] Section 75(1)(d) of the Sexual Offences Act 2003 now provides that where a person is unconscious, it will be presumed that consent is absent. This would include where a person is unconscious through drink, although this is not expressly stated. Presumptions are rebuttable which means that even though C is proved to have been unconscious at the time, the defence is able to bring forward evidence to argue that she was consenting. In situation (g), where an intoxicant capable of overpowering the complainant is administered to her without consent, it is also presumed under section 75(1)(f) that consent is absent.[19] However, in the case of self-induced intoxication, where C is not rendered unconscious, no presumption applies as far as consent is concerned, however intoxicated C was at the time and whatever the degree of impairment of her cognitive state. This means that in situations (a)–(e), section 74, the basic consent provision, applies. This states, 'A person consents if he agrees by choice and has the freedom and capacity to make that choice'.

The Sex Offences Review

The Sex Offences Review proposed that there should also be a presumption of non-consent where a person was too affected by alcohol to give free agreement (Home Office, 2000a: vol 1, 19). This would apply to self-induced intoxication. However, the Home Secretary rejected this suggestion in the following terms:

> I have rejected the suggestion that someone who is inebriated could claim they were unable to give consent – as opposed to someone who is unconscious for whatever reason, including because of alcohol – on the ground that we do not want mischievous accusations. (Office for Criminal Justice Reform, 2006: 12)

This statement is itself a prime endorsement of several key rape myths, namely that false rape allegations are common and that women who allege rape having

---

[17] [1998] 2 Cr App R 447. The court went on usefully to state 'What occurred in those circumstances – not wishing to have intercourse but being unable to do anything about it – [. . .] would plainly, as a matter of common sense, be against her will'. The defendant's guilt in these circumstances will depend on his state of mind.

[18] *Camplin* (1845) 1 Cox CC 220.

[19] S 61 of the SOA 2003 also addresses this situation by making it a separate offence intentionally to administer a substance to C, knowing that she does not consent and with the intention of stupefying or overpowering her so as to enable any person to engage in a sexual activity involving her. As a preparatory offence it can be used where no sexual activity in fact ensues.

drunk too much are in fact likely to have consented and then regretted it after-wards. In the absence of any evidence whatever to support these propositions, this statement is hard to defend.

The 2006 Consultation Paper

Concern has arisen that issues relating to consent in cases where C was drunk are not being given proper consideration by the courts. It is thought that the Act is insufficiently clear about consent where drink is involved. The consultation paper has therefore raised the question whether there should be a statutory def-inition of capacity which would be of assistance in cases where C was very drunk. While superficially an attractive idea, there is clearly a danger that any such definition would add a further level of complexity to the existing law and also be interpreted, mistakenly, to require the prosecution to prove a lack of such capacity in all cases where C was very drunk. As was pointed out in *Malone*, this would be erroneous. The issue is whether the complainant did consent, not whether she had the capacity to consent. A person who retains capacity may nevertheless not consent.

The consultation paper tentatively puts forward a suggestion for a definition of capacity based on a proposal by Rook and Ward who have sought to adapt the common law on capacity to the definition of consent in section 74. They sug-gest that 'a complainant will not have had the capacity to agree by choice where their understanding and knowledge were so limited that they were not in a posi-tion to decide whether or not to agree' (Office for Criminal Justice Reform, 2006: 13). However, it is not clear that this well-intentioned proposal would be helpful. Key elements of the suggested definition of capacity would be 'under-standing and knowledge' (Office for Criminal Justice Reform, 2006: 14). But questions arise as to the intended meaning of these concepts in this context. The requirement that consent be based on 'understanding and knowledge' was articulated in the old case of *Howard*[20] in which the consent of young girls was considered, the complainant herself being only six. It was held that in such cases, lack of consent must be proved by showing that the girl's 'understanding and knowledge were such that she was not in a position to decide'. Where chil-dren are concerned, understanding and knowledge clearly refer to understand-ing and knowledge about sex and the 'facts of life'. However, in the case of adults, the meaning is less evident and it is not set out in the consultation paper. If it is supposed that, in the case of an adult, 'understanding and knowledge' refer to awareness and understanding of what is going on, then such a definition of capacity would be uncontroversial. It is obvious that in situation (b) above, a person who is not aware of what is going on, or does not understand what she is consenting to, does not give a valid consent. If C is so drunk that, although

[20] [1965] 3 All ER 684.

conscious, she is unaware that D is having intercourse with her, she cannot be said to be consenting. Similarly, there is no consent to sexual intercourse where C thinks that D is inviting her to dance the lambada when in fact he is proposing they have sex. C must understand the nature of the act proposed.

However, the Rook and Ward proposal would appear to be about more than simple awareness and understanding of the facts. It implies that C would lack capacity where her understanding and knowledge were so limited *that she was not in a position to decide whether or not to agree* (Office for Criminal Justice Reform, 2006: 13). This suggests that 'understanding and knowledge' is also about understanding the implications of consent and exercising judgment; it is referring to the situation where C's cognition is so impaired that she cannot make a proper decision. It is thus about the *quality* of her decision-making in a situation where she knows what is on offer.

But, if this is what 'understanding and knowledge' is intended to mean, this would raise a problem too practically and philosophically complex to be capable of resolution in the courtroom or arguably anywhere. For, if C does express her consent, at what point can it be said that C's judgment is too impaired to make that consent valid, at what point does it cease to be a true or free consent and how, in any case, it might further be asked, is D supposed to know this. In practice, it is likely to be impossible to secure a conviction in these circumstances. There is a strong case for saying that a person who is aware of what she is consenting to and gives her consent at the time, as in situation (c), should be regarded as consenting. It is an altogether different matter where, as in (d), she does not consent but fails to communicate this by word or deed for here the *Malone* principle applies, as discussed above.

A New Presumption?

The consultation paper does not favour the creation of a further presumption of lack of consent in circumstances where alcohol is involved. It argues that the presumptions 'all relate to circumstances where C is not able to freely consent due to factors outside her control' (Office for Criminal Justice Reform, 2006: 15) and assumes that where alcohol is concerned this does not apply, save where it is administered without consent. 'Factors outside her control' is another way of stating that the presumptions should apply only where C herself is not at fault. However, the list in its present form includes the situation where C is unconscious. Unconsciousness through drink may be entirely the fault of the complainant, taking place where she was in full control of her alcohol consumption.

The consultation paper invokes the former Home Secretary's words, cited above, in support of the idea that the presumptions should, in effect, apply only where C has been blameless (Office for Criminal Justice Reform, 2006: 15). But, to suggest that blamelessness on the part of the complainant should be at the heart of the list of presumptions is to pander to the very stereotypes and moralistic assumptions which bedevil this area of law and which have nothing to do with the issue of consent. It is also entirely contrary to basic principle in criminal law which has no place for notions of contributory negligence on the part of the victim. In neither *Setting the Boundaries* nor *Protecting the Public* was blamelessness thought to be the entry qualification for admission to the list of presumptions. Indeed, in *Protecting the Public* it was stated that the list is designed to 'send a clear signal to the public about the circumstances in which sexual activity is likely to be wrong' (Home Office, 2002: para 32). Even assuming that the presumptions are used infrequently (Home Office, 2006e), the addition of a further presumption relating to intoxication is one way of addressing this issue given the present structure of the Act. On the other hand, a separate provision making a number of statements about intoxication could be a more satisfactory way forward.

An Alternative Solution

Several things need to be made clear as far as intoxication is concerned which apparently are not clear enough. The first is that where a person is unconscious through drink, a situation which is not unusual, then consent is not possible. People who are highly intoxicated are prone to drift in and out of consciousness. In the unconscious moments, consent cannot be given or continue to exist if it was given previously. The law should spell this out. In *R v Dougal*,[21] the case of the Aberystwyth University student which has rightly exercised the media and to which the consultation paper refers, the student concerned was apparently unconscious when sexual intercourse took place.[22] If this were the case, the prosecution should have been pursued on this basis. The only legal question which arises is why this situation does not give rise to an irrebuttable presumption of absence of consent as it did at common law rather than a rebuttable one as at present under the Sexual Offences Act. It can only be assumed that what the draftsman had in mind when creating a rebuttable presumption was the hypothetical situation where the parties agree beforehand that C should be rendered unconscious and that during this state D should have intercourse with C. Since *ex hypothesi* both parties are in agreement, it is most unlikely that the matter would come before the prosecuting authorities.[23] But there is a serious objection to the alteration of the common law on this ground. This is because the fundamental principle which should operate in the law of sexual offences is that consent must be present at the moment of the sexual act and remain present thereafter for as long as sexual intercourse or other sexual activity continues.[24] There should be no such thing as a valid consent to future sexual acts. For this

---

[21] [2005] Swansea Crown Court, Office for Criminal Justice Reform, 2006: 13.
[22] See *The Observer* (25 June 2006).
[23] Cf *Laskey v UK* (1997) 24 EHRR 39.
[24] See Sexual Offences Act 2003, s 79 (2).

reason the presumption of non-consent where C is unconscious should revert to an irrebuttable one as it was at common law.

The second point which needs to be made clear is that consent is based on awareness and on understanding of the nature of the act. C cannot consent to something of which, through intoxication or for any other reason, she is unaware or as to whose nature she is mistaken. The Sex Offences Review included mistakes as to the nature of the act in its list of situations in which consent would be vitiated (Home Office 2000a: vol 1, para 2.10.9), but there is no provision concerning mistakes other than those induced by fraud in the 2003 Act.

Finally, the *Malone* principle needs to be set out for all to see.[25] It needs to be made clear that 'there is no requirement that the absence of consent be demonstrated or communicated'. Thus, if D has sex with a drunken person who does not express consent, he will be treading a dangerous path.

It has been suggested here that the Sexual Offences Act 2003 should be amended to make it plain that there can be no consent when the complainant was or becomes unconscious, or where she is mistaken as to the nature of the proposed act and that the Act should also spell out the *Malone* principle. These three legislative changes, in combination with expert evidence, would assist in challenging some of the beliefs and rape myths associated with drink without unfairness to the accused. They are preferable to the enactment of the definition of capacity proposed in the consultation paper.[26]

8.3 SUMMARY AND CONCLUSIONS

This chapter has suggested that there is still room for further law reform in the area of sexual offences in order to assist in the task of dismantling the stereotypes of rape which involve derogatory beliefs about rape victims and their credibility and serve to cloud the issues in rape cases. As far as the law of evidence is concerned, it has suggested that the prosecution should be allowed to make use of expert evidence as a means of educating both the jury and the public about rape. It has reiterated the need for proper enforcement of the law on sexual history and the implementation of the recommendations contained in the evaluation report on the operation of section 41 (Kelly *et al*, 2006). It has proposed that the rules on corroboration and third party disclosure be strengthened and that evidence of the good character of the complainant become admissible. Regarding the law of rape itself, it has recommended some amendments to the

---

[25] It is a pity that in *R v Bree*, the Court of Appeal sought to downplay this highly valuable decision, see [2007] 2 All ER 676, at para 28.

[26] The Government has now rejected the idea of enacting a definition of capacity on the ground that the judgement in *R v Bree* (see n 16 above) has rendered this unnecessary. However, it will invite the Judicial Studies Board to consider whether a new specimen direction would be helpful for the judges when directing juries (Office for Criminal Justice Reform 2007: 11).

Sexual Offences Act 2003 along the original lines of the common law in order to strengthen the concept of consent in cases where alcohol is involved, an area in which stereotypes abound. All these changes, if properly implemented and enforced, have a role to play in tackling attrition in rape cases, but they need to be boosted by further improvements to rape trials which are considered in the next chapter.

9

Improving Rape Trials

CHAPTER EIGHT CONSIDERED the steps which could be taken through law reform to challenge some of the misconceptions and stereotypes about rape. This chapter will discuss a number of possibilities for further improving rape trials. As this book has sought to demonstrate, juries formed of members of the public can frequently be a problem in sexual assault cases because of the prejudiced attitudes that some of its members may bring to bear on their judgments about rape allegations. The first and most radical proposal which is canvassed in this chapter is to abolish jury trial in sexual assault cases. However, such is the commitment to this form of trial in the common law world that a step of this kind is highly unlikely in the foreseeable future. Moreover, this book has revealed that the stage has not yet been reached at which it can be claimed that judges are necessarily free from the very same biases and stereotypical views of which juries may be accused. The chapter will therefore assume that, for the time being, jury trial will remain the method by which serious sexual assault is dealt with. It will discuss jury selection and screening, and steps which could be taken to help juries to focus on the facts and the evidence in the case. Suggestions for making juries more accountable for their decisions will also be explored. The chapter will then go on to consider the education of legal professionals as a further means of improving rape trials. Finally, it will discuss whether, given the problems of bias and stereotyping which work against complainants in rape trials, the appointment of more female judges would be likely to make a difference.

9.1 ABOLISHING THE JURY IN SEXUAL ASSAULT CASES

In chapter five we demonstrated that some members of the public are heavily biased against rape victims and that their biases are brought to bear on the assessments they make about situations where a rape occurs. In the Study 3 sample comprising over 2000 participants, it was found that while the majority did not score high on rape myth acceptance, a substantial minority did. On the female precipitation measure, 25.3 per cent and on the modern rape myth measure, 44.4 per cent had scores above the midpoint of the scale. Our studies show that people who score high on scales which measure adherence to rape myths are less likely to make judgments about rape which are based on the facts and the evidence. Rather, their judgments are likely to be based on reasoning which relies on their biased assumptions. These findings coincide with the impressions of key players in the criminal justice system. Thus, as one barrister noted in the interview study, skilled defence counsel do not necessarily have to do a great deal to secure an acquittal in a non-stranger rape case. It is frequently sufficient to invoke ideas about risky behaviour or that the victim brought what happened on herself by her conduct or dress. In psychological terms, cross-examination of this sort will act as a prime (see chapter five) to those members of the jury who strongly adhere to stereotypical views about rape by bringing these attitudes to the fore and pushing them into play. It is likely to ensure that such jurors employ schematic reasoning to arrive at their judgment of the case rather than making an assessment based on the facts and the evidence.

Jurors with a strong belief in rape myths are problematic in more ways than one. First, in a non-stranger rape case, it may well require only three people on a jury of 12 who score high on rape myth acceptance to ensure that the defendant is acquitted. Secondly, they are likely to express their stereotypical beliefs in the course of the jury's deliberations, giving them prominence and potential influence on those members who might not otherwise have looked at the case from that point of view. Just as defence counsel may 'prime' the stereotypes of those already endorsing them, biased members of the jury may channel the interpretation of the evidence as a whole in a direction that undermines the complainant's position. Finally, the difficulty posed by juries in rape cases is an important factor in the attrition problem throughout the system since police and prosecutors will inevitably second-guess juries in the decisions they make as to whether prosecutions should be pursued. Unjustified acquittals serve to reinforce existing stereotypes.

Thus, overall, there would seem to be a good case for arguing that the best solution for the time being would be to abolish jury trial in sexual assault cases in the interest of procuring justice for victims as well as defendants.[1] Rape-ticketed judges are far less likely to be led astray by defence counsel or, perhaps, by a victim's incongruent emotional expression (see Wessel, Drevland, Eilertsen and Magnusen, 2006, discussed in chapter two). Unlike inexperienced jurors, they will be familiar with patterns of sexual aggression and are more likely to be able to draw the inferences which can and should be drawn from the evidence (see chapter six). Kalven and Zeisel (1966) showed that when both judges and juries were asked to make decisions about the same rape charges, judges were seven times more likely to convict than juries in those cases particularly susceptible to rape myths, ie acquaintance rapes without aggravating factors. Moreover, while training judges is not unproblematic, structures are now in place and can be built on whereas no such opportunities to educate juries could

---

[1] A recent Australian study with actual jurors carried out immediately after child sexual abuse trials does not inspire confidence. It found that some jurors were 'confused, unclear, uncertain' as to the verdict which they had just delivered (Cashmore and Trimboli, 2006: 12).

ever be built into the system. It also seems likely that in the absence of a jury, the tone and quality of rape trials would improve substantially as counsel, free from the need to convince juries by fair means or foul, would be less inclined to indulge in some of the excesses which even now characterise rape trials. A strong cross-examination of complainants would still be necessary, but the experience of victims should nonetheless become less painful and traumatic.[2]

In chapter six it was seen that many of the judges and barristers who were interviewed offered some criticism of jury decision-making in sexual assault trials. Indeed, with three exceptions, all interviewees seemed to think that convictions would increase with judge-only trials.[3] At the time of interviewing, the Criminal Justice Bill 2003 contained a provision, which was later dropped, which would have enabled defendants to choose trial by judge alone. Most interviewees were convinced that defendants would never opt for this. Indeed, B3 considered that the proposal was 'mad' and that counsel would always advise a man accused of rape to opt for jury trial: 'I can't believe any defendant would ever go for it. It's madness'. B2 expressed a similar view:

> To put all your eggs in one basket in having it determined by one mind rather than 12, and a mind who hears the same sort of account again and again in the various cases that come before him, I would be very surprised if that was invoked in this sort of situation.

But, despite the belief of most interviewees that convictions would rise with judge-only trials, all but two were firmly against abolishing the jury in sexual assault cases, either because they were believers in the jury system or because they feared the consequences of trial by judge alone.

Judge 5 considered that judges become too hardened and would be likely to convict in cases where the jury would not, which would not necessarily be a good thing, as the jury reflects the views of the general public:

> Over the years I think to a certain extent you do get a shell, you do get a bit hardened. You try not to. I don't think that it is a good idea at all to have a professional judiciary. I think that the input of the jury is very important because it reflects in a way that we can't what actually the general public thinks about things.

Judge 1 said juries give legitimacy and majesty to a verdict: 'I think people trust the juries. And there's something quite majestic about a jury verdict'.

It was felt that juries are trusted by the public in a way that judges are not, that juries bring to the task of decision-making a unique combination of common sense and judgment: 'Somehow the common sense and judgement that you get out of twelve people, is, I think, amazing and amazingly valuable'. (Judge 6)

---

[2] Orth and Maercker (2004) found no evidence of retraumatisation in sexual assault victims who had gone through court proceedings in Germany where there is a mixed court system consisting of two lay and three professional judges for most serious crimes (see Bliesener, 2006).

[3] One of those who did not share this view was B5 who considered that judges were 'far more male, middle-class, far more removed from the circumstances'.

Judge 1 considered that juries are useful because they take the responsibility for the decision. Judges would otherwise be blamed:

> I wouldn't want to get rid of juries in rape cases. On the whole I believe in the jury system. And quite frankly I'd prefer them to take the responsibility.

It was felt that judges would face the criticism of the media in a way that juries never do. As Judge 1 went on to state:

> I mean you can see what would happen if a judge acquitted, for example. And you'd hear about, white, middle-class, middle-aged, Oxbridge-educated, who don't know what's happening in society.

Similarly, Judge 6 commented: 'One of the great things about jury verdicts is that they are not open to the same criticism in the media as decisions made by judges'.

Quite apart from the firm opposition of interviewees to abolishing juries in rape trials, it remains the case that there is no solid data from which to conclude that judge-only trials would lead to decisions that are less influenced by rape schemata. The Kalven and Zeisel analysis was carried out in the 1950s. Without more recent data and without being able to tell whether the judges' higher conviction rates reflected more data-driven processing of the evidence, their findings provide at best tentative support for the idea that judge-only trials might reduce the justice gap. More research in this area, while hard to carry out, would clearly be desirable. There are alternatives to judge-only trials (for different European models see Vidmar 2000), but any proposal to abolish the existing jury system in sexual assault trials would be likely to meet fierce opposition. This chapter therefore continues by exploring other possible means of bridging the justice gap by improving the quality of decision-making within the framework of the jury system.[4]

9.2 SCREENING AND SELECTING JURORS

A possible solution for reducing the operation of biases and stereotypes would be to screen potential jurors for their acceptance of rape myths. Screening for attitudes, such as misconceptions about rape, which may result in bias against one party or another is permitted in some states of America as part of the *voir dire* procedure and can lead to the disqualification of individual jurors (Lieberman and Sales, 2007; United States Department of Justice, 2007b). Screening can take place either in the form of direct face to face questioning or in the form of written responses to questionnaires. The National Center on Domestic and Sexual Violence has issued 'Voir dire and prosecution tips for

[4] In recent years, a far-reaching departure from jury trial has been suggested by scholars advocating restorative justice procedures in specified cases of sexual assault. See eg Koss (2006) for a critical analysis and the RESTORE programme (Koss, Bachar, Hopkins and Carlson, 2004). A discussion of these proposals is beyond the scope of the present book.

sexual assault cases' that explain to prosecutors what to look out for as indications of bias in jurors (National Center on Domestic and Sexual Violence, 2007). Similar question lists have been prepared by the National District Attorneys Association (2007). Their purpose is to identify prospective jurors who might be biased in their approach to the case, either in favour of the complainant (eg because of previous rape experiences) or in favour of the defendant (eg because of adherence to rape stereotypes or myths). However, as Kovera, Dickinson and Cutler (2003) have pointed out, there is little evidence to prove that juror selection improves the quality of decision-making. They concluded from the few studies which have been carried out that the process might make little difference (Kovera *et al*, 2003: 171). Hans and Jehle (2003) have concluded, on the basis of their review of the evidence, that traditional *voir dire* procedures involving a limited set of questions posed to prospective jurors in a group setting are often ineffective because jurors may be reluctant to disclose personal information or attitudes they think are socially undesirable. The authors favour an expansive *voir dire* in which a broader range of questions is used than at present and prospective jurors are questioned individually and in confidence. It is suggested here that a first step would be to design and test attitude scales specifically for the purpose of individual screening.

Screening for juror attitudes is not widely used in legal systems outside the United States and is not permitted in England and Wales. Research is needed into how and whether it could be implemented effectively and in a way that is fair to both sides.

9.3 ASSISTING THE JURY

This book has demonstrated the widespread existence of biases against rape victims, and that juries may well share these biases. A key question which arises, therefore, is whether juries can be steered away from stereotypical thinking and made to focus more strongly and without prejudice on the facts of the case. It would seem obvious that the more juries are guided as to the agreed issues in the case and assisted in recalling the facts and applying the law to them, the better equipped they will be to engage in rational decision-making. The oral tradition which has dominated jury trial in England and Wales for centuries has not been entirely conducive to the achievement of this goal. Psychological research demonstrates that when information is presented in oral form it is forgotten soon after it is heard (Miller and Mauet, 1999: 562). By contrast, written material has the advantage that it may be reviewed as necessary to aid both comprehension and memory. Today the criminal trial has departed substantially from the principle of orality. Pre-trial procedures have also been developed and improved in ways that should enhance the quality of jury decision-making. These advances should be of some assistance in sex cases. It will be suggested here that further steps need to be taken in this direction.

Pre-Trial Procedure

There is now extensive case management by the judges, part of which is designed to assist the jury in understanding the case. Under the Criminal Procedure Rules 2005,[5] the court is instructed to engage in active case management. One aspect of this is to ensure that evidence is presented in the shortest and clearest way and that use is made of technology. In fulfilling its duty actively to manage the case, the court may give any direction and take any step unless this would be inconsistent with legislation. Thus, judges are given a very free hand, and this freedom could be put to good use in the task of ensuring that juries focus fully on the facts and are in a position to make judgments on the basis of the evidence alone in sex cases.

Starting the Case

It is now routine for the jury to be given a copy of the indictment at the outset of prosecution counsel's opening. Some judges direct that they should have that copy at an earlier stage when they are put in charge of the defendant,[6] which is preferable as it gives a little more time to focus on the case. In Scotland, each potential juror is handed a copy of the indictment on entering the jury box (Auld, 2001: para. 21).

Some judges provide a short introduction to the case and set out the issues that need to be decided. In his review of the criminal justice system, Lord Justice Auld proposed that the judge should give a much fuller introduction to jurors as to their task than is currently the norm and should provide an objective summary of the case, spelling out the questions the jury has to decide. Some judges oppose these proposals on the ground that the task of providing an outline of the case and the nature of the allegations is best performed, as it is at present, by prosecuting counsel lest the judge be thought to have given a slanted view. However, the judge's introduction could be agreed with counsel beforehand. Auld further proposed that the judge's oral introduction should be supported with a written aide-memoire, referred to as 'a case and issues summary' (paras 22–24). This document would set out the nature of the charges, the evidence about which there is no dispute between the parties, the matters of fact which are at issue and a list of the likely questions for their decision. It would be updated as the trial progressed.

The system has now moved some way in this direction. Currently, as part of the case management process, the parties are enjoined to consider what issues can be agreed between them and to draw up admissions and schedules of agreed

---

[5] SI 2005 No 384, pt 3.
[6] That is to say, after having been sworn in.

matters. Juries may also, in cases deemed appropriate, be given at the start of the case a *Schedule of Facts* which are agreed, an *Agreed Chronology*, a *Summary of the Issues* and any other document that will assist its understanding of the trial. As the case progresses, they will be given any other agreed documents, all of which can be taken with them into the jury room when they retire to consider their verdict. But it is not clear to what extent these useful measures are used in routine sex cases. Also of potential value in sex cases are the enacted provisions applying now only to fraud. Under section 9 of the Criminal Justice Act 1987, in complex fraud cases, the judge may order the prosecution to supply the court with a case statement setting out the principle facts of the prosecution case, the witnesses who will speak to those facts and any proposition of law on which the prosecution proposes to rely. It may also order the prosecution to prepare evidence in such a way as to aid comprehension by the jury.

In the New Zealand jury study, which involved real as against mock jurors, a significant number of interviewees (62.2 per cent of a total of 312) stated that they would have appreciated a written summary of the law at the start of the trial (Young, Cameron, and Tinsley, 1999: 62). In two cases, jurors were supplied with an outline of the elements of the offence and a flowchart showing a sequential list of questions designed around those elements as a guide to the direction which deliberations should take. All jurors found them extremely useful (Young *et al*, 1999: 63). The New Zealand Law Commission (2001: 5) has since recommended the use of such flowcharts.

Notebooks have become increasingly popular in the United States following the recommendation of the American Bar Association in 1989 that they be used in lengthy or complex trials (Dann, 1993: 1250). The idea is that a single source of reference is produced for individual jurors to use throughout the trial and their deliberations. The provision of appropriate material by the lawyers for each side is supervised by the judge as part of the pre-trial case management. Additions can be made as the trial continues. Typical contents would include: space for jurors' notes, forms for asking questions, preliminary jury instructions, a list of witnesses together with identifying information, copies of key exhibits used in evidence, a glossary of technical terms, a seating plan of those involved in the trial and the judge's final written directions. Juror notebooks have the advantage of allowing jurors to organise, understand, recall and evaluate important information as the trial progresses and ultimately enhance their decision-making (Dann, Hans and Kaye, 2005: 20). There is a danger that in lengthy or complex trials jurors may become overwhelmed with material, but this can be guarded against with efficient case management. There has been limited empirical research into the use and value of juror notebooks, but pilot studies in a number of US states have shown high levels of juror satisfaction. The key reasons reported for finding the notebooks helpful were that they helped jurors both understand and remember the evidence (Dann *et al*, 2005: 21).

There is much to be said in rape and sexual assault cases, however straightforward they may be deemed to be by lawyers, for employing one or other of the approaches discussed above, whether it is juror notebooks, flowcharts, or a written aide-memoire. At the very least, jurors should be given a written statement of the law, particularly that relating to consent as set out in section 74, so that they can focus on this from the start. There is no reason, moreover, why a judge should not give any general warnings that are felt to be appropriate at the outset of the case. This commonly occurs where, for example, a case is likely to attract publicity and the jury will be warned to decide the case only on the evidence and not what they may read in the press or see on television. Moreover, a judge is now required to warn the jury not to seek any assistance from the internet.[7] It is suggested that in sex cases the judge should always give a neutral reminder to the jury to focus on the facts and the law and to try to leave all preconceptions at the door of the courtroom. This could be set out in writing and included with the rest of the materials.

Witness Statements

The New Zealand study found that where juries were given written material, eg witness statements, extensive use was made of it during deliberations, particularly as a means of clarifying the sequence of events, resolving conflicting evidence or identifying contradictions in the defendant's evidence (Young *et al*, 1999: 21). Furthermore, Bourgeois, Horowitz and ForsterLee (1993) showed that jurors were better able to focus on the evidence in a complex trial when they were given a trial transcript. The criminal trial in England and Wales has now moved in the direction of permitting the jury to see witness statements in certain circumstances. Statements made by the accused when questioned by the police are given to the jury, and these may be taken into the jury room. Moreover, as a result of sections 119 and 120 of the Criminal Justice Act 2003, previous inconsistent statements of witnesses as well as certain other previous statements of witnesses are now admissible as evidence of the truth of their contents where certain requirements are fulfilled. Under section 122 of the Act, the jury will be able to see these documents which are treated as exhibits. However, the jury cannot take them into the jury room when it retires to consider its verdict unless the judge considers it appropriate or all the parties agree to this.[8] It is similarly the case that where a child's evidence is given in court by means of a video recording and a transcript of the video is supplied to the jury while it is listening to the evidence, this transcript cannot generally be taken into the jury room because it is thought to be unfair to have the child's evidence in writing but not the defendant's.[9] All the judge can do, therefore, is to sum up the child's

---

[7] See *R v K* [2005] EWCA Crim 346; [2005] 2 Cr App R 5.

[8] In *R v Hulme* [2006] EWCA Crim 2899, the Court of Appeal decided that the judge was wrong to have allowed the jury to take the statement into the jury room on the ground that the jury might give its contents disproportionate weight.

[9] *R v Welstead* [1996] 1 Cr App R 59; *R v Morris* [1998] Crim LR 416.

evidence slowly so that the jury can make a note of it. If the jury, having retired, comes back to ask the judge what is in the transcript, the judge can then read it out but the jury cannot have the document that best reminds it of the evidence. Many judges are appalled by this state of affairs. If juries are to reach reasoned decisions based on the evidence, it is important that they be permitted to take with them into the jury room the documents which they are allowed to see in court.

Asking Questions

While jurors in England and Wales are permitted to ask questions if they have a problem understanding any part of the proceedings or evidence, research studies show a distinct inhibition about doing so (Darbyshire, Maughan and Stewart, 2001: 47). A survey undertaken for the Home Office found a significant percentage of jurors (67 per cent) reported that they would have liked to have asked questions but felt that the procedure was unclear or were deterred in case they held up the trial (Matthews, Hancock and Briggs, 2004: 40). Other reasons given by jurors for not asking questions included a feeling of intimidation by the courtroom setting, that they felt it was the lawyers' job not theirs or that the procedure (of passing a written question via the jury foreperson to the court usher to pass to the judge) was too cumbersome (Matthews *et al*, 2004: 31). Researchers believe that asking questions allows jurors to be actively engaged and involved with the trial process (Dann, 1993: 1253; Penrod and Heuer, 1997), and as such the procedure for doing so should be made clear at the outset. Recommendations have included that guidance be given in the introductory video for jurors, or more radically, that a short period be given at the end of each day of the trial for jurors to pose questions to the judge (Matthews *et al*, 2004: 68).

The Summing-up

In England and Wales, the judge gives a summing-up to the jury at the end of the case which involves going through the evidence and giving the jury an explanation of the law and how their findings of fact must fit within the law. In the research review for the Auld Report, Darbyshire *et al* (2001: 25) reported that there was a consensus among researchers that juries have a great deal of difficulty understanding and applying oral judicial instructions. One consequence of this is that jurors may fall back on their own perceptions of what the law is (Darbyshire *et al*, 2001: 26; see also Ogloff and Rose, 2005).

Auld (2001) proposed that 'the case and issues summary' be used as an integral part of the summing-up, that this be supplemented where necessary with other written or visual aids, including PowerPoint presentations, and that the judge should relate his oral address methodically to the written material (para 42). Another approach designed to assist the jury which is becoming more common in complex cases is the use of a written list of directions as a supplement to the summing-up. These have to be submitted to counsel before their closing speeches to the jury and 'the judge should then use them as an integral part of the summing-up, referring the jury to them one by one as he deals with the points orally' (Archbold, 2007: para 4-356). However, since many sexual assault cases are not regarded as complicated, they may be less likely to receive this treatment.[10] While some judges might be resistant, there is every reason to insist that in sex cases (and arguably in all cases) the judge's directions on the law referable to each count on the indictment should be given in writing. Moreover, in setting out the law, the issues in relation to each count should be identified and what the prosecution has to prove in relation to each issue should be clearly specified in writing as well. Following current practice, the judge would have to discuss these written directions with counsel beforehand in order to avoid errors, to include any matters that the judge has overlooked and to avoid appeals.

9.4 MAKING THE JURY ACCOUNTABLE

Auld considered that jury directions were too cumbersome. He recommended instead that the judge should, so far as possible, not direct the jury on the law, but should present a series of written factual questions to the jury which corresponded to those set out in the updated case and issues summary. Each question would be tailored to the law and the issues and evidence in the case. The answers to these questions would logically lead only to a verdict of guilty or not guilty. Auld further proposed that the judge, in appropriate cases, could be permitted to require a jury to answer publicly each of the questions and to declare a verdict in accordance with those answers (Auld, 2001: para. 55). In this way, it would be made to justify its verdict.

It may be true that written questions would have certain advantages in the battle to ensure that juries do not decide cases simply in accordance with their own biases.[11] By delivering precise factual questions to the jury to which it is required to respond, rather than simply allowing it to return a guilty or not guilty verdict, there is a greater chance that minds will be focused and verdicts returned which are based on the facts.

There are, however, obvious objections to the Auld proposals which would constitute a major departure from the present system in the direction of the

---

[10] See also *R v Lawson* [1998] Crim LR 883, in which the jury requested that the judge set out in writing the difference in law between murder and manslaughter. This the judge declined to do and the Court of Appeal upheld his decision.

[11] The problem of bias has been met by a degree of denial: see eg *R v Abdroikov* [2005] EWCA Crim 1986; [2005] 1WLR 3538.

continental jury systems. They would add a new level of complexity to the system given that there may be disagreements among jury members on different questions. In addition, perfectly relevant matters may occur to a jury which are not covered in the questions. If the jury is to be held to a verdict on the basis of its answers, these answers may themselves be deliberately given by a determined jury so as to correspond to their eventual chosen verdict. The separation of law and fact which Auld advocates is also not necessarily easy or desirable in sex cases. It is important that juries should apply to their deliberations the definition of consent which Parliament has laid down rather than their own versions. Moreover, many would object that the proposal would involve a radical shift of power from jury to judge. Indeed, Vogler (2005: 239) has pointed out that the use of a list of questions is one of the methods traditionally used in European countries to weaken juries and render them pliant. The jury would be impeded from returning perverse verdicts. Recently, the House of Lords has made it clear that judges are not to tell juries that they have to return guilty verdicts given the evidence in the case.[12]

Social psychological research also highlights the potential drawbacks of requiring juries to answer specific questions about a case if question lists are long and complex since they can create a state of cognitive overload in jurors (see Kaplan, Martin and Hertel, 2006, for a review). Social cognition research has shown that where cognitive overload occurs, decision-makers organise information into pre-existing cognitive schemata to make sense of them (Bodenhausen and Lichtenstein, 1987). In the case of sexual assault, this means that they are likely to fall back on their stereotypes about rape, rather than embarking on a more systematic appraisal of the available evidence.

It is noteworthy that Auld favoured asking the jury to answer questions, rather than requiring it simply to give reasons for its decision, as is the case, for example, in Spain. There, juries are required 'to give a succinct rationale for their verdict, indicating the evidence on which it is based and the reasons for finding particular propositions proved or not proved' (Thaman, 2000: 345). Thaman (2000: 345) comments: 'This is the clearest attempt yet by a legislature to require that juries justify their verdicts' and it is a way of seeking to comply with the presumption of innocence under Article 6(2) of the European Convention on Human Rights. While this might appear to have certain attractions, the Spanish experience suggests that asking juries to provide reasons for their verdicts is often unproductive and is likely to give rise to unenlightening responses. It was found that although some juries gave elaborate explanations, others simply provided the briefest of answers, such as 'Witnesses' or 'Testimony of witnesses and experts' (Thaman, 2000: 345). While there would be ways of ensuring less laconic responses, reasons are still likely to be given formulaically in such a way as to ensure that the verdict passes muster.

---

[12] *R v Wang* [2005] UK HL 9; [2005] 2 Cr App R 8.

But the Spanish experience need not necessarily be determinative of the matter. Research by Tetlock (1992) on accountability shows that individuals who were asked to form an impression of another person, engaged in more careful and systematic information processing when they expected to have to explain and justify their impression afterwards. Importantly, however, this was only the case when they were told they would be held accountable prior to being given the information. Similarly, in a study by Krahé, Temkin and Bieneck (2007), participants were asked to make judgments about a set of case scenarios involving sexual assault. Before being given these scenarios, one group was told that they might have to justify their judgments afterwards, whereas a control group was not given this instruction. It was found that where the instruction was given, this reduced the impact of rape myth acceptance in situations most at odds with the real rape stereotype, namely those involving rape by an ex-partner. This research suggests that there might be some mileage in informing the jury at the outset of the trial that it will be asked to give reasons for its decision as a method of ensuring that the evidence in the case is carefully processed. Further research is needed to substantiate the benefits of introducing accountability for jury decision-making.

9.5 EDUCATING LEGAL PROFESSIONALS

Juries are not alone in requiring more assistance if sexual assault trials are to be improved. There is also a need for further education of lawyers involved in such trials. Judges, however, are notoriously difficult to educate. When the Judicial Studies Board (JSB) was founded in 1979 to provide continuing education for judges in England and Wales, this was considered by the judges at the time to be a questionable development (Malleson, 1997). Training organised by outsiders has been firmly resisted in many jurisdictions. Judicial independence is often invoked as a reason for keeping training to the profession itself, although this contention is less than convincing (Malleson, 1997). In the United States a training manual for judges has noted:

> Mandatory judicial education is highly controversial and must be approached cautiously. Many judges resent the notion that they need or could benefit from education. Appellate judges are particularly hostile, asserting that education is only for trial judges. [. . .] Two myths must be overcome: First, that 'only judges can teach judges', second, that judges should not take into account social science data. [. . .] In fact, judges often do not have all the expertise they need for their own decision-making or to teach other judges. They need to hear from the experts who can provide this critical background. (Schafran and Wikler, 2001: 30)

Training about gender and gender bias is particularly controversial and this remains to be firmly established as part of the curriculum throughout the common law world.

Judicial Education in the United States and Canada

The United States led the way in the 1970s in developing an understanding of judicial gender bias (Stewart, 2001). The enactment of the Equal Justice for Women in the Courts Act 1994 provided a substantial impetus for judicial training about rape and sexual assault. Section 40411 provides that 'the State Justice Institute may award grants for the purpose of developing, testing, presenting, and disseminating model programs to be used by States in training judges and court personnel'. Section 40412 which specifies the possible content of such programmes is set out in table 9.1.

Table 9.1

Judicial training about rape and sexual assault
(Equal Justice for Women in the Courts Act 1994, s 40412)[13]

> Training provided pursuant to grants may include current information, existing studies, or current data on
>
> (1) the nature and incidence of rape and sexual assault by strangers and non-strangers, marital rape, and incest;
> (2) the underreporting of rape, sexual assault, and child sexual abuse;
> (3) the physical, psychological, and economic impact of rape and sexual assault on the victim, the costs to society, and the implications for sentencing;
> (4) the psychology of sex offenders, their high rate of recidivism, and the implications for sentencing;
> (5) the historical evolution of laws and attitudes on rape and sexual assault;
> (6) sex stereotyping of female and male victims of rape and sexual assault, racial stereotyping of rape victims and defendants, and the impact of such stereotypes on credibility of witnesses, sentencing, and other aspects of the administration of justice;
> (7) application of rape shield laws and other limits on introduction of evidence that may subject victims to improper sex stereotyping and harassment in both rape and non-rape cases, including the need for *sua sponte* judicial intervention in inappropriate cross-examination;
> (8) the use of expert witness testimony on rape trauma syndrome, child sexual abuse accommodation syndrome, post-traumatic stress syndrome, and similar issues;
> (9) the legitimate reasons why victims of rape, sexual assault, and incest may refuse to testify against a defendant.

Section 40413 provides that:

> the State Justice Institute shall ensure that model programs carried out pursuant to grants [. . .] are developed with the participation of law enforcement officials, public

[13] See: http://usinfo.stste.gov/usa/infousa/laws/majorlaw/gun94.pdf, p 148.

and private non-profit victim advocates, legal experts, prosecutors, defense attorneys, and recognized experts on gender bias in the courts.

Section 40421 further provides:

> In order to gain a better understanding of the nature and the extent of gender bias in the Federal courts, the circuit judicial councils are encouraged to conduct studies of the instances, if any, of gender bias in their respective circuits.

Section 40421b (11) specifically suggests that such studies may include the effects of gender on 'the admissibility of the victim's past sexual history in civil and criminal cases'.

In the wake of this legislation, 45 states set up special task forces on gender bias in the courts and some states have produced Codes of Judicial Conduct. The National Judicial Education Program (NJEP) in co-operation with the National Association of Women Judges conducts training and develops model curricula for work with judges, lawyers, bar associations and prosecutors. It claims to have increased awareness about the ways that gender bias undermines fairness in decision-making and court interactions. It promotes education on gender bias through curricula, videos and DVDs, publications in journals and the popular press and by supporting gender bias task forces. It has also produced a substantial training manual (Schafran and Wikler, 2001). While there has been some judicial hostility to the idea of gender bias, many judges have been supportive of this type of education and commentators believe that a change in the judicial climate has resulted (Stewart, 2001).

Where the United States led, Canada, Australia and New Zealand have followed (Stewart 2001). In Canada, judicial training has included 'social context' with a specific programme on violence against women. At the time of writing, a course specifically on gender was planned for 2007. The Social Context Education Project (SCEP) was a special project of the National Judicial Institute between 1996–2003 (National Judicial Institute, 2006). SCEP was designed, *inter alia*, to assist judges 'to explore their own assumptions, biases and views of the world with a view to reflecting on how these may interact with judicial process' (Dawson, 2004). A lengthy and comprehensive planning process took place to devise the programme. The project placed emphasis on securing the involvement of the most senior judges both in planning and delivery of the programmes in order to send a strong message that involvement in the project was to be seen as a high priority for all judges, with members of the Supreme Court of Canada specifically endorsing it. Thus, for example, Justice L'Heureux-Dubé has pointed to 'the importance of ensuring that courts remain attentive to historical patterns of discrimination in determining whether a particular rule, inference, or presumption is based on myth or stereotype and therefore violates constitutional guarantees of equality' (L'Heureux-Dubé, 2001: 94). The impetus for this type of education has undoubtedly been the Canadian Constitution, particularly the fundamental principle of equality which it incorporates.

Judicial Education in England and Wales

Chapter seven of this book has demonstrated that not all judges in the interview study were fully conversant with or had a proper understanding of aspects of the evidential law relating to sexual offences. Some judges also shared common stereotypical beliefs about rape. In England and Wales, all judges who try rape cases are 'rape-ticketed' which means they are obliged to attend the serious sexual assault seminars provided by the Judicial Studies Board (JSB). The watchword of the JSB is education by judges for judges, and therein lies both its strength and its weakness.

The serious sexual assault seminars are devised by experienced judges who determine their content and arrange speakers. The content is weighed heavily in the direction of those matters which most concern the trial judges themselves. The 2004 residential programme, for example, was organised over two days. There were lectures provided by academics or judges on changes to the law of evidence and practice relating to sexual offences, changes to the substantive law, the use of special measures such as video and television link, and sentencing powers in relation to sexual offences. In addition, there was a lecture on the assessment and treatment of sex offenders in the community provided by a probation officer, a lecture on police practice in investigating sexual assault provided by a very senior police officer and one on the policy and practice of the Crown Prosecution Service provided by the Director of Public Prosecutions. The course divides up between lectures and discussion groups where practical exercises take place.

It might have been expected that, given the compulsory nature of these courses, judges would be better informed at the very least on the legal side. However, there is no obligation to do anything other than attend. Knowledge is not tested. Those attending lectures are asked to evaluate them by filling in comment and evaluation forms. There is no external quality control.

While the provision is in many ways strong, organisers of the JSB seminars have struggled to inject some broader content which would provide judges with an overview of the social, criminological and statistical aspects of rape. A single 45-minute overview lecture has been used on occasions to cover these matters. However, the negative judicial response to receiving such instruction has ensured that this lecture does not necessarily take place. Instead, a judge may give a personal overview of some of the issues involved in serious sexual assault cases. Challenging stereotypes and judgmental attitudes has not been part of the curriculum. However, in a letter to the *Times* in 1996, the secretary of the JSB wrote that in the general training of judges, 90-minute sessions on human awareness had been introduced which 'aimed to show how to avoid preconceptions about individuals because of race or gender'.[14]

---

[14] *The Times* (9 July 1996). It is not known whether these sessions are now an established part of the programme.

The JSB also has an *Equal Treatment Bench Book* which is distributed to all judges and which deals, *inter alia*, with gender stereotyping, sexual harassment and violence against women (Judicial Studies Board, 2005). There is a section on sexual offences which is one and a half pages in length and deals with some selected issues in very brief paragraphs. Whether judges read these sections of the handbook is a matter for speculation and some doubt. In addition, the JSB has an *Equal Treatment Advisory Committee* (ETAC) whose stated role is to:

1. Provide training and supporting materials which enable judges and magistrates to:

   • perform their judicial functions in a manner that is fair and free from bias or discrimination;
   • identify their own prejudices and preconceptions and how these can affect their decision-making and interpersonal relationships; and
   • acquire relevant knowledge about race, culture, religion, gender, disability, sexual orientation and other diversity issues.

2. Advise the JSB Board and Committees on the ways in which judges and magistrates can be assisted in addressing equality/diversity and fair treatment issues.
3. Assist in reviewing and keeping under review the content of the JSB seminars to ensure they reflect the aims and objectives of ETAC (Judicial Studies Board, 2006).

ETAC has been active on race issues, but the extent of its involvement as far as gender is concerned is less clear. Stewart (2001) has pointed out that despite the considerable knowledge which exists in Britain about the way in which gender bias works across the legal system, the judiciary has not been prepared to take this on board in the same way as the judiciary in the United States, Canada, Australia and New Zealand. It has instead confined its attention to bias in relation to race. She speculates that this is because of a wider gulf between academic lawyers and practitioners, the absence of a Bill of Rights or written constitution and acute judicial anxiety about perceived interference[15] with judicial independence and also about media reactions (Stewart, 2001).

There can be no doubt that the JSB has achieved much in setting up a compulsory course for judges who try serious sexual assault cases but the package, while pedagogically unimpeachable in many respects, does not appear sufficiently to reflect the aims and objectives of ETAC or to be entirely fit for purpose in the twenty-first century. Strong education for judges about race and about domestic violence has been introduced. If judges are to continue to be in charge of their own continuing education, those responsible for training will need to be bolder and firmer in their determinations of what goes into the cur-

---

[15] The dark references to pressure groups by some interviewees offer some support for this thesis: see ch 6, section 6.3.

riculum in sexual assault training. This should include an overview of the social, criminological and statistical aspects of rape, and be capable of challenging stereotypical assumptions and judgmental attitudes about it. Consideration also needs to be given to assessment and to evaluation of courses other than by participants themselves.[16]

Performance Appraisal, Monitoring and Mentoring

Trial judges in England and Wales, unlike magistrates, are not subject to performance appraisal, although this is now being contemplated.[17] Resistance to this is understandable, although performance appraisal has become routine in other walks of life. Trial judges sit alone. They have the opportunity to discuss cases over lunch or at the end of the day, but there is no established system of monitoring or even mentoring. Judges do not sit in on trials to see how fellow judges are handling them or to offer friendly advice. Counsel for both sides can advise the judge or may be invited to give their opinion on certain matters, such as whether a particular jury direction should be given, but otherwise there is little feedback other than by the Court of Appeal in those cases where an appeal is brought. But counsel's knowledge cannot always be relied on. Two judges in the interview study said that they were regularly hearing applications to include sexual history in open court even though this is not permitted under the legislation.[18]

One way of giving teeth to judicial training on serious sexual assault would be to instigate a mentoring system in which experienced judges would observe several trials conducted by fellow judges. The emphasis would be on assistance rather than evaluation. This modest proposal would not offend against the desire to keep training within the judiciary itself and would at least go some way towards following training through into the courtroom.[19] Mentoring does involve the cost of judicial time but, if carefully chosen, recently retired judges who are up to date and have a wealth of experience, could be brought in to assist.

CPS Training and Training for Barristers

The CPS has appreciated the importance of specific training about sexual assault for crown prosecutors. It claims to have trained 520 specialist rape

---

[16] It appears that 'training for judges who sit in rape cases has recently been overhauled' (Office for Criminal Justice Reform, 2007: 11). No information is provided as to the nature of the overhaul but see n 19 below.

[17] See *The Times*, 17 September 2007.

[18] See also *R v V* [2006] EWCA Crim 1901.

[19] Twenty-six judges currently involved in the JSB serious sexual offences training seminars have indicated a willingness to act as mentors to less experienced ticketed judges (Judicial Studies Board 2007). If this is a precursor to the introduction of a formal mentoring system, it would be a welcome step forward.

prosecutors 'to ensure that all rape cases are prepared by experts' (Office for Criminal Justice Reform, 2006: 10). Training is compulsory for rape specialists. The training consists of a number of courses covering the law and procedure in sex cases. There are also quarterly seminars covering the Sexual Offences Act 2003, special measures, disclosure and the myths surrounding rape. In addition, there is an annual rape conference and a serious sexual offences newsletter. A recent report has revealed the gaps in the training currently offered and has made recommendations for improving it (Her Majesty's Crown Prosecution Service Inspectorate, 2007: 98).

Training for Barristers

Until recently, there has been no compulsory training specially for barristers who deal with sexual assault cases. The Bar Vocational Course does not include specific training in handling sexual assault and the issues surrounding it, although some courses will cover aspects of the substantive and evidential law relating to sex offences. Practising barristers are obliged to undergo continuing professional development, but this has not required barristers who deal with sex cases to undertake specific training in dealing with them. The CPS has, however, liased with the Bar Council to introduce comprehensive training on rape issues and quality assurance of barristers prosecuting rape cases in court (Office for Criminal Justice Reform, 2006: 10). This is a welcome development. Some training seminars have been held on section 41 (the sexual history provisions) and have been monitored by the CPS. An accreditation scheme has been agreed with the CPS so that only trained barristers will now be able to prosecute sexual offence cases. The circuits to which barristers belong have responded by setting up training days so that their members will receive accreditation. However, it is not clear how far the CPS is engaged in specifying their precise content and actively monitoring them. It is further intended that accreditation will depend on an evaluation of court performance after attendance at training courses.[20] But the recent HMCPSI report noted that 'formal monitoring of rape advocates is still not generally undertaken' (Her Majesty's Crown Prosecution Service Inspectorate 2007: 135). Ideally, those who are accredited should continue to be monitored, and follow-up courses should equally be made compulsory.

There are no plans for an accreditation scheme for those who only defend in these cases. It is suggested that all barristers appearing in sex cases require training. Reliance on the myths and stereotypes surrounding rape should be as unacceptable for defence barristers as are the myths and stereotypes of race. Compulsory education is the best way of moving towards this goal.

---

[20] This had not been implemented at the time of writing.

9.6 APPOINTMENT OF MORE FEMALE JUDGES?

In the United States, studies have provided 'overwhelming evidence that gender-based myths, biases and stereotypes are deeply embedded in the attitudes of many male judges' (Wilson, 1990: 512). Some American judges themselves have not been slow to recognise this. Judge Shientag of the Appellate Division of the New York Supreme Court, for example, in a 1975 handbook for judges, warned his fellow judges of the way in which judges can so easily believe themselves to be acting with cold neutrality when in fact they are prey to biases of which they are often unconscious (Shientag, 1975).[21] The response to this awareness in the United States has been not merely to seek to address the problem through intensive educational programmes as outlined above, but to increase the number of women judges and lawyers (Wilson, 1990: 512). Part of the reason for doing so is to increase confidence in the criminal justice system: 'The public must perceive its judges as fair, impartial and representative of the diversity of those who are being judged'.[22]

In England and Wales, there were 623 circuit judges in post on 30 September 2005 of whom 66 or 11 per cent were women (Department for Constitutional Affairs, 2006: 18.) It is to be anticipated that this statistic will slowly be improved now that the independent Judicial Appointments Commission has taken over the task of making judicial appointments.[23] But the question remains whether more female judges would have any effect on rape trials. English judges are wont to say that it is women on juries who often are responsible for acquittals in rape cases because of their judgmental attitudes towards the behaviour of other women (see chapter six). Some are also wont to follow up this observation with the comment that more female judges would do nothing to enhance the conviction rates in rape cases. However, in chapter two it was pointed out that a large number of studies show that in fact men are more disposed than women to blame the victim. It might be thought, therefore, that if there were more women judges trying rape cases, this could indeed make some difference to case outcomes. But, as was also pointed out in chapter two and further demonstrated in the studies in chapter four, the crucial factor here is the extent to which a person subscribes to rape myths. Women subscribe to rape myths as well as men, albeit less frequently, and those who do are indistinguishable from men in the extent to which they blame complainants and are disinclined to view the defendant as criminally liable. The studies discussed in chapter two illustrating a gender difference in rape myth acceptance (RMA) were mostly carried out with students or in some cases with the general public. It cannot necessarily be assumed that female judges will generally be less inclined to accept rape myths than male judges. The socialisation process which women go through as

---

[21] Cited by Wilson (1990: 510).
[22] *Ibid.*
[23] This took place in April 2006.

barristers and then as judges could well reduce the gender difference in RMA, but this possibility remains speculative in the absence of empirical data. Our own data with prospective lawyers showed no gender differences on either rape-supportive attitudes or perceptions of defendants and complainants in rape cases (see chapter four, Study 2).

In order to ensure that those with rape-supportive attitudes do not try rape cases, the obvious step forward would be to screen judges before they are rape-ticketed. If this is not an option, the alternative is to appoint more female judges since studies mainly show that women are less likely than men to have stereo-typical views about rape. However, this strategy carries with it the risk that some of the women appointed would be among those who do endorse rape myths. As suggested above, judicial education aimed at dispelling rape myths held by both male and female judges would seem to be essential.

9.7 SUMMARY AND CONCLUSIONS

This chapter has canvassed a range of different approaches to tackling the attitude problem which besets the processing of rape cases within the criminal jus-tice system. It has discussed abolishing the jury in rape trials, concluding that this was not an option in the immediate future. It has looked at the possibility of jury screening as a potential method of ensuring that those who are particularly biased against rape victims do not sit on the jury in rape cases. A number of suggestions for enhancing rational decision-making in the jury room have also been made. In addition, this chapter has recommended further research into the efficacy of telling juries at the outset of the trial that they will be asked to give reasons for their decisions. The purpose would be to test this as a method of promoting care-ful rather than schematic processing of the evidence in the case.

Those involved with sex offences within the criminal justice system require special training. In England and Wales, training about serious sexual assault is compulsory for trial judges who hold the rape ticket. This in itself is a con-siderable achievement since compulsory training is by no means the norm in the common law world. Moreover, this training is not conducted exclusively by judges. But the course content remains narrow in comparison with that which is available in North America. The absence of any follow-up in the courtroom or any means of assessing whether judges have assimilated the material is a fur-ther problem. The CPS provides training for crown prosecutors who deal with sexual assault, but further steps need to be taken to improve it. Progress has been made with the training of barristers who prosecute in sex cases, but this does not extend to those who only defend in such cases. Thus, education of the legal profession in the many serious issues arising in sexual assault cases is at present patchy. While the importance of training to address stereotypical think-ing about rape and sexual assault is now increasingly recognised, such training has yet to be firmly embedded in England and Wales.

It has been suggested in this chapter that while the appointment of more women as rape-ticketed judges is a laudable aim in itself, it is not clear that this would necessarily make a difference to rape trials. In terms of the evidence reviewed in chapter two and two of the original studies reported in this book, it is true to say that women were generally found to be less accepting of rape myths than men. However, no systematic research has as yet been carried out on gender differences in rape-supportive attitudes among the judiciary itself. Therefore, while there is some reason to hope that, on the basis of statistical probability, increasing the number of female judges would assist in reducing the impact of rape stereotypes in the courtroom, such an approach carries with it the risk that those appointed would be women who do subscribe to rape myths. Rape-ticketed judges need to be people without rape-supportive attitudes and, unless judges are screened for their attitudes, the only way forward is through more intensive education.

10

Changing Public Attitudes

T HERE IS EVIDENCE from multiple sources that misconceptions about rape abound and that they influence the way in which victims are treated by the criminal justice system. To the extent that members of the public are called on to render verdicts in rape cases, their attitudes and judgmental biases are relevant to the outcome of rape trials and may explain attrition in rape cases. As shown throughout this book, in particular in our study with over 2000 members of the public set out in chapter five, rape myths are widely accepted in society and affect perceptions of defendants and complainants in rape cases. Therefore, designing effective strategies for changing these misconceptions is an urgent task, not only to improve the fate of rape victims in the criminal justice system and avoid 'secondary victimisation', but to reduce the prevalence of sexual assault in the first place.[1] This chapter reviews existing approaches designed to challenge rape myths and outlines directions for future efforts towards this goal.

10.1 RAPE PREVENTION PROGRAMMES FOR COLLEGE STUDENTS

There has been considerable alarm at the high incidence of sexual assault among students in the United States which was first uncovered on a large scale by Koss and her colleagues (Koss, Gidycz and Wisniewski, 1987; Koss and Oros, 1982). Universities have responded by implementing rape education programmes, and many have made attendance compulsory for their male students (Bachar and Koss, 2001). Challenging rape myths is almost always the objective of these programmes (see Krahé, 2001: ch 8; and Schewe, 2002, for reviews). In terms of reducing the rate of sexual assault, men are the primary target group for these interventions (Berkowitz, 2002). However, from the point of view of dispelling rape myths in society at large so as to reduce their impact on decision-making in legal contexts, it has been recognised that interventions need to be directed at both men and women. This has led to the development of mixed-gender and also women-only interventions (Yeater and O'Donohue, 1999). Rape myths have been addressed in these programmes in a number of different ways. One is

---

[1] The need to raise 'levels of public awareness [as to] what is acceptable and what is unacceptable sexual behaviour' has been recognised by the Home Office (2006e: 290).

to use written material presenting facts and figures about rape which contradict rape myths. Another is to ask participants to answer 'true or false' to a series of statements about rape containing rape myths. This is followed by discussion and explanation (eg Gidycz, *et al*, 2001). In addition, many interventions use educational videotapes in which rape myths are challenged by factual information and interviews with rape survivors (eg Johansson-Love and Geer, 2003).

Many studies have been conducted over the last two decades which address the effectiveness of rape prevention programmes. In terms of reducing rape myth acceptance, they do not paint a positive picture (see reviews by Anderson and Whiston, 2005; Bachar and Koss, 2001; Schewe, 2002; Yeater and O'Donohue, 1999). Rape myth acceptance is typically measured immediately before and after participation in the intervention, with some studies including follow-ups taking place up to two months post-intervention. A meta-analysis by Flores and Hartlaub (1998) found evidence of short-term reductions in rape myth acceptance, and more recent studies have shown that the effects of the programmes are stronger on those with high rape myth acceptance prior to the intervention (Pacifici, Stoolmiller and Nelson, 2001; Schewe and O'Donohue, 1996) or on men with a prior history of sexual aggression (O'Donohue, Yeater and Fanetti, 2003). However, the reviews also concluded that the effects tended to disappear within a few weeks post-intervention, with attitudes showing a rebound to the original level (see also Anderson, Stoelb, Duggan, Hieger, Kling and Payne, 1998; Heppner, Humphreys, Hillenbrand-Gunn and DeBord, 1995; Lonsway and Kothari, 2000). Bachar and Koss (2001) even questioned whether the immediate post-intervention decline in rape myth acceptance reflected a genuine change of attitude, or whether participants were simply giving responses which they believed would be regarded as socially acceptable. One of the reasons for these disappointing results is the short duration of the interventions, usually consisting of a single session (Schewe, 2002). Interventions extending over longer periods of time are likely to produce more lasting effects (Anderson and Whiston, 2005; Lonsway, *et al*, 1998), but there may be practical constraints on providing longer interventions even with a captive audience such as college students.

10.2 SCHOOL-BASED INTERVENTIONS

Many adolescents become sexually active in their mid-teens or younger (eg YouGov, 2006), and their sexual scripts often contain the use of pressure or even force as normative elements of sexual interactions (Krahé, Bieneck and Scheinberger-Olwig, 2007). It follows that interventions aimed at reducing the acceptance of sexual aggression and challenging myths about rape should start as early as possible. The school setting provides a context in which more extensive and longer interventions could be implemented which have been shown to be more successful than single-shot attempts at changing rape-supportive attitudes. However, compared with the burgeoning number of rape prevention schemes directed at undergraduate students, school-based interventions are few and far between (eg Hilton, Harris, Rice, Krans and Lavigne, 1998). One study by Pacifici *et al* (2001) exposed 15 and 16-year-old high school students to a multimedia curriculum on preventing coercive sexual behaviour in dating situations. It consisted of three 80-minute periods of class instruction and the additional presentation of a video. One period was designed to address beliefs and attitudes about sexual coercion, including common myths about rape. When measured in the period following the last session, acceptance of rape myths was found to be significantly reduced among those participants with high initial levels of rape myth acceptance, as compared with a control group which had not attended the sessions. While this is an encouraging result, this study in line with others (eg Hilton *et al*, 1998), says nothing about the longevity of the effect since no follow-up research took place. In an impressive longitudinal project, eighth-grade students who participated in a 10-week dating violence prevention programme were followed up over a period of four years (Foshee, Bauman, Ennett, Linder, Benefield and Schindran, 2004). Compared with a control group, participants in the intervention had significantly lower rates of sexual aggression (male participants) and sexual victimisation (female participants) over the four-year period. Even though the study did not specifically address changes in attitudes about sexual violence, its findings demonstrate that it is possible to achieve lasting effects with carefully planned and extensive interventions targeting young adolescents.

In Britain, the 'Personal, Social and Health Education' (PSHE) module of the National Curriculum defines as one of its central objectives in years 10 and 11 (Key Stage 4) the teaching of knowledge, skills and understanding for 'Developing good relationships and respecting the differences between people' (National Curriculum Online, 2006). At present, sexual aggression and myths surrounding sexual assault are not mentioned under this heading, even though learning 'to be aware of exploitation in relationships' comes close to it. Given that lasting effects can be achieved provided that the programme is long enough, implementing a rape awareness module appears a promising strategy. It is essential, however, that the content and format of such an intervention should be grounded in a theoretical understanding of the principles of attitude change through persuasive communication, and that there should be an emphasis on changing behaviour as well as attitudes (see Bohner and Wänke, 2002).

10.3 EDUCATING THE GENERAL PUBLIC ABOUT RAPE: USING THE MEDIA

Offering rape education courses to members of the general public on a voluntary basis is unlikely to have much impact because it is likely that they would be preaching to the converted. Thus, alternative ways of dispelling rape myths need to be found which have a higher chance of reaching those who would be otherwise disinclined to address the issue. Public service announcements (PSAs) have been employed as one method of raising awareness in society at large about the problem of sexual assault, as have advertising campaigns using posters, print media and the web.[2]

In England and Wales, the Consent Campaign run by the Home Office (Home Office, 2006c) which included the use of posters was described in chapter five. Posters have also been used to raise women's awareness of the risk of sexual assault when intoxicated as for example in a campaign by the Portman Group in 2004 to promote responsible drinking (Portman Group, 2006) and in a campaign by Greater Manchester Police (2006). In the United States, a poster campaign by the Los Angeles Commission on Assaults against Women (LACAAW, 2006) is designed to challenge the attitudes that support rape and sexual assault. The campaign includes a range of posters portraying women and girls, all bearing the slogan 'This is not an invitation to rape me'.

The National Commission of Women (NWC, 2006) 'End violence against women' initiative in the United States has used its website to present facts about rape and sexual assault. At the European level, the Rape Crisis Network Europe (RCNE, 2006) supported by the European Commission has a website that offers facts about rape and challenges rape myths. In the United States, an example of a website addressing rape myths is the Rape, Abuse and Incest National Network (RAINN, 2006).[3]

Evaluating the Effectiveness of the Media

Evaluating the effectiveness of mass media campaigns designed to change attitudes and knowledge about rape is far more difficult than assessing the effects of intervention programmes delivered face to face to a definable audience with the possibility of taking pre- and post-intervention measures. We were unable to find any systematic evaluations of such campaigns. However, the literature on evaluating information campaigns in the health domain is informative about the potential limitations of this approach. A meta-analysis by Derzon and Lipsey (2002) of 72 studies evaluating campaigns directed at changing knowledge, attitudes and behaviour related to substance abuse revealed little overall change from pre- to post-intervention levels. Although attitudes were more amenable to

---

[2] A Google search produces a large number of poster campaigns against rape, the discussion of which is beyond the scope of this chapter. Examples include: http://www.sdcda.org/helping/rapeposter.php; http://www.voicesnotvictims.org/campaigns.html; http://www.voicesnotvictims.org/campaigns.html; http://www.mencanstoprape.org/info-url2698/info-url.htm An extensive list of programmes can be found at: http://www.vawnet.org/

[3] A Google search under 'rape awareness websites' comes up with a large number of pertinent sites across the world.

change than behaviours, the effects were small. Video messages were more successful than print media, and messages presented over longer periods of time were most successful. The implications of these results for poster campaigns directed at changing attitudes about rape are that their impact is likely to be marginal at best in terms of the magnitude and the duration of the effects. However, Derzon and Lipsey (2002) also found that when mass communication messages are supplemented by other forms of intervention, such as face to face instruction, their effectiveness is enhanced. Therefore, it is possible that rape awareness posters could be more effective if combined with other methods, such as the class-based programmes discussed above.

The success of mass media campaigns designed to influence attitudes critically depends on the content of the message (Perloff, 1993: ch 12). Messages should be tailored to the target audience, and those with high sensation value have been found to be more successful (eg Harrington, *et al*, 2003; Morgan, Palmgreen, Stephenson, Hoyle and Lorch, 2003). Both requirements were met by the Home Office Consent campaign (see chapter five). The campaign, which was directed at men between 18 and 24, included radio broadcasts, stickers on condom vending machines as well as posters, all emphasising the need to obtain consent. The posters contained eye-catching images (see chapter five, figure 5.5) but were criticised for objectifying women and for being more concerned with protecting men from accusations of rape than protecting women from men's sexual violence.[4] Our experimental evaluation of these posters in Study 3 (see chapter five) revealed that they failed to make viewers more attentive to a woman's expression of non-consent or to reduce the tendency to blame the victim. This was true despite the fact that participants were constantly exposed to the posters as they read and judged the rape scenarios, thus creating a higher level of attention than the posters would be likely to attract in the natural context of the campaign.

Poster campaigns also run the risk of being misunderstood, as a comment from a recently retired judge on a BBC radio programme illustrates:

> I think the Government's present campaign of advertising to advise women what may happen if they continue binge drinking and wearing revealing clothes is a proper advertising scheme for ignorant people to make them aware of the dangers.[5]

If the judge was referring to the Home Office campaign, he clearly failed to grasp its stated objective which was 'to reduce incidents of rape by ensuring that men know they need to gain consent before they have sex' (Home Office, 2006c). Alternatively, if he was confusing it with the Portman Group campaign which stressed the vulnerability of women when they are drunk, that too was not aimed at warning women about the dangers of wearing revealing clothes.

---

[4] For critical comments posted on the web, see: http://mindthegapcardiff.blogspot.com/2006/03/campaign-in-need-of-some-awareness.html, retrieved 21 November 2006.

[5] *Unreliable Evidence*, BBC Radio 4 (25 April 2006).

Clearly the judge's own stereotypical understandings of rape were brought to bear on his interpretation of one or other or both poster campaigns.

The evaluation conducted by the Home Office of the posters in the Consent Campaign revealed that some respondents had misperceived the message of the prison poster (see chapter five) as suggesting that if a man rapes he gets raped in prison. Similarly, the posters from the Los Angeles (LACAAW) campaign while well intentioned could be open to misunderstanding. In addition to depicting particularly vulnerable groups, such as young girls, the elderly or the homeless, some of the posters portray women in sexually explicit poses, as shown in figure 10.1.

These posters could potentially reinforce the view that women are responsible for rape because of the way they put their sexuality on display. The slogan 'This is not an invitation to rape' could be misread as implying that there is such a thing as an invitation to rape under different circumstances. Mass media communication does not offer the opportunity to correct such misperceptions, so the potential for messages to backfire cannot be remedied once the campaign has started. Moreover, mass communication researchers are well aware of

Figure 10.1 *Examples from the 'This is not an invitation to rape me' poster campaign by the Los Angeles Commission on Assaults against Women*

(Reprinted with permission from Peace Over Violence, formerly Los Angeles Commission on Assaults Against Women).

the problem of 'assimilation', ie the tendency by recipients to distort campaign messages in line with their pre-existing attitudes (Perloff, 1993). It is possible, therefore, that those with strong rape-supportive beliefs who are most in need of being educated will see their stereotypes reinforced rather than questioned by such images and are least likely to be reached by the campaign's message. While the LACAAW campaign organisers are satisfied that the posters have generated intense and sustained interest from the public, there has been no evaluation so far of the effectiveness of the posters in changing attitudes.[6]

In conclusion, available evidence on mass media campaigns to raise public awareness about health-related issues as well as an analysis of some poster campaigns designed specifically to combat rape suggest that this approach will need to be considerably finessed. Campaigns should be based on established knowledge about attitude change and need to be carefully piloted and systematically evaluated if they are to be effective.

10.4 CHANGING NORMS ABOUT SEXUAL AGGRESSION

A number of initiatives have been launched by men opposed to sexual violence. The perspective underlying these initiatives is exemplified by the *Men Can Stop Rape* (MCSR) Campaign, based in Washington, DC, which 'empowers young men to join women as allies in preventing rape and other forms of men's violence' (Men Can Stop Rape, 2006).[7] Another example is the White Ribbon Campaign initiated in Canada in 1991 (www.whiteribbon.com). Members of the campaign wear a white ribbon as a personal pledge never to commit, condone or remain silent about violence against women.

Such initiatives challenge acceptance of the use of coercion to obtain sex by publicly rejecting any form of violence against women. A study by Fabiano, Perkins, Berkowitz, Linkenbach and Stark (2003) has shown that men misperceive the social norms of other men in relation to sexual violence. They asked students to rate the importance they personally attached to ensuring consent in sexual interactions as well as the importance they thought the typical male students at their university would attach to the issue. The results showed that men misperceived the norm of consent in their group, thinking that their fellow students would rate consent as being less important than they actually did. Importantly, the authors also showed a significant link between personal commitment to consent and perceived norms about consent in the peer group: the less men felt that consent was deemed important in their peer group, the lower the importance they personally gave to the issue.

---

[6] Email communication from the Director of Communications, Media and Community Relations, Peace Over Violence (formerly LACAAW), 22 November 2006.

[7] Further examples include *Men against Violence* (MAV; http://www.menagainstviolence.org/); *Men Against Sexual Violence* (MASV; http://www.menagainstsexualviolence.org/); *Stand Up Guys* (http://standupguys.org/index.html)

In a study by Bohner, Siebler and Schmelcher (2006), some male participants were informed that the acceptance of rape myths among fellow students was high, while other participants were told that it was low. It was found that those who were led to believe that rape myth acceptance was high among fellow students showed higher ratings of rape proclivity, ie the estimated likelihood that they would rape a woman, than those who were led to believe that rape myth acceptance was low.

Based on evidence that perceived norms about the acceptability of sexual aggression against women play an important role in guiding men's personal norms and behaviour, Fabiano *et al* (2003) have proposed a 'social norms approach' to rape prevention. The aim of this approach is to counter the rape-supportive normative environment by engaging men as social justice allies in correcting misperceptions through communicating their rejection of rape and rape myths. It has long been established in other areas of intervention designed to change problem behaviours that normative information about the attitudes and behaviours of peers and other important reference groups is an important predictor of change (see Krahé, Abraham and Scheinberger-Olwig, 2005, for AIDS prevention interventions, or Perkins, 2002, for promoting safe drinking). These studies suggest that changing misperceptions about the acceptability of sexual aggression as well as rape-supportive attitudes should be given greater attention in rape awareness campaigns.

Evidence of the effectiveness of interventions to promote the normative rejection of sexual assault and rape-supportive attitudes through information about peer attitudes is summarised on the website of the National Social Norms Resource Center (2006). It describes programmes showing that perceptions of support for sexual aggression in the peer group declined, whereas perceived importance of consent went up in participants in the intervention groups compared with those in the no-intervention control groups. One example is the 'A Man Campaign' developed at James Madison University.[8] Flyers were distributed campus-wide, advertising three messages:

1. A Man Respects a Woman: 9 out of 10 JMU men stop the first time their date says no to sexual activity.
2. A Man Always Prevents Manipulation: 3 out of 4 men think it's NOT okay to pressure a date to drink alcohol in order to improve their chances of getting their date to have sex; and
3. A Man Talks Before Romance: Most JMU men believe talking about sex doesn't destroy the romance of the moment. Talking about it can make sure you have consent.

An evaluation was conducted with 340 men who were surveyed before the start of the campaign and again one year later. It showed a decrease in the

---

[8] See http://www.higheredcenter.org/socialnorms/violence/jamesmadison.html for a description of the campaign and http://www.jmu.edu/healthctr/ohp/wm_library/Year%20Two%20Implementation%20summary.pdf for a summary of the findings.

number of men who believed that an average fellow student would press on with sexual activity despite being asked to stop, and would believe that talking about sex destroys the romance of the moment. The number of men who thought it was okay to pressure a date to drink alcohol to make them engage in sex and who believed that talking about sex destroyed the romance of the moment also decreased. Unfortunately, no data are available as to changes in the incidence of sexual aggression from pre- to post-campaign. Nonetheless, the findings are encouraging in showing that media campaigns can be successful in challenging men's misperceptions about the normative acceptance of sexual aggression in relevant peer groups.

10.5 SUMMARY AND CONCLUSIONS

It has been widely recognised that progress in reducing the justice gap depends on displacing common misconceptions about rape which affect all levels of society. Rape prevention programmes have become routine at many American colleges, but few have been able to produce lasting effects. The short duration of these programmes is one reason for this, as is the fact that by the time people reach college, their rape-related attitudes may already be firmly embedded. Rape education, therefore, needs to start at an earlier age and be made an integral part of the curriculum, exploiting the possibility provided by the school setting for more extensive and continuous programmes.

Media campaigns have been designed to raise awareness about rape through posters, radio messages and printed advertisements. In our evaluation of posters which were part of a Home Office Consent Campaign (see chapter five), we found no evidence that exposure to the two visual images highlighting the importance of consent affected perceivers' attitudes towards consent. However, other studies suggest that material of this kind may be more successful when combined with other elements of rape awareness interventions, such as school-based information campaigns which provide information and challenge myths about sexual assault.

Finally, this chapter has emphasised the importance of initiatives by men opposed to sexual violence. A critical aspect of these initiatives is to correct the misperception that sexual violence and myths about rape are widely accepted by men, and to substitute these beliefs and myths with social norms emphasising consent.

11

Conclusion

T HERE CAN BE no doubt that for women in the twenty-first century in many parts of the Western world a dangerous situation prevails. As large-scale surveys show, the risk of being sexually assaulted is a tangible threat in women's lives. At the same time, victims of sexual assault can expect little in the way of redress or assistance. A large number of rapes go unreported, and of those that do come to the attention of the police, only a tiny fraction end in conviction. The message from the criminal justice system could not be clearer. Women must put strict limits on their behaviour, must trust no one and take no risks. And, since even this is not at all a guarantee of safety, they must learn to live with rape.

Evidence from a range of sources brought together in this book clearly shows that in contrast to the normative model of legal decision-making as data-driven, judgments about rape cases are influenced by schematic processing, relying on stereotypic beliefs about rape which contain a restrictive and inaccurate understanding of what 'real rape' is. By reducing the range of what is considered a genuine rape complaint, these stereotypes are a contributory factor in the justice gap. Rape stereotypes affect the judgments made by individuals dealing with rape cases, for example as police officers, judges or members of a jury, and thereby shape the understanding of rape as it is represented and dealt with in the criminal justice system.

Despite all the efforts and undoubted improvements over the past thirty years, the rape trial as it is configured in the common law world is frequently not up to the task of delivering justice for rape victims (see also Ellison, 2001). This book has demonstrated that attitudes which are undermining of the complainant are a major reason for this. It is often said that the problem in rape cases is simply the lack of evidence, or that it is just one person's word against another. Our analysis shows that it is not necessarily the *lack* of evidence but the *attitude* towards the evidence which matters. Not only are rape myths widely shared in many countries across the world, they are also endorsed by members of professional groups involved in different stages of the prosecution of rape complaints. The more a person holds to misconceptions about rape, including the belief that women precipitate rape by the way they behave or dress, the more they see an alleged victim as responsible for her fate and the less likely they are to think that the defendant should be held liable for rape.

In a sample of over 2000 members of the public whose views were ascertained in our third study (see chapter five), it was found that many participants adhered to stereotypical beliefs about rape. Our studies with prospective lawyers showed that they, too, were by no means immune from such beliefs. Moreover, our three quantitative studies illustrate that people rely on their general attitudes about rape when making judgments about specific cases. Those who scored high on measures of rape myth acceptance allowed these myths to influence their assessments even of clear-cut cases of rape rather than making evidence-based judgments. In a rape trial, defence cross-examination is likely to act as a prime to members of the jury who hold such beliefs by invoking ideas about risky behaviour and unsuitable dress. In this way their biases are brought to the fore and activated.

Adherence to rape stereotypes that bias judgments is not the only problem. As one judge in our interview study noted, jurors, particularly first timers, are disinclined to draw the obvious inferences from the evidence they have heard. They want, metaphorically, to see blood on the knife and frequently feel unable to say they are sure unless they have seen it. Jury decision-making is affected by many of the well-documented shortcomings in processing information which occur when evidence appears incomplete or is contested. Jurors seem frequently unable to disregard inadmissible evidence once it has come to light and may selectively attend to the evidence which fits with their own storyline. It might be thought that a possible answer to the jury problem would be judge-only trials in rape cases. This might seem to be the best way of increasing the chances of evidence-based decisions, given judges' experience, expertise and greater familiarity with patterns of sexual aggression. On the other hand, our qualitative study demonstrates how progressive law reform in the area of rape has been undermined by judicial interpretation and how some judges are not entirely free from the same stereotypical beliefs and assumptions held by members of the public. Another option is trial by a mixed panel of lay and professional judges. More research is needed comparing judges' and jurors' decisions in order to arrive at firm conclusions.

There is no simple solution to the justice gap. Some obvious suggestions may well be blind alleys. However, this book has suggested different ways in which the problem could be approached, both within the criminal justice system and by challenging the acceptance of rape myths in society.

In terms of rape trials, the rules relating to sexual history, corroboration and third party disclosure need to be strengthened, and their enforcement should be secured by affording greater prosecution rights of appeal. Expert evidence should be allowed both as a way of educating the public and for the difference that it may make in some cases. Evidence of the complainant's good character should be admissible. Measures of potential value in many criminal trials which assist the jury to focus on the evidence should be adopted. At the same time, jury screening needs to be explored and debated with a view to deciding whether those who are likely to be implacably biased against the complainant or the defendant should serve. The education of judges and barristers has to be improved so that it challenges stereotypical assumptions and judgmental attitudes about rape. It should be bolstered with evaluation, mentoring and monitoring.

Attention should also be given to public education, starting in school at an appropriate age. It should focus on the need for consent in sexual interactions and on changing the misperception that sexual coercion is acceptable. These efforts should be supported by public information campaigns which need to be grounded in a theoretical understanding of persuasive communication and launched only after careful piloting.

As the human rights of victims come increasingly to be articulated, it is likely that the present system for dealing with rape will come under more persistent scrutiny. The view taken here is that changing attitudes, preventing stereotypical notions from infiltrating decision-making and replacing these notions with a realistic understanding of the problem of rape is one of the keys to achieving justice for its victims.

References

Abrams, D, Viki, GT, Masser, B and Bohner, G (2003) 'Perceptions of stranger and acquaintance rape: The role of benevolent and hostile sexism' 84 *Journal of Personality and Social Psychology* 111–25.

Adler, Z (1987) *Rape on trial* (London and New York, Routledge and Kegan Paul).

Alicke, MD (2000) 'Culpable control and the psychology of blame' 126 *Psychological Bulletin* 556–74.

Allison, JA (1996) 'The law and information processing: Implications for verdicts in rape cases' 26 *Journal of Applied Social Psychology* 1961–77.

American Psychiatric Association (ed) (1994) *Diagnostic and statistical manual of mental disorders*, 4th edn (Washington, DC). Retrieved 20 October 2006, from: http://www.psychnet-uk.com/dsm_iv/posttraumatic_stress_disorder.htm

Amnesty International UK (2005) *Sexual assault research summary report*. Retrieved 22 December 2005, from: http://www.amnesty.org.uk/news/press/16618.shtml

Anderson, CA, Benjamin, AL and Bartholow, BD (1998) 'Does the gun pull the trigger? Automatic priming effects of weapon pictures and weapon names' 9 *Psychological Science* 308–14.

Anderson, KB, Cooper, H and Okamura, L (1997) 'Individual differences and attitudes toward rape: A meta-analytic review' 23 *Personality and Social Psychology Bulletin* 295–315.

Anderson, LA, Stoelb, MP, Duggan, P, Hieger, B, Kling, KH and Payne, JP (1998) 'The effectiveness of two rape prevention programs in changing the rape-supportive attitudes of college students' 39 *Journal of College Student Development* 131–42.

Anderson, LA and Whiston, SC (2005) 'Sexual assault education programs: A meta-analytic examination of their effectiveness' 29 *Psychology of Women Quarterly* 374–88.

Anderson, WP and Cummings, K (1993) 'Women's acceptance of rape myths and their sexual experiences' 34 *Journal of College Student Development* 53–57.

Archbold, JF (2006) *Criminal pleading, evidence and practice* (London, Sweet and Maxwell).

—(2007) *Criminal pleading, evidence and practice* (London, Sweet and Maxwell).

Arkes, HR and Mellers, BA (2002) 'Do juries meet our expectations?' 26 *Law and Human Behavior* 625–39.

Aromäki, AS, Haebich, K and Lindman, RE (2002) 'Age as a modifier of sexually aggressive attitudes in men' 43 *Scandinavian Journal of Psychology* 419–23.

Auld, R (2001). *Review of the criminal courts in England and Wales*. Retrieved 20 December 2005, from: http:// www.criminal-courts-review.org.uk

Bachar, K and Koss, MP (2001) 'From prevalence to prevention: Closing the gap between what we know about rape and what we do' in CM Renzetti and JL Edelson (eds), *Sourcebook of violence against women* (Thousand Oaks, CA, Sage) 117–42.

Bachman, R (1998) 'The factors related to rape reporting behavior and arrest: New evidence from the National Crime Victimization Survey' 25 *Criminal Justice and Behavior* 8–29.

Baldry, AC (1996) 'Rape victims' risk of secondary victimization by police officers' 25 *Issues in Criminological and Legal Psychology* 65–68.

Baron, RM and Kenny, DA (1986) 'The moderator-mediator variable distinction in social psychological research' 51 *Journal of Personality and Social Psychology* 1173–82.

Ben-David, S and Schneider, O (2005) 'Rape perceptions, gender role attitudes, and victim-perpetrator acquaintance' 53 *Sex Roles* 385–99.

Berkowitz, AD (2002) 'Fostering men's responsibility for preventing sexual assault' in PA Schewe (ed), *Preventing violence in relationships* (Washington, DC, American Psychological Association) 163–96.

Best, CL, Dansky, BS and Kilpatrick, DG (1992) 'Medical students' attitudes about female rape victims' 7 *Journal of Interpersonal Violence* 175–88.

Biggers, JR (2003) 'Rape trauma syndrome: An examination of standards that determine the admissibility of expert witness testimony' 3 *Journal of Forensic Psychology Practice* 61–77.

Binder, R (1981) 'Why women don't report sexual assault' 42 *Journal of Clinical Psychiatry* 437–38.

Birch, D (2000) 'A better deal for vulnerable witnesses' *Criminal Law Review* (April) 223.

Birch, D (2002) 'Rethinking sexual history evidence: proposals for fairer trials' *Criminal Law Review* 531.

Bliesener, T (2006) 'Lay judges in the German criminal court: Social psychological aspects in the German criminal justice system' in MF Kaplan and AM Martin (eds), *Understanding world jury systems through social psychological research* (Hove, Psychology Press) 179–97.

Block, AP (1990) 'Rape trauma syndrome as scientific expert testimony' 19 *Archives of Sexual Behavior* 309–23.

Bodenhausen, GV and Lichtenstein, M (1987) 'Social stereotyping and information-processing strategies: The impact of task complexity' 51 *Journal of Personality and Social Psychology* 1032–43.

Boeschen, LE, Sales, BD and Koss, MP (1998) 'Rape trauma experts in the courtroom' 4 *Psychology, Public Policy and Law* 414–32.

Bohner, G, Jarvis, CI, Eyssel, F and Siebler, F (2005) 'The causal impact of rape myth acceptance on men's rape proclivity: Comparing sexually coercive and noncoercive men' 35 *European Journal of Social Psychology* 819–28.

Bohner, G, Reinhard, MA, Rutz, S, Sturm, S, Kerschbaum, B and Effler, D (1998) 'Rape myths as neutralizing cognitions: Evidence for a causal impact of anti-victim attitudes on men's self-reported likelihood of raping' 28 *European Journal of Social Psychology* 257–68.

Bohner, G, Siebler, F and Schmelcher, J (2006) 'Social norms and the likelihood of raping: Perceived rape myth acceptance of others affects men's rape proclivity' 32 *Personality and Social Psychology Bulletin* 286–97.

Bohner, G and Wänke, M (2002) *Attitudes and attitude change* (Hove, Psychology Press).

Bornstein, BH (1999) 'The ecological validity of jury simulations: Is the jury still out?' 23 *Law and Human Behavior* 75–91.

Bourgeois, MJ, Horowitz, IA and ForsterLee L (1993) 'Effects of technicality and access to trial transcripts on verdicts and information processing in a civil trial' 19 *Personality and Social Psychology Bulletin* 220–27.

Branscombe, NR, Owen, S, Garstka, TA and Coleman, J (1996) 'Rape and accident counterfactuals: Who might have done otherwise and would it have changed the outcome?' 26 *Journal of Applied Social Psychology* 1042–67.

Branscombe, NR and Weir, JA (1992) 'Resistance as stereotype inconsistency: Consequences for judgments of rape victims' 11 *Journal of Social and Clinical Psychology* 80-102.

Brekke, NJ and Borgida, E (1988) 'Expert psychological testimony in rape trials: A social cognitive analysis' 55 *Journal of Personality and Social Psychology* 372–86.

Brekke, NJ, Enko, PJ, Clavet, G and Seelau, E (1991) 'Of juries and court-appointed experts: The impact of nonadversarial versus adversarial expert testimony' 15 Law and Human Behavior 451–75.

Bridges, JS and McGrail, CA (1989) 'Attributions of responsibility for date and stranger rape' 21 *Sex Roles* 273–86.

Bright, DA and Goodman-Delahunty, J (2006) 'Gruesome evidence and emotion: Anger, blame, and jury decision-making' 30 *Law and Human Behavior* 183–202.

Brown, B, Burman, M and Jamieson, L (1992) *Sexual history and sexual character evidence in Scottish sexual offence trials* (Edinburgh, Scottish Office Central Research Unit).

Brown, JM, Hamilton, C and O'Neill, D (2007) 'Characteristics associated with rape attrition and the role played by scepticism or legal rationality by investigators and prosecutors' 13 *Psychology, Crime and Law* 355–70.

Brown, JM and King, J (1998) 'Gender differences in police officers' attitudes towards rape: Results of an exploratory study' 4 *Psychology, Crime and Law* 265–79.

Buddie, AM and Miller, AG (2001) 'Beyond rape myths: A more complex view of perceptions of rape victims' 45 *Sex Roles* 139–60.

Bundeskriminalamt (2006) *Kriminalstatistik. PKS-Zeitreihen 1987–2005* (Wiesbaden, BKA). Retrieved 4 October 2006, from: http://www.bka.de/pks/zeitreihen/index.html

Bundesministerium des Inneren (Hg) (2001) *Erster periodischer Sicherheitsbericht der Bundesregierung* (Berlin, BMI).

Bunting, AB and Reeves, JB (1983) 'Perceived male sex-role orientation and beliefs about rape' 4 *Deviant Behavior* 281–95.

Burgess, AW and Holmstrom, LL (1985) 'Rape trauma syndrome and post traumatic stress response' in AW Burgess (ed), *Rape and sexual assault: A research handbook* vol I (New York, Garland) 46–60.

Burt, MR (1980) 'Cultural myths and support for rape' 38 *Journal of Personality and Social Psychology* 217–30.

Burt, MR and Albin, RS (1981) 'Rape myths, rape definitions, and probability of conviction' 11 *Journal of Applied Social Psychology* 212–30.

Burton, M, Evans, R and Sanders, A (2007) 'Vulnerable and intimidated witnesses and the adversarial process in England and Wales' 11 *The International Journal of Evidence and Proof* 1–24.

Calhoun, LG, Cann, A, Selby, JW and Magee, DL (1981) 'Victim emotional responses. Effects on social reactions to victims of rape' 20 *British Journal of Social Psychology* 17–21.

Campbell, R (2005) 'What really happened? A validation study of rape survivors' help-seeking experiences with the legal and medical systems' 20 *Violence and Victims* 55–68.

Campbell, R (2006) 'Rape survivors' experience with the legal and medical systems: Do rape victim advocates make a difference?' 12 *Violence against Women* 30–45.

Campbell, R, Sefl, T, Barnes, HE, Ahrens, CE, Wasco, SM and Zaragoza-Diesfeld, Y (1999) 'Community services for rape survivors: Enhancing psychological well-being or increasing trauma?' 67 *Journal of Consulting and Clinical Psychology* 847–58.

Campbell, R, Wasco, S M, Ahrens, CE, Sefl, T, and Barnes, HE (2001) 'Preventing the "second rape": Rape survivors experiences with community service providers' 16 *Journal of Interpersonal Violence* 1239–59.

Cann, A, Calhoun, G and Selby, JW (1979) 'Attributing responsibility to the victim of rape: Influence of information regarding past sexual experience' 32 *Human Relations* 57–67.

Carli, LL (1999) 'Cognitive reconstruction, hindsight, and reactions to victims and per-petrators' 25 *Personality and Social Psychology Bulletin* 966–79.

Carli, LL and Leonard, JB (1989) 'The effect of hindsight on victim derogation' 8 *Journal of Social and Clinical Psychology* 331–43.

Carlson, KA and Russo, JE (2001) 'Biased interpretation of evidence by mock jurors' 7 *Journal of Experimental Psychology: Applied* 91-103.

Carmody, DC and Washington, LM (2001) 'Rape myth acceptance among college women' 16 *Journal of Interpersonal Violence* 424–36.

Caron, SL and Carter, DB (1997) 'The relationship among sex role orientation, attitudes toward sexuality, and attitudes toward violence against women' 137 *Journal of Social Psychology* 568–87.

Cashmore, J and Trimboli, L (2006) 'Child sexual assault trials: A survey of juror per-ceptions' 102 (September) *Crime and Justice Bulletin*. NSW Bureau of Crime Statistics and Research. Retrieved 28 June 2007, from: http://www.lawlink.nsw.gov. au/lawlink/bocsar/ll_bocsar.nsf/vwFiles/CJB102.pdf/$file/CJB102.pdf

Check, JVP and Malamuth, NM (1985) 'An empirical assessment of some feminist hypotheses about rape' 8 *International Journal of Women's Studies* 414–23.

Chen, S and Chaiken, S (1999) 'The heuristic-systematic model in its broader context' in S Chaiken and Y Trope (eds), *Dual-process theories in social psychology* (New York, Guilford Press) 73–96.

Chiroro, P, Bohner, G, Viki, GT and Jarvis, CI (2004) 'Rape myth acceptance and rape proclivity' 19 *Journal of Interpersonal Violence* 427–42.

Clancy, A, Hough, M, Aust, A and Kershaw, C (2001) *Crime, policing, and justice: The experience of ethnic minorities*. Home Office Research Study No 223 (London, Home Office). Retrieved 5 October 2006, from: http://www.homeoffice.gov.uk/rds/pdfs/ hors223.pdf

Clark, L, and Lewis, D (1977) *Rape: The price of coercive sexuality* (Toronto, The Women's Press).

Clifford, B (2003) 'Methodology: Law's adopting and adapting to psychology's methods and findings' in D Carson and R Bull (eds), *Handbook of psychology in legal contexts*, 2nd edn (Chichester, Wiley) 605–24.

Coleman, K, Jansson, K, Kaiza, P and Reed, E (2007) *Homicide, firearm offences and inti-mate violence 2005/2006*. (Supplementary Volume 1 to Crime in England and Wales 2005/2006). Retrieved 26 January 26 2007, from: http://www.homeoffice.gov.uk/ rds/pdfs07/hosb0207.pdf

Collett, ME and Kovera, MB (2003) 'The effects of British and American trial procedures on the quality of juror decision-making' 27 *Law and Human Behavior* 403–22.

Costin, F (1985) 'Beliefs about rape and women's social roles' 4 *Archives of Sexual Behavior* 319–25.

Costin, F and Kaptanoglu, C (1993) 'Beliefs about rape and women's social roles: A Turkish replication' 23 *European Journal of Social Psychology* 327–30.

Council of Europe (1999) *European sourcebook of crime and criminal justice statistics* (Strasbourg, Council of Europe). Retrieved 15 January 2007, from: http://www.europeansourcebook.org/

Cowan, G and Quinton, W (1997) 'Cognitive style and attitudinal correlates of the perceived causes of rape scale' 21 *Psychology of Women Quarterly* 227–45.

Criminal Bar Association (2006) *Report on behalf of the CBA on the Consultation Paper on 'Convicting Rapists and Protecting Victims–Justice for Victims of Rape'*. Retrieved 18 June 2007, from: www.criminalbar.com/86/records/153/Annex%20B%20-%20CBA%20Report%20on%20CRPV%20Consultation%20Paper.doc

Criminal Cases Review Commission (2005) *Annual report and accounts 2004/2005*. Retrieved 4 Oct 2006, from: http://www.ccrc.gov.uk/CCRC_Uploads/420165_CCRC_AR_V9lo.pdf

Criminal Statistics for England and Wales (1987). Retrieved 4 October 2006, from: http://www.archive.official-documents.co.uk/document/cm53/5312/cm5312.htm

Criminal Statistics for England and Wales (2000). Retrieved 4 October 2006, from: http://www.archive.official-documents.co.uk/document/cm53/5312/crimestats.pdf

Crown Prosecution Service (2004) *Policy for prosecuting cases of rape* (London, CPS). Retrieved 5 December 2006, from: www.cps.gov.uk/publications/docs/prosecuting_rape.pdf

—— (2005) *Domestic violence good practice guidance*. Retrieved 11 May 2007, from: http://www.cps.gov.uk/publications/docs/dv_protocol_goodpractice.pdf

Dann, B (1993) '"Learning lessons" and "speaking rights": Creating educated and democratic juries' 68 *Indiana Law Journal* 1229–79.

Dann, B, Hans, VP and Kaye, D (2005) *Testing the effects of selected jury trial innovations on juror comprehension of contested DNA evidence: Final technical report* (Rockville, MD, National Criminal Justice Reference Service). Retrieved 20 October 2006, from: www.ncjrs.gov/pdffiles1/nij/grants/211000.pdf

Darbyshire, P, Maughan, A and Stewart, A (2001) *What can the English legal system learn from jury research published up to 2001?* Retrieved 20 October 2006, from: www.kingston.ac.uk/~ku00596/elsres01.pdf

Davies, M and Rogers, P (2006) 'Perceptions of male victims in depicted sexual assaults: A review of the literature' 11 *Aggression and Violent Behavior* 367–77.

Dawson, TB (2004) *The social context education project* (unpublished report, National Judicial Institute Canada).

Deitz, SR, Blackwell, KT, Daley, PC and Bentley, BJ (1982) 'Measurement of empathy toward rape victims and rapists' 43 *Journal of Personality and Social Psychology* 372–84.

Deitz, SR and Byrnes, LE (1981) 'Attribution of responsibility for sexual assault: The influence of observer empathy and defendant occupation and attractiveness' 108 *The Journal of Psychology* 17–29.

Deitz, SR, Littman, M and Bentley, BJ (1984) 'Attribution of responsibility for rape: The influence of observer empathy, victim resistance, and victim attractiveness' 10 *Sex Roles* 261–81.

Department for Constitutional Affairs (2006) *Judicial Appointments 7th Annual Report 2004–2005*. Retrieved 22 October 2006, from: http://www.dca.gov.uk/judicial/ja-arep2005/parttwo.htm

Department for Constitutional Affairs (2007) *Criminal procedure rules. Notes to accompany 4th update, March 2007*. Retrieved 11 May 2007, from: http://www.justice.gov.uk/criminal/procrules_fin/contents/notes_and_tables/notes_crim4.htm

Derzon, JH and Lipsey, MW (2002) 'A meta-analysis of the effectiveness of mass-communication for changing substance-use knowledge, attitudes, and behavior' in WD Crano and M Burgoon (eds), *Mass media and drug prevention* (Mahwah, NJ, L Erlbaum) 231–58.

Diamond, SS (1997) 'Illuminations and shadows from jury simulations' 21 *Law and Human Behavior* 561–71.

Du Mont, J, Miller, KL and Myhr, TL (2003) 'The role of "real rape" and "real victim" stereotypes in the police reporting practices of sexually assaulted women' 9 *Violence against Women* 466–86.

Eagly, AH and Chaiken, S (1993) *The psychology of attitudes* (New York, Harcourt, Brace, Jovanovich).

Ellison, L. (2001) *The Adversarial Process and the Vulnerable Witness* (Oxford, OUP).

—— (2005) 'Closing the credibility gap: The prosecutorial use of expert witness testimony in sexual assault cases' 9 *The International Journal of Evidence and Proof* 239–68.

Ellsworth, PC (1993) 'Some steps between attitudes and verdicts' in R Hastie (ed), *Inside the juror* (Cambridge, Cambridge University Press) 42–64.

Emmers-Sommer, TM and Allen, M (1999) 'Variables related to sexual coercion: A path model' 16 *Journal of Social and Personal Relationships* 659–78.

Etter, J-F and Laszlo, E (2005) 'Evaluation of a poster campaign against passive smoking for World No-Tobacco Day' 57 *Patient Education and Counseling* 190–98.

Eyssel, F, Bohner, G and Siebler, F (2006) 'Perceived rape myth acceptance of others predicts rape proclivity: Social norm or judgmental anchoring?' 65 *Swiss Journal of Psychology* 93–99.

Fabiano, PM, Perkins, HW, Berkowitz, A, Linkenbach, J and Stark, C (2003) 'Engaging men as social justice allies in ending violence against women: Evidence for a social norms approach' 52 *Journal of American College Health* 105–12.

Faigman, DL (2003) 'Expert evidence: The rules and the rationality of the law applies (or should apply) to psychological expertise' in D Carson and R Bull (eds), *Handbook of psychology in legal contexts*, 2nd edn (Chichester, Wiley) 367–400.

Federal Bureau of Investigation (1980–1985) *Crime in the United States: Uniform Crime Reports (Annual Volumes 1980–1985)* (Washington, DC, United States Department of Justice).

—— (1983) *Crime in the United States: Uniform Crime Reports 1982* (Washington, DC, United States Department of Justice).

—— (1993) *Crime in the United States: Uniform Crime Reports 1992* (Washington, DC, United States Department of Justice).

—— (2005) *Crime in the United States: Uniform Crime Reports 2004* (Washington, DC, United States Department of Justice). Retrieved 4 October 2006, from: www.fbi.gov/ucr/cius_04/offenses_reported/violent_crime/forcible_rape.html

—— (2006) *Crime in the United States: Uniform Crime Reports 2005* (Washington, DC, United States Department of Justice). Retrieved 20 October 2006, from: http://www.fbi.gov/ucr/ucr.htm#cius

Federal Ministry for Family Affairs, Senior Citizens, Women, and Youth (2005) *Health, well-being, and personal safety of women in Germany*. Retrieved 4 October 2006, from:

http://www.bmfsfj.de/RedaktionBMFSFJ/Abteilung4/Pdf-Anlagen/kurzfassung-gewalt-frauen-englisch,property=pdf,bereich=,rwb=true.pdf

Feigenson, N (2000) *Legal blame* (Washington, DC, American Psychological Association).

Feigenson, N and Park, J (2006) 'Emotions and attributions of legal responsibility and blame: A research review' 30 *Law and Human Behavior* 141–63.

Feild, HS (1978) 'Attitudes toward rape: A comparative analysis of police, rapists, crisis counselors, and citizens' 36 *Journal of Personality and Social Psychology* 156–79.

Finch, J (1987) 'Research note: The vignette technique in survey research' 21 *Sociology* 105–14.

Finch, E and Munro, VE (2005a) 'Juror stereotypes and blame attribution in rape cases involving intoxicants' 45 *British Journal of Criminology* 25–38.

—— (2005b) 'Of bodies, boundaries and borders: Intoxicated consent under the law of Scotland and England' 1 *Juridical Review* 53–73.

—— (2006) 'Breaking boundaries: Sexual consent in the jury room' 26 *Legal Studies* 303–20.

Finney, A (2006) *Domestic violence, sexual assault and stalking: Findings from the 2004/05 British Crime Survey* Home Office Online Report 12/06. Retrieved 20 October 2006, from: http://www.homeoffice.gov.uk/rds/pdfs06/rdsolr1206.pdf

Fischer, G (1986) 'College student attitudes towards forcible date rape: I. Cognitive predictors' 15 *Archives of Sexual Behavior* 457–66.

Fischer, K (1989) 'Defining the boundaries of admissible expert psychological testimony on rape trauma syndrome' *University of Illinois Law Review* 691–734.

Fischhoff, B (2002) 'Heuristics and biases in application' in T Gilovich, D Griffin and D Kahneman (eds), *Heuristics and biases: The psychology of intuitive judgment* (New York, Cambridge University Press) 730–48.

Fisher, BS, Cullen, FT and Daigle, LE (2005) 'The discovery of acquaintance rape: The salience of methodological innovation and rigor' 20 *Journal of Interpersonal Violence* 493–500.

Fisher, BS, Cullen, FT and Turner, MG (2000) 'The sexual victimization of college women. Research Report NJC 182369'. US Department of Justice. Retrieved 4 October 2006, from: http://www.ncjrs.gov/pdffiles1/nij/182369.pdf

Fisher, BS, Daigle, LE, Cullen, FT and Turner, MG (2003) 'Reporting sexual victimization to the police and others: Results from a national-level study of college women' 30 *Criminal Justice and Behavior* 6–38.

Flores, SA and Hartlaub, MG (1998) 'Reducing rape-myth acceptance in male college students: A meta-analysis of intervention studies 39 *Journal of College Student Development* 438–48.

Flowe, HD, Ebbesen, EB and Putcha-Bhagavatula, A (2007) 'Rape shield laws and sexual behavior evidence: Effects of consent levels and women's sexual history on rape allegations' 31 *Law and Human Behavior* 159–75.

Foa, EB and Rothbaum, BO (1998) *Treating the trauma of rape* (New York, Guilford Press).

Foley, LA, Evancic, C, Karnik, K, King, J and Parks, A (1995) 'Date rape: Effects of race of assailant and victim and gender of subjects on perceptions' 21 *Journal of Black Psychology* 6–18.

Follingstad, DR, Shillinglaw, RD, DeHart, DD and Kleinfelter, KJ (1997) 'The impact of elements of self-defense and objective vs. subjective instructions on jurors' verdicts for battered women defendants' 12 *Journal of Interpersonal Violence* 729–47.

Försterling, F (2001) *Attribution* (Hove, Psychology Press).

Foshee, VA, Bauman, KE, Ennett, ST, Linder, GF, Benefield, T and Schindran, C (2004) 'Assessing the long-term effects of the safe dates program and a booster in preventing and reducing adolescent dating violence victimization and perpetration' 94 *American Journal of Public Health* 619–24.

Foster, J, Newburn, T and Souhami, A (2005) *Assessing the impact of the Stephen Lawrence Inquiry.* Home Office Research Study 294 (Home Office Research, Development and Statistics Directorate). Retrieved 27 June 2007, from: www.home-office.gov.uk/rds/pdfs05/hors294.pdf

Frazier, PA and Borgida, E (1988) 'Juror common understanding and the admissibility of rape trauma syndrome evidence in court' 12 *Law and Human Behavior* 101–23.

—— (1992) 'Rape trauma syndrome: A review of case law and psychological research' 16 *Law and Human Behavior* 293–311.

Frazier, PA, Candell, S, Arikian, N and Tofteland, A (1994) 'Rape survivors and the legal system' in M Costanzo and S Oskamp (eds), *Violence and the law* (Thousand Oaks, CA, Sage) 135–58.

Frazier, PA and Haney, B (1996) 'Sexual assault cases in the legal system: Police, prosecutor, and victim perspectives' 20 *Law and Human Behavior* 607–28.

Frese, B, Moya, M and Megías, JL (2004) 'Social perception of rape: How rape myth acceptance modulates the influence of situational factors' 19 *Journal of Interpersonal Violence* 143–61.

Gabora, NJ, Spanos, NP and Joab, A (1993) 'The effects of complainant age and expert psychological testimony in a simulated sexual abuse trial' 18 *Law and Human Behavior* 103–19.

Garrison, AH (2000) 'Rape trauma syndrome: A review of a behavioral science theory and its admissibility in criminal trials' 23 *American Journal of Trial Advocacy* 591–657.

George, WH and Martinez, LJ (2002) 'Victim blaming in rape: Effects of victim and perpetrator race, type of rape, and participant racism' 26 *Psychology of Women Quarterly* 110–19.

Gerber, GL, Cronin, JA and Steigman, H (2004) 'Attributions of blame in sexual assault to perpetrators and victims of both genders' 34 *Journal of Applied Social Psychology* 2149–65.

Gerger, H, Kley, H, Bohner, G and Siebler, F (2007) 'The Acceptance of Modern Myths About Sexual Aggression (AMMSA) Scale: Development and validation in German and English' 33 *Aggressive Behavior* 422–40.

Giacopassi, DJ and Dull, RT (1986) 'Gender and racial differences in the acceptance of rape myths within a college population' 15 *Sex Roles* 63–75.

Gidycz, CA and Layman, MJ (1996) 'The crime of acquaintance rape' in TL Jackson (ed), *Acquaintance rape* (Sarasota, FL, Professional Resources Press) 17–54.

Gidycz, CA, Layman, MJ, Rich, CL, Crothers, M, Gylys, J, Matorin, A and Jacobs, CD (2001) 'An evaluation of an acquaintance rape prevention program' 16 *Journal of Interpersonal Violence* 1120–38.

Glass, GV, McGraw, B and Smith, ML (1981) *Meta-analysis in social research* (Beverly Hills, CA, Sage).

Gölge, ZB, Yavuz, MF, Müderrisoglu, S and Yavuz, MS (2003) 'Turkish university students' attitudes toward rape' 49 *Sex Roles* 653–61.

Greater Manchester Police (2006) 'Palm trees and urinal stickers to raise rape awareness'. Retrieved 20 November 2006, from: http://www.gmp.police.uk/mainsite/pages/B27D52297894F17D802571CE002A80F1.htm

Greene, E and Wrightsman, L (2003) 'Decision making by juries and judges: International perspectives' in D Carson and R Bull (eds), *Handbook of psychology in legal contexts*, 2nd edn (Chichester, Wiley) 401–22.

Hall, ER, Howard, JA and Boezio, SL (1986) 'Tolerance of rape: A sexist or antisocial attitude?' 10 *Psychology of Women Quarterly* 101–18.

Hall, RE (1985) *Ask any woman. A London inquiry into rape and sexual assault* (Bristol, Falling Wall Press).

Hall RE and Longstaff, L (1999) 'Sexism still part of new rape law' *The* Times (13 July).

Hannon, R, Hall, DS, Kuntz, T, Van Laar, S and Williams, J (1995) 'Dating characteristics leading to unwanted vs. wanted sexual behavior' 33 *Sex Roles* 767–83.

Hans, VP and Jehle, A (2003) 'Avoid bald men and people with green socks? Other ways to improve the voir dire process in jury selection' 78 *Chicago-Kent Law Review* 1178–201.

Harrington, NG, Lane, DR, Donohew, L, Zimmerman, RS, Norling, GR, An, JH, Chea, WH, McLure, L, Buckingham, T, Garofalo, E and Bevins, CC (2003) 'Persuasive strategies for effective anti-drug messages' 70 *Communication Monographs* 16–38.

Harris, J and Grace, S (1999) *A question of evidence? Investigating and prosecuting rape in the 1990s*. Home Office Research Study 196. Retrieved 20 October 2006, from: http://www.homeoffice.gov.uk/rds/pdfs/hors196.pdf

Hart, AJ (1995) 'Naturally occurring expectation effects' 68 *Journal of Personality and Social* Psychology 109–15.

Heaton-Armstrong, A, Shepherd, E, Gudjonsson, G and Wolchover, D (2006) *Witness testimony: Psychological, investigative and evidential perspectives* (Oxford, Oxford University Press).

Heenan, M and McKelvie, H (1997) *Evaluation of the Crime (Rape) Act 1991. Executive Summary*. Attorney General's Legislation and Policy Branch (Melbourne, Department of Justice).

Heider, F (1958) *The psychology of interpersonal relations* (New York, Wiley).

Henning T and Bronitt S (1998) 'Rape victims on trial: Regulating the use and abuse of sexual history evidence' in P Easteal (ed), *Balancing the scales: Rape, law reform and Australian culture* (Sydney, The Federation Press) 76–93.

Heppner, MJ, Humphreys, CF, Hillenbrand-Gunn, TL and DeBord, KA (1995) 'The differential effects of rape prevention programming on attitudes, behavior, and knowledge' 42 *Journal of Counseling Psychology* 508–18.

Her Majesty's Crown Prosecution Service Inspectorate (2002) *A report on the joint inspection into the investigation and prosecution of cases involving allegations of rape* (London, HMCPSI).

Her Majesty's Crown Prosecution Service Inspectorate (2007) *Without consent. A report on the joint review of the investigation and prosecution of rape offences*. Retrieved 9 February 2007, from: http://inspectorates.homeoffice.gov.uk/hmic/inspect_reports1/thematic-inspections/wc-thematic/them07-wc.pdf?view=Binary

Hilton, NZ, Harris, GT, Rice, ME, Krans TS and Lavigne, SE (1998) 'Antiviolence education in high schools: Implementation and evaluation' 13 *Journal of Interpersonal Violence* 726–42.

Hinck, SS and Thomas, RW (1999) 'Rape myth acceptance in college students. How far have we come?' 40 *Sex Roles* 815–32.

Home Office (1975) *Report of the advisory group on the law of rape* Cmnd 6352 (London, Home Office).

—— (1980–2000, Annual Volumes) *Criminal Statistics England and Wales Supplementary Tables* (vols 1 and 2) (London, Government Statistical Service).

—— (1986) *Violence against women* Circular 69 (London, Home Office).

—— (1998a) *Speaking up for justice: Report of the interdepartmental working group on the treatment of vulnerable or intimidated witnesses in the criminal justice system* (London, Home Office). Retrieved 22 October 2006, from: http://www.homeoffice. gov.uk/documents/sufj.pdf?view=Binary

—— (1998b) *Criminal Statistics England and Wales 1997*. Cm4162 (London, The Stationery Office).

—— (1999a). *Explanatory notes: Youth Justice and Criminal Evidence Act 1999* (London, The Stationery Office). Retrieved 28 June 2007, from: http://www.opsi.gov. uk/ACTS/en1999/1999en23.htm

—— (1999b) *Recorded crime statistics England and Wales, April 1998–March 1999* (London, Home Office). Retrieved 21 September 2007, from: http://www.homeoffice. gov.uk/rds/pdfs/hosb1899.pdf

—— (2000a) *Setting the boundaries: Reforming the law on sex offences* (vols 1 and 2). Home Office Communication Directorate (London, Home Office). Retrieved 22 October 2006, from:http://www.homeoffice.gov.uk/documents/vol1main.pdf? view=Binary

—— (2000b) *Criminal Statistics England and Wales 1999*. Cm 5001 (London, The Stationery Office).

—— (2002) *Protecting the public*. CM 5668. Retrieved 22 October 2006, from: http://www.homeoffice.gov.uk/documents/protecting-the-public.pdf?view= Binary

—— (2004) *Criminal Statistics, England and Wales 2003*. Retrieved 17 May 2007, from: www.homeoffice.gov.uk/rds/crimstats03.html

—— (2005a) *Criminal Statistics, England and Wales 2004. Home Office Statistical Bulletin* 19 May 2005 (London, Home Office). Retrieved 4 October 2006, from: http://www.homeoffice.gov.uk/rds/crimstats04.html

—— (2005b) *Crime in England and Wales 2004/5. Home Office Statistical Bulletin 11/05* (London, Home Office). Retrieved 15 May 2007, from: http://www.homeoffice.gov. uk/rds/pdfs05/hosb1105.pdf

—— (2006a) *Crime Statistics in England and Wales. Long-term trends*. Retrieved 4 October 2006, from: http://www.crimestatistics.org.uk/output/Page27.asp

—— (2006b) *Crime in England and Wales 2005/06. Home Office Statistical Bulletin 12/06* (London, Home Office). Retrieved 4 October 2006, from: http://www.homeoffice. gov.uk/rds/pdfs06/hosb1206.pdf

—— (2006c) *Consent campaign*. Retrieved 19 November 2006, from: http://www. homeoffice.gov.uk/documents/consent-campaign/

—— (2006d) *Consent Awareness Campaign–summary of evaluation*. Unpublished report.

—— (2006e) *Sexual Offences Act 2003- A stocktake* (London, Home Office). Retrieved 20 October 2006, from: http://www.crimereduction.gov.uk/sexual/sexual24.pdf

—— (2006f) *Criminal Statistics England and Wales 2005. Home Office Statistical Bulletin* 19/06 (London, Home Office). Retrieved 15 May 2007, from: www. homeoffice.gov.uk/rds/crimstats05.html#vol5

Horowitz, IA, Kerr, NL, Park, ES and Gockel, C (2006) 'Chaos in the courtroom reconsidered: Emotional bias and juror nullification' 30 *Law and Human Behavior* 163–81.

Howells, K, Shaw, F, Greasley, M, Robertson, J, Gloster, D and Metcalfe, N (1984) 'Perceptions of rape in a British sample: Effects of relationship, victim status, sex, and attitudes to women' 23 *British Journal of Social Psychology* 35–40.

Hoyano, L and Keenan, C (2007) *Child abuse* (Oxford, Oxford University Press).

Iyengar, S and McGrady, J (2005) 'Mass media and political persuasion' in TC Brock and MC Green (eds), *Persuasion. Psychological insights and perspectives* (Thousand Oaks, CA, Sage) 225–48.

Janoff-Bulman, R, Timko, C and Carli, LL (1985) 'Cognitive biases in blaming the victim' 21 *Journal of Experimental Social Psychology* 161–77.

Jenkins, MJ and Dambrot, FH (1987) 'The attribution of date rape: Observer's attitudes, sexual experiences, and the dating situation' 17 *Journal of Applied Social Psychology* 875–95.

Jimenez, JA and Abreu, JM (2003) 'Race and sex effects on attitudinal perceptions of acquaintance rape' 50 *Journal of Counseling Psychology* 252–56.

Johansson-Love, J and Geer, JH (2003) 'Investigation of attitude change in a rape prevention program' 18 *Journal of Interpersonal Violence* 84–99.

Johnson, JD (1994) 'The effect of rape type and information admissibility on perceptions of rape victims' 30 *Sex Roles* 781–92.

Johnson, BD, Kuck, DL and Schander, PR (1997) 'Rape myth acceptance and sociodemographic characteristics: A multidimensional analysis' 36 *Sex Roles* 693–707.

Johnson, H and Sacco, V (1995) 'Researching violence against women: Statistics Canada's national survey' 37 *Canadian Journal of Criminology* 281–304.

Johnson, JD, Jackson, LA, Gatto, L and Nowak, A (1995) 'Differential male and female responses to inadmissible sexual history information regarding a rape victim' 16 *Basic and Applied Social Psychology* 503–13.

Jordan, J (2001) 'Worlds apart? Women, rape and the police reporting process' 41 *British Journal of Criminology* 679–706.

—— (2004) 'Beyond belief? Police, rape, and women's credibility' 4 *Criminal Justice* 29–59.

Judicial Studies Board (2005) *Equal treatment bench book*. Retrieved 8 September 2007, from: http://www.jsboard.co.uk/etac/index.htm

—— (2006) *Equal Treatment Advisory Committee Information*. Retrieved 4 November 2006, from: http://www.jsboard.co.uk/committees/equal.htm

Judicial Studies Board (2007) *Annual Report 2006/07*. Retrieved 19 December 2007, from: http://www.jsboard.co.uk/downloads/JSB_Annual_Report_2007_web%20new%2045.pdf

Kahn, AS, Mathie, VA and Torgler, C (1994) 'Rape scripts and rape acknowledgement' 18 *Psychology of Women Quarterly* 53–66.

Kalven, H and Zeisel, H (1966) *The American jury* (Boston, Little, Brown).

Kapardis, A (1997) *Psychology and the law* (Cambridge, Cambridge University Press).

Kaplan, MF, Martin, AM and Hertel, J (2006) 'Issues and prospects in European juries: An overview' in M Kaplan and AM Martin (eds), *Understanding world jury systems through social psychological research* (Hove, Psychology Press) 111–24.

Kaplan, MF and Simon, R (1972) 'Latitude and severity of sentencing options: Race of the victim and decisions of simulated juries' 7 *Law and Society Review* 87–98.

Kaufmann, G, Drevland, GCB, Wessel, E, Overskeid, G and Magnussen, S (2003) 'The importance of being earnest: Displayed emotions and witness credibility' 17 *Applied Cognitive Psychology* 21–34.

Kelly, L (2002) *A research review on the reporting, investigation, and prosecution of rape cases* (London, Her Majesty's Crown Prosecution Service Inspectorate).

Kelly, L, Lovett, J and Regan, L (2005) *A Gap or a chasm? Attrition in reported rape cases*. Home Office Research Study 293. Retrieved 26 December 2006, from: http://www.homeoffice.gov.uk/rds/pdfs05/hors293.pdf

Kelly, L, Temkin, J and Griffiths, S (2006) *Section 41: An evaluation of new legislation limiting sexual history evidence in rape trials* (London, Home Office). Retrieved 20 October 2006, from: http://www.homeoffice.gov.uk/rds/pdfs06/rdsolr2006.pdf

Kennedy, MA and Gorzalka, B (2002) 'Asian and non-Asian attitudes toward rape, sexual harassment, and sexuality' 46 *Sex Roles* 227–38.

Kerr, NL (1978) 'Severity of prescribed penalty and mock jurors' verdicts' 36 *Journal of Personality and Social Psychology* 1431–42.

Kerr, NL and Bray, RM (2005) 'Simulation, realism, and the study of the jury' in N Brewer, and KD Williams (eds), *Psychology and law* (New York, Guilford Press) 322–64.

Kerstetter, WA and Van Winkle, B (1990) 'Who decides? A study of the complainant's decision to prosecute in rape cases' 17 *Criminal Justice and Behavior* 268–83.

Kibble, N (2001) The relevance and admissibility of prior sexual history with the defendant in sexual offence cases *Cambrian Law Review* 27–63.

—— (2004) *Judicial perspectives on Section 41 of the Youth Justice and Criminal Evidence Act 1999*. A Research Report sponsored by the Criminal Bar Association of England and Wales, jointly funded by the University of Wales, Aberystwyth (London, Criminal Bar Association).

Kopper, BA (1996) 'Gender, gender identity, rape myth acceptance, and time of initial resistance on the perception of acquaintance rape blame and avoidability' 34 *Sex Roles* 81–93.

Koss, MP (2006) 'Restoring rape survivors. Justice, advocacy, and a call for action' 1087 *Annals of the New York Academy of Sciences* 206–34.

Koss, MP, Bachar, KJ, Hopkins, CQ and Carlson, C (2004) 'Expanding a community's justice response to sex crimes through advocacy, prosecutorial, and public health collaboration: Introducing the RESTORE program' 19 *Journal of Interpersonal Violence* 1435–63.

Koss, MP and Cleveland, H (1997) 'Stepping on toes: Social roots of date rape lead to intractability and politicisation' in M Schwartz (ed), *Researching sexual violence against women. Methodological and personal perspectives* (Newbury Park, CA, Sage) 4–21.

Koss, MP, Gidycz, CA and Wisniewski, N (1987) 'The scope of rape: Incidence and prevalence of sexual aggression and victimization in a national sample of higher education students' 55 *Journal of Consulting and Clinical Psychology* 162–70.

Koss, MP, Goodman, LA, Browne, A, Fitzgerald, LF, Keita, GP and Russo, NF (1994) *No safe haven: Male violence against women at home, at work, and in the community* (Washington, DC, American Psychological Association).

Koss, MP and Oros, CJ (1982) 'Sexual experiences survey: A research instrument investigating sexual aggression and victimization' 50 *Journal of Consulting and Clinical Psychology* 455–57.

Kovera, MB, Dickinson, JJ and Cutler, BL (2003) 'Voir dire and jury selection' in AM Goldstein (ed), *Handbook of psychology: Forensic psychology* (vol 11) (Hoboken, NJ, Wiley) 161–75.

Kovera, MB, Levy, RJ, Borgida, E and Penrod, SD (1994) 'Expert testimony in child sexual abuse cases' 18 *Law and Human Behavior* 653–74.

Krahé, B (1985) 'Verantwortungszuschreibungen in der sozialen Eindrucksbildung über Vergewaltigungsopfer und -täter' 16 *Gruppendynamik* 169–78.

—— (1988) 'Victim and observer characteristics as determinants of responsibility attributions to victims of rape' 18 *Journal of Applied Social Psychology* 50–58.

—— (1991a) 'Police officers' definitions of rape: A prototype study' 1 *Journal of Community and Applied Social Psychology* 223–44.

—— (1991b) 'Social psychological issues in the study of rape' in W Stroebe and M Hewstone (eds), *European Review of Social Psychology* (vol 2) (Chichester, Wiley) 279–309.

—— (1992) 'Coping with rape: A social psychological perspective' in L Montada, SH Filipp and MJ Lerner (eds), *Life crises and experiences of loss in adulthood* (Hillsdale, NJ, L Erlbaum) 477–96.

—— (2001) *The social psychology of aggression* (Hove, Psychology Press).

Krahé, B, Abraham, C and Scheinberger-Olwig, R (2005) 'Can safer-sex promotion leaflets change cognitive antecedents of condom use? An experimental evaluation' 10 *British Journal of Health Psychology* 203–20.

Krahé, B, Bieneck, S and Scheinberger-Olwig, R (2007) 'The role of sexual scripts in sexual aggression and victimization' 36 *Archives of Sexual Behavior* 687–701.

Krahé, B, Scheinberger-Olwig, R and Schütze, S (2001) 'Risk factors of sexual aggression and victimization among homosexual men' 31 *Journal of Applied Social Psychology* 1385–1408.

Krahé, B, Schütze, S, Fritsche, I and Waizenhöfer, E (2000) 'The prevalence of sexual aggression and victimization among homosexual men' 37 *The Journal of Sex Research* 142–50.

Krahé, B, Temkin, J and Bieneck, S (2007) 'Schema-driven information processing in judgements about rape' 21 *Applied Cognitive Psychology* 601–19.

Krahé, B, Temkin, J, Bieneck, S and Berger, A 2007 in press 'Prospective lawyers' rape stereotypes and schematic decision-making about rape cases' *Psychology, Crime and Law*.

Krug, EG, Dahlberg, LL, Mercy, JA, Zwi, AB and Lozano, R (2002) *World report on violence and health* (Geneva, World Health Organisation). Retrieved 20 October 2006, from: http://whqlibdoc.who.int/hq/2002/9241545615.pdf

Krulewitz, JE (1982) 'Reactions to rape victims: Effects of rape circumstances, victim's emotional response, and sex of helper' 29 *Journal of Counseling Psychology* 645–54.

Kruse, K and Sczesny, S (1993) 'Vergwaltigung und sexuelle Nötigung–bagatellisierende Auslegung und Scheitern einer Reform' 26 *Kritische Justiz* 336–51.

Kunda, Z (1999) *Social cognition* (Cambridge, MA, MIT Press).

L'Heureux-Dubé, C (2001) 'Beyond the myths: Equality, impartiality and justice' 10 *Journal of Social Distress and Homelessness* 87-104.

LaFree, GD (1981) 'Official reactions to social problems: Police decisions in sexual assault cases' 28 *Social Problems* 581–94.

—— (1989) *Rape and criminal justice: The social construction of sexual assault* (Belmont, CA, Wadsworth).

Lea, SJ, Lanvers, U and Shaw, S (2003) 'Attrition in rape cases: Developing a profile and identifying relevant factors' 43 *British Journal of Criminology* 583–99.

Lee, J, Pomeroy, EC, Yoo, SK and Rheinboldt, KT (2005) 'Attitudes toward rape: A comparison between Asian and Caucasian college students' 11 *Violence Against Women* 177–98.

Lees, S (2002) *Carnal knowledge: Rape on trial*, rev edn (London, The Women's Press).

Lerner, JS, Goldberg, JH and Tetlock, PE (1998) 'Sober second thought: The effects of accountability, anger, and authoritarianism on attributions of responsibility' 24 *Personality and Social Psychology Bulletin* 563–74.

Lewis, P (2006) 'A comparative examination of corroboration and caution warnings in prosecutions of sexual offences' (October) *Criminal Law Review* 889–901.

Lieberman, JD and Sales, BD (2007) 'In-court questioning of prospective jurors' in JD Lieberman and BD Sales (eds), *Scientific jury selection* (Washington, DC, American Psychological Association) 103–23.

London, K and Nunez, N (2000) 'The effect of jury deliberations on jurors' propensity to disregard inadmissible evidence' 85 *Journal of Applied Psychology* 932–39.

Lonsway, KA (2005) *The use of expert witnesses in cases involving sexual assault.* Violence against Women Online Resources. Retrieved 12 October 2006, from: http://www.mincava.umn.edu/documents/commissioned/svandexpertwitnesses/svandexpertwitnesses.pdf

Lonsway, KA and Fitzgerald, LF (1994) 'Rape myths' 18 *Psychology of Women Quarterly* 133–64.

Lonsway, KA, Klaw, EL, Berg, DR, Waldo, CR, Kothari, C, Mazurek, CJ and Hegeman, KE (1998) 'Beyond "no means no". Outcomes of an intensive program to train peer facilitators for campus acquaintance rape education' 13 *Journal of Interpersonal Violence* 73–92.

Lonsway, KA and Kothari, C (2000) 'First year campus acquaintance rape education' 24 *Psychology of Women Quarterly* 220–32.

Los Angeles Commission on Assaults against Women (2006) *'This is not an invitation to rape me' campaign*. Retrieved 19 November 2006, from: http://www.lacaaw.org/notinvitation.html

Luginbuhl, J and Mullin, C (1981) 'Rape and responsibility: How and how much is the victim blamed?' 7 *Sex Roles* 547–59.

Malleson, K (1997) 'Judicial training and performance appraisal: The problem of judicial independence' 60 *Modern Law Review* 655–67.

Marable, BE (1999) 'Influence of expert testimony and victim resistance on mock jurors' decisions and judgments concerning acquaintance rape' 59(9-B) *Dissertation Abstracts International: Section B: The Sciences and Engineering* 5096.

Marciniak, LM (1998) 'Adolescent attitudes toward victim precipitation of rape' 13 *Violence and Victims* 287–300.

Mason, GE, Riger, S and Foley, LA (2004) 'The impact of past sexual experiences on attributions of responsibility for rape' 19 *Journal of Interpersonal Violence* 1157–71.

Matthews, R, Hancock, L and Briggs, D (2004) *Jurors' perceptions, understanding, confidence and satisfaction in the jury system: a study in six courts*. Home Office Online Report 05/04. Retrieved 20 October 2006, from: www.homeoffice.gov.uk/rds/pdfs2/rdsolr0504.pdf

Mattinson, J (1998) *Criminal appeals England and Wales, 1995 and 1996*. Home Office Statistical Bulletin, 3/1998. Retrieved 4 October 2006, from: http://www.homeoffice. gov.uk/rds/pdfs/hosb398.pdf

McAuliff, BD, Nemeth, RJ, Bornstein, BH and Penrod, SD (2003) 'Juror decision-making in the twenty-first century: Confronting science and technology in court' in D Carlson and R Bull (eds), *Handbook of psychology in legal contexts*, 2nd edn (Chichester, Wiley) 303–27.

McDonald, TW and Kline, LM (2004) 'Perceptions of appropriate punishment for committing date rape: Male college students recommend lenient punishments' 38 *College Student Journal* 44–56.

McEwan, J (2003) *The verdict of the court: Passing judgment in law and psychology* (Oxford, Hart Publishing).

McGowan, MG and Helms, JJ (2003) 'The utility of the expert witness in a rape case: Reconsidering rape trauma syndrome' 3 *Journal of Forensic Psychology Practice* 51–60.

Men Can Stop Rape (2006) *Who we are*. Retrieved 21 November 2006, from: http://www.mencanstoprape.org/info-url_nocat2701/info-url_nocat_show.htm?doc_id=48503

Miller, M and Mauet, T (1999) 'The psychology of jury persuasion' 22 *American Journal of Trial Advocacy* 549–70.

Mitchell, TL, Haw, RM and Pfeifer, JE and Meissner, CA (2005) 'Racial bias in mock juror decision-making: A meta-analytic review of defendant treatment' 29 *Law and Human Behavior* 621–37.

Mohler-Kuo, M, Dowdall, GW, Koss, MP and Wechsler, H (2004) 'Correlates of rape while intoxicated in a national sample of college women' 65 *Journal of Studies on Alcohol* 37–45.

Morgan, SE, Palmgreen, P, Stephenson, MT, Hoyle, RH and Lorch, EP (2003) 'Associations between message features and subjective evaluations of the sensation value of antidrug public service announcements' 53 *Journal of Communication* 512–26.

Mori, L, Bernat, JA, Glenn, PA and Selle, LL (1995) 'Attitudes toward rape: Gender and ethnic differences across Asian and Caucasian college students' 32 *Sex Roles* 457–67.

Morry, MM and Winkler, E (2001) 'Student acceptance and expectation of sexual assault' 33 *Canadian Journal of Behavioral Science* 188–92.

Munday, R (2005) *Evidence*, 3rd edn (Oxford, Oxford University Press).

National Center on Domestic and Sexual Violence (2007) *Voir dire and prosecution tips for sexual assault cases*. Retrieved 14 January 2007, from: http://www.ncdsv.org/ images/SexualAssault—VOIRDIREANDPROSECUTIONTIPS.pdf

National Commission of Women (2006) *End violence against women*. Retrieved 19 November 2006, from: http://www.endviolenceagainstwomen.org.uk/home.asp

National Curriculum Online (2006) *PSHE. Knowledge, skills and understanding*. Retrieved 21 November 2006, from: http://www.nc.uk.net/webdav/harmonise?Page/ @id=6001andSession/@id=D_m8LlAwFv8w9XMgigJA0LandPOS[@stateId_eq_main]/@id=4361andPOS[@stateId_eq_note]/@id=4361

National District Attorneys Association (2007) *Voir dire questions*. Retrieved 2 February 2007, from: http://www.ndaa-apri.org/apri/programs/vawa/voir_dire_questions.html #samplequestion

National Judicial Institute (2006) *Criminal law seminar: Sexual assault.* Retrieved 4 November 2006, from: http://www.nji.ca/nji/postings/criminal_law_06/index. htm

National Social Norms Resource Center (2006) *Social norms and sexual assault prevention.* Retrieved 23 November 2006, from: http://www.socialnorms.org/CaseStudies/ sexassaultprev.php

Nayak, MB, Byrne, CA, Martin, MK and Abraham, AG (2003) 'Attitudes toward violence against women: A cross-nation study' 49 *Sex Roles* 333–42.

New Zealand Law Commission (2001) *Report 69: Juries in criminal trials* (Wellington, New Zealand). Retrieved 22 October 2006, from: www.lawcom.govt.nz/UploadFiles/ Publications/Publication_76_161_R69.pdf

Nicol, D (2006) 'Law and politics after the Human Rights Act' (Winter) *Public Law* 722–51.

Neitzel, MT, McCarthy, DM and Kern, MJ (1999) 'Juries. The current state of the empirical literature' in R Roesch, SD Hart and JRP Ogloff (eds), *Psychology and law: The state of the discipline* (New York, Kluwer Academic Publishing) 23–52.

Norris, J and Cubbins, LA (1992) 'Dating, drinking, and rape' 16 *Psychology of Women Quarterly* 179–91.

O'Donohue, W, Yeater, EA and Fanetti, M (2003) 'Rape prevention with college males' 18 *Journal of Interpersonal Violence* 513–31.

Office for Criminal Justice Reform (2006) *Convicting rapists and protecting victims. Justice for victims of rape. A consultation paper.* Retrieved 7 November 2006, from: http://www.homeoffice.gov.uk/documents/cons-290306-justice-rape-victims? view=Binary

Office for Criminal Justice Reform (2007). *Convicting rapists and protecting victims: Response to consultation November 2007.* Retrieved December 18, 2007, from: http://www.cjsonline.gov.uk/the_cjs/whats_new/news-3624.html

Ogloff, JRP and Rose, VG (2005) 'The comprehension of judicial instructions' in N Brewer and KD Williams (eds), *Psychology and law* (New York, Guilford Press) 407–44.

Olson-Fulero, L and Fulero, SM (1997) 'Common sense rape judgments: An empathy-complexity theory of rape juror story making' 3 *Psychology, Public Policy, and Law* 402–27.

Ong, AS and Ward, CA (1999) 'The effects of sex and power schemas, attitudes toward women, and victim resistance on rape attributions' 29 *Journal of Applied Social Psychology* 362–76.

Ormerod, D (2005) *Smith and Hogan Criminal Law* (New York, Oxford University Press).

Orth, U and Maercker, A (2004) 'Do trials of perpetrators retraumatize crime victims?' 19 *Journal of Interpersonal Violence* 212–27.

Osland, JA, Fitch, M and Willis, EE (1996) 'Likelihood to rape in college males' 35 *Sex Roles* 171–83.

Pacifici, C, Stoolmiller, M and Nelson, C (2001) 'Evaluating a prevention program for teenagers on sexual coercion: A differential effectiveness approach' 69 *Journal of Consulting and Clinical Psychology* 552–59.

Payne, DL, Lonsway, KA and Fitzgerald, LF (1999) 'Rape myth acceptance: Exploration of its structure and its measurement using the Illinois Rape Myth Acceptance Scale' 33 *Journal of Research in Personality* 27–68.

Pechmann, C and Reibling, ET (2006) 'Antismoking advertisements for youths: An independent evaluation of health, counter-industry, and industry approaches' 96 *American Journal of Public Health* 906-13.

Pennington, N and Hastie, R (1992) 'Explaining the evidence: Tests of the story model for juror decision making' 62 *Journal of Personality and Social Psychology* 189–206.

Penrod, SD and Heuer, L (1997) 'Tweaking commonsense: Assessing guides to jury decision making' 3 *Psychology, Public Policy, and Law* 259–84.

Perkins, HW (2002) 'Social norms and the prevention of alcohol misuse in collegiate contexts' 14 *Journal of the Study of Alcohol* 164–72.

Perloff, RM (1993) *The dynamics of persuasion* (Hillsdale, NJ, L Erlbaum).

Peterson, ZD and Muehlenhard, CL (2004) 'Was it rape? The function of women's rape myth acceptance and definitions of sex in labeling their own experiences' 51 *Sex Roles* 129–44.

Petty, RE and Cacioppo, JT (1986) *Communication and persuasion: Central and peripheral routes to attitude change* (New York, Springer).

Petty, RE, Cacioppo, JT, Strathman, AJ and Priester, JR (2005) 'To think or not to think: Exploring two routes to persuasion' in TC Brock and MC Brown (eds), *Persuasion: Psychological insights and perspectives*, 2nd edn (Thousand Oaks, CA, Sage) 81-116.

Pfeifer, JE and Ogloff, JRP (1991) 'Ambiguity and guilt determinations: A modern racism perspective' 21 *Journal of Applied Social Psychology* 1713–25.

Pollard, P (1992) 'Judgements about victims and attackers in depicted rapes: A review' 31 *British Journal of Social Psychology* 307–26.

Portman Group (2006) *Promoting responsible drinking*. Retrieved 20 November 2006, from: http://www.portmangroup.org.uk/campaigns/271.asp

Raitt, FE and Zeedyck, MS (2000) *The implicit relation of psychology and law: Women and syndrome evidence* (London, Routledge).

Rape Crisis Network Europe (2006) *The myths and facts about rape*. Retrieved 20 November 2006, from: http://www.rcne.com/

Rape, Abuse and Incest National Network (2006) *Statistics*. Retrieved 20 November 2006, from: http://www.rainn.org/statistics/index.html

Redmayne, M (2003) 'Myths, relationships and coincidences: The new problems of sexual history' 7 *The International Journal of Evidence and Proof* 75-101.

Regan, L and Kelly, L (2001) *Teenage tolerance. The hidden lives of Irish young people* (Dublin, Women's Aid). Summary retrieved 28 December 2006, from: http://www.womensaid.org/

—— (2003) *Rape: Still a forgotten issue* (London, Child and Women Abuse Studies Unit). Retrieved 20 November 2006, from: http://www.rcne.com/downloads/RepsPubs/Attritn.pdf

Rempala, DM and Bernieri, F (2005) 'The consideration of rape: The effect of target information disparity on judgments of guilt' 35 *Journal of Applied Social Psychology* 536–50.

Rose, MP, Nadler, J and Clark, J (2006) 'Appropriately upset? Emotion norms and perceptions of crime victims' 30 *Law and Human Behavior* 203–19.

Rose, VM and Randall, SC (1982) 'The impact of investigator perceptions of victim legitimacy on the processing of rape/sexual assault cases' 5 *Symbolic Interaction* 23–36.

Rozee, P (1999) 'Stranger rape' in MA Paludi (ed), *Sexual victimization* (Westport, CT, Greenwood Press) 97–115.

Rumney, P (2006) 'False allegations of rape' 65 *Cambridge Law Journal* 128–58.

Rumney, P and Morgan-Taylor, M (2002) 'The use of syndrome evidence in rape trials' 13 *Criminal Law Forum* 471–506.

Russell, DEH (1984) *Sexual exploitation. Rape, child sexual abuse and workplace harassment* (Beverly Hills, CA, Sage).

—— (1990) *Rape in marriage*, 2nd edn (Bloomington, IN, Indiana University Press).

Ryan, KM (1988) 'Rape and seduction scripts' 12 *Psychology of Women Quarterly* 237–45.

Ryckman, RM, Graham, SS, Thornton, B, Gold, JA and Lindner, MA (1998) 'Physical size stereotyping as a mediator of attributions of responsibility in an alleged date-rape situation' 28 *Journal of Applied Social Psychology* 1876–88.

Sapp, M, Farrell, WC and Johnson, JR (1999) 'Attitudes toward rape among African American male and female college students' 77 *Journal of Counseling and Development* 204–08.

Schafran, LH and Wikler, NJ (2001) *Gender fairness in the courts: Action in the new millennium*. State Justice Institute, National Judicial Education Program. Retrieved 22 October 2006, from: http://womenlaw.stanford.edu/genderfairness-strategiesproject.pdf

Schewe, PA (2002) 'Guidelines for developing rape prevention and risk reduction interventions' in PA Schewe (ed), *Preventing violence in relationships* (Washington, DC, American Psychological Association) 107–36.

Schewe, PA and O'Donohue, W (1996) 'Rape prevention with high-risk males: Short-term outcome of two interventions' 25 *Archives of Sexual Behavior* 455–71.

Schnopp-Wyatt, EN (2000) 'Expert testimony in rape trials: Prejudicial or probative?' 60 *Dissertation Abstracts International: Section B: The Sciences and Engineering* 6425.

Schuller, RA and Hastings, PA (2002) 'Complainant sexual history evidence: Its impact on mock jurors' decisions' 26 *Psychology of Women Quarterly* 252–61.

Schuller, RA and Klippenstine, MA (2004) 'The impact of complainant sexual history evidence on jurors' decisions: Considerations from a psychological perspective' 10 *Psychology, Public Policy, and Law* 321–42.

Schuller, RA and Stewart, A (2000) 'Police responses to sexual assault complaints: The role of perpetrator/complainant intoxication' 24 *Law and Human Behavior* 535–51.

Schuller, RA and Wall, AM (1998) 'The effects of defendant and complainant intoxication on mock jurors' judgments of sexual assault' 22 *Psychology of Women Quarterly* 555–73.

Schult, DG and Schneider, LJ (1991) The role of sexual provocativeness, rape history, and observer gender in perceptions of blame and sexual assault 6 *Journal of Interpersonal Violence* 94–101.

Schwartz, MD (ed) (1997) *Researching sexual violence against women* (Thousand Oaks, CA, Sage).

Schwarz, N (2002) 'Feelings as information: Judgments and information processing strategies' in T Gilovich, D Griffin and D Kahneman (eds), *Heuristics and biases: The psychology of intuitive judgment* (Cambridge, Cambridge University Press) 534–47.

Schwendinger, JR and Schwendinger, H (1974) 'Rape myths: In legal, theoretical and everyday practice' 1 *Crime and Social Justice* 18–26.

Semmler, C and Brewer, N (2002) 'Effects of mood and emotion on juror processing and judgments' 20 *Behavioral Sciences and the Law* 423–36.

Shaw, JL and Skolnick, P (2004) 'Effects of prejudicial pretrial publicity from physical and witness evidence on mock jurors' decision making' 34 *Journal of Applied Social Psychology* 2132–48.

Sheldon, JP and Parent, SL (2002) 'Clergy's attitudes and attributions of blame toward female rape victims' 8 *Violence against Women* 233–56.

Shientag, BL (1975) 'The virtue of impartiality' in GR Winters (ed), *Handbook for judges* (Des Moines, IA, The American Judicature Society) 57–62.

Sidani, S (2006) 'Random assignment: A systematic review' in RR Bootzin and PE McKnight (eds), *Strengthening research methodology: Psychological measurement and evaluation* (Washington, DC, American Psychological Association) 125–41.

Simonson, K and Subich, LM (1999) 'Rape perceptions as a function of gender-role traditionality and victim-perpetrator association' 40 *Sex Roles* 617–34.

Sinclair, HC and Bourne, LE (1998) 'Cycle of blame or just world: Effects of legal verdicts on gender patterns in rape-myth acceptance and victim empathy' 22 *Psychology of Women Quarterly* 575–88.

Sleed, M, Durrheim, K, Kriel, A, Solomon, V and Baxter, V (2002) 'The effectiveness of the vignette methodology: A comparison of written and video vignettes in eliciting responses about rape' 32 *South African Journal of Psychology* 21–28.

Smith, LJF (1989) *Concerns about rape.* Home Office Research Study No 106 (London, Home Office). Retrieved 20 October 2006, from: http://www.homeoffice.gov.uk/rds/pdfs05/hors106.pdf

Smith, VL (1991) 'Prototypes in the courtroom: Lay representations of legal concepts' 61 *Journal of Personality and Social Psychology* 857–72.

Smith, AC and Greene, E (2005) 'Conduct and its consequences: Attempts at debiasing jury judgments' 29 *Law and Human Behavior* 505–26.

Smith, RE, Keating, JP, Hester, RK and Mitchell, HE (1976) 'Role and justice considerations in the attribution of responsibility to a rape victim' 10 *Journal of Research in Personality* 346–57.

Smith, SM, Martin, LL and Kerwin, JL (2001) 'Inhibition and disinhibition of male aggression against females: A personality moderator approach' 31 *Journal of Applied Social Psychology* 170–90.

Snell, WE and Godwin, L (1993) 'Social reactions to depictions of casual and steady acquaintance rape: The impact of AIDS exposure and stereotypic beliefs about women' 29 *Sex Roles* 599–616.

Sobel, ME (1982) 'Asymptotic intervals for indirect effects in structural equations models' in S Leinhart (ed), *Sociological methodology 1982* (San Francisco, Jossey-Bass) 290–312.

Sommers, SR and Ellsworth, PC (2001) 'White juror bias: An investigation of prejudice against Black defendants in the American courtroom' 7 *Psychology, Public Policy, and Law* 201–29.

Spanos, NP, Dubreuil, SC and Gwynn, MI (1991–92) 'The effects of expert testimony concerning rape on the verdicts and beliefs of mock jurors' 11 *Imagination, Cognition and Personality* 37–51.

Statistics Canada (1993) *Violence against women. Survey highlights and questionnaire package.* Retrieved 22 October 2006, from: http://www.statcan.ca/cgi-bin/imdb/

p2SV.pl?Function=getSurveyandSDDS=3896andlang=enanddb=IMDBanddbg=fandadm=8anddis=2

Steblay, NM, Hosch, HM, Culhane SE and McWethy, A (2006) 'The impact on juror verdicts of judicial instruction to disregard inadmissible evidence: A meta-analysis' 30 *Law and Human Behavior* 469–92.

Stephan, C (1974) 'Sex prejudice in jury simulation' 88 *Journal of Psychology: Interdisciplinary and Applied* 305–12.

Stephenson, GW (1992) *The psychology of criminal justice* (Oxford, Blackwell).

Stewart, A (2001) 'Judicial attitudes to gender justice in India: The contribution of judicial training' 1 *Law, Social Justice and Global Development Journal* 1–20. http://elj.warwick.ac.uk/global/issue/2001-1/stewart.html

Stewart, MW, Dobbin, SA and Gatowski, SI (1996) '"Real rapes" and "real victims": The shared reliance on common cultural definitions of rape' 4 *Feminist Legal Studies* 159–77.

Stormo, KJ, Lang, AR and Stritzke, WGK (1997) 'Attributions about acquaintance rape: The role of alcohol and individual differences' 27 *Journal of Applied Social Psychology* 279–305.

Struckman-Johnson, C and Struckman-Johnson, D (1992) 'Acceptance of male rape myths among college men and women' 27 *Sex Roles* 85–100.

Tapper, C (2007) *Cross and Tapper on evidence*, 11th edn (Oxford, Oxford University Press).

Temkin, J (1993) 'Sexual history evidence: The ravishment of Section 2' (January) *Criminal Law Review* 3–20.

—— (1997) 'Plus ça change: Reporting rape in the 1990s' 37 *British Journal of Criminology* 507–28.

—— (1998) 'Medical evidence in rape cases: A continuing problem for criminal justice' 61 *Modern Law Review* 821–48.

—— (1999) 'Reporting rape in London: A qualitative study' 38 *The Howard Journal* 17–41.

—— (2000) 'Prosecuting and defending rape: Perspectives from the Bar' 27 *Journal of Law and Society* 219–48.

—— (2002a) *Rape and the legal process*, 2nd edn (Oxford, Oxford University Press).

—— (2002b) 'Digging the dirt: Disclosure of records in sexual assault cases' 61 *Cambridge Law Journal* 126–45.

—— (2003) 'Sexual history evidence: Beware the backlash' 49 *Criminal Law Review* 217–43.

Terrance, CA, Matheson, K and Spanos, NP (2000) 'Effects of judicial instructions and case characteristics in a mock jury trial of battered women who kill' 24 *Law and Human Behavior* 207–29.

Tetlock, PE (1992) 'The impact of accountability on judgment and choice: Toward a social contingency model' 22 *Advances of Experimental Social Psychology* 331–76.

Tetreault, PA (1989) 'Rape myth acceptance: A case for providing educational expert testimony in rape jury trials' 7 *Behavioral Sciences and the Law* 243–57.

Tetreault, PA and Barnett, MA (1987) 'Reactions to stranger and acquaintance rape' 11 *Psychology of Women Quarterly* 353–58.

Thaman, SC (2000) 'Europe's new jury systems: The cases of Spain and Russia' in N Vidmar (ed), *World Jury Systems* (New York, Oxford University Press) 319–51.

Toner, B (1982) *The facts of rape* (London, Arrow Books).

Truman, DM, Tokar, DM and Fischer, AR (1996) 'Dimensions of masculinity: Relations to date rape supportive attitudes and sexual aggression in dating situations' 74 *Journal of Counseling and Development* 555–62.

Ugwuegbu, DC (1979) 'Racial and evidential factors in juror attribution of legal responsibility' 15 Journal of Experimental Social Psychology 133–46.

United States Department of Justice (2005) *Criminal victimization in the United States, 2003.* Retrieved 4 October 2006, from: http://www.ojp.usdoj.gov/bjs/pub/pdf/cvus03.pdf

—— (2006) *Criminal offender statistics.* Retrieved 5 October 2006, from: http://www.ojp.usdoj.gov/bjs/crimoff.htm#lifetime

—— (2007a). *Bureau of Justice Statistics Crime & Justice Online Data.* Retrieved November 30, 2007, from http://bjsdata.ojp.usdoj.gov/dataonline/Search/Crime/State/statebystaterun.cfm?stateid=52

—— (2007b) *125 Sample Voir Dire Questions-Fair Housing-Racial Discrimination.* Retrieved 14 January 2007, from: http://www.usdoj.gov/usao/eousa/foia_reading_room/usam/title9/crm00532.htm

Van Knippenberg, A, Dijksterhuis, A and Vermeulen, D (1999) 'Judgement and memory of a criminal act: The effects of stereotypes and cognitive load' 29 *European Journal of Social Psychology* 191–201.

Vidmar, N (ed) (2000) *World Jury Systems* (New York, Oxford University Press)

Vidmar, N (2005) 'Expert evidence, the adversary system, and the jury' 95 *American Journal of Public Health* 137–43.

Viki, GT, Abrams, D and Masser, B (2004) 'Evaluating stranger and acquaintance rape: The role of benevolent sexism in perpetrator blame and recommended sentence length' 28 *Law and Human Behaviour* 295–303.

Vogler, RK (2005) *A world view of criminal justice* (Aldershot, Ashgate).

Vrij, A and Firmin, HR (2001) 'Beautiful thus innocent? The impact of defendants' and victims' physical attractiveness and participants' rape beliefs on impression formation in alleged rape cases' 8 *Review of Victimology* 245–55.

Wakelin, A and Long, KM (2003) 'Effects of victim gender and sexuality on attributions of blame to rape victims' 49 *Sex Roles* 477–87.

Walby, S and Allen, J (2004) *Domestic violence, sexual assault, and stalking. Findings from the British Crime Survey.* Home Office Research Study 276 (London, The Home Office). Retrieved 4 October 2006, from: http://www.homeoffice.gov.uk/rds/pdfs04/hors276.pdf

Ward, C (1988) 'The Attitudes toward Rape Victims Scale: Construction, validation, and cross-cultural applicability' 12 *Psychology of Women Quarterly* 127–46.

—— (1995) *Attitudes toward rape* (London, Sage).

Weiner, B (1985) 'Spontaneous causal thinking' 97 *Psychological Bulletin* 74–84.

Weir, JA and Wrightsman, LS (1990) 'The determinants of mock jurors' verdicts in a rape case' 20 *Journal of Applied Social Psychology* 901–19.

Wenger, AA and Bornstein, BH (2006) 'The effects of victim's substance use and relationship closeness on mock jurors' judgments in an acquaintance rape case' 54 *Sex Roles* 547–55.

Wessel, E, Drevland, GCB, Eilertsen, DE and Magnussen, S (2006) 'Credibility of the emotional witness: A study of ratings by judges' 30 *Law and Human Behavior* 221–30.

Whatley, MA (1996) 'Victim characteristics influencing attributions of responsibility to rape victims: A meta-analysis' 1 *Aggression and Violent Behavior* 81–95.

Whatley, MA (2005) 'The effect of participant sex, victim dress, and traditional attitudes on causal judgments for marital rape victims' 20 *Journal of Family Violence* 191–200.

White, BH and Kurpius, SE (1999) 'Attitudes toward rape victims' 14 *Journal of Interpersonal Violence* 989–95.

Williams, JE and Holmes, KA (1981) *The second assault: Rape and public attitudes* (Westport, CT, Greenwood Press).

Willis, CE (1992) 'The effect of sex role stereotype, victim and defendant race, and prior relationship on rape culpability attributions 26 *Sex Roles* 213–26.

Wilson, B (1990) 'Will women judges really make a difference?' 28 *Osgoode Hall Law Journal* 507–22.

Winkel, FW and Koppelaar, L (1991) 'Rape victims' style of self-presentation and secondary victimization by the environment' 6 *Journal of Interpersonal Violence* 29–40.

Women's National Commission (1985) *Violence against women. Report of an ad hoc working group* (London, Women's National Commission).

Woods, DG (1981) *Sexual assault law reforms in New South Wales* (Sydney, Department of the Attorney General and of Justice).

Workman, JE and Freeburg, EW (1999) 'An examination of date rape, victim dress, and perceiver variables within the context of attribution theory' 41 *Sex Roles* 261–77.

Workman, JE and Orr, RL (1996) 'Clothing, sex of subject, and rape myth acceptance as factors affecting attributions about an incident of acquaintance rape' 14 *Clothing and Textiles Research Journal* 276–84.

Yarmey, AD (1985) 'Older and younger adults' attributions of responsibility toward rape victims and rapists' 17 *Canadian Journal of Behavioural Science* 327–28.

Yeater, EA and O'Donohue, W (1999) 'Sexual assault prevention programs' 19 *Clinical Psychology Review* 739–71.

Yescavage, K (1999) 'Teaching women a lesson: Sexually aggressive and nonaggressive men's perceptions of acquaintance and date rape' 5 *Violence against Women* 796–812.

YouGov (2006) *Sex lives.* Survey Results November 2006. Retrieved 22 November 2006, from: http://www.yougov.com/archives/pdf/SexLivesThisMorning.pdf

Young, W, Cameron, N and Tinsley, Y (1999) *Juries in criminal trials. Part 2: A summary of the research findings.* New Zealand Law Commission Preliminary Paper 37. Retrieved 20 October 2006, from: www.lawcom.govt.nz/UploadFiles/Publications/Publication_76_159_PP37Vol2.pdf

Zander, M and Henderson, P (1993) *The Royal Commission on Criminal Justice: The Crown Court Study.* Research Study No 19 (London, HMSO).

Zeedyck, MS and Raitt, FE (1998) 'Psychological evidence in the courtroom: Critical reflections on the general acceptance standard' 8 *Journal of Applied and Community Psychology* 23–39.

Appendix 1

Evidential and Procedural Issues in the Law Relating to Sexual Offences in England and Wales

THIS APPENDIX IS designed to provide some further details and discussion of the law relating to corroboration, sexual history and third party disclosure as a background to chapters one, seven and eight.

CORROBORATION

Generally, in all criminal cases in England and Wales, the evidence of a single witness, if believed, is sufficient to prove the case against the accused. By way of exception, judges in rape and sexual assault trials were formerly compelled to issue a warning to juries about the danger of convicting without corroboration.[1] There was thus a requirement that a corroboration *warning* be given but there was no requirement that there be actual corroboration, and indeed the judge could tell the jury that it was perfectly entitled to convict the defendant in the absence of corroboration if the defendant's guilt was clear beyond reasonable doubt.

After the abolition of the requirement for a corroboration warning (see section 32(1) of the Criminal Justice Act 1994), Lord Taylor held in *R v Makanjuola*[2] that while *in some cases* it *might* still be appropriate for the judge to warn the jury to exercise caution before acting on the unsupported evidence of a witness, that would not be so simply because the witness was a complainant of a sexual offence. There would need to be an evidential basis for suggesting that the evidence of the witness might be unreliable which went beyond mere suggestions in cross-examination by counsel.[3]

In cases where some sort of warning is regarded as necessary, the Court of Appeal has stated in several cases[4] that the complainant's evidence could not be

---

[1] A corroboration warning was also required in a limited number of other cases as well, such as where accomplices or mental patients were involved.

[2] [1995] 2 Cr App R 469.

[3] At p 473.

[4] *R v Islam* [1999] 1 Cr App R 22; *R v Churchill* [1999] Crim LR 664; *R v Croad* [2001] EWCA Crim 644, [2001] All ER (D) 241 (Mar).

said to be supported by evidence that she complained of rape to a third party immediately or very soon after the rape took place since such complaints do not constitute independent evidence. More recently, as a result of section 120 of the Criminal Justice Act 2003, previous complaints concerning the same incident of rape which comply with certain conditions[5] will be admissible as evidence that what the complainant complained about actually happened. But, despite this, the view has been expressed that the complaint is unlikely to be regarded as supporting evidence (see Archbold, 2007, para 8-106). If this is correct, it will be highly confusing for juries which is unhelpful in the prosecution of rape cases.

SEXUAL HISTORY

Legislation to control the use in rape trials of evidence of the complainant's previous sexual behaviour has been on the statute book since 1976. Section 2 of the Sexual Offences (Amendment) Act 1976 forbade any evidence to be adduced and any question to be asked in cross-examination by or on behalf of any defendant about any of the complainant's sexual experiences other than with the accused himself, but permitted the defence to apply, in the absence of the jury, for leave to do so. The judge was left to decide whether it would be unfair to the accused to exclude such evidence or questions and, if it was thought to be unfair, the judge had to accede to the defence's request to admit it.[6]

Section 2 was soon given a broad interpretation favourable to the defence. In the leading case of *Viola*, the Court of Appeal held that 'if the questions (about the complainant's sexual history) are relevant to an issue in the trial in the light of the way the case is being run, for instance relevant to the issue of consent as opposed merely to credit, they are likely to be admitted'.[7] Thus, all was left to depend on what view the trial judge took as to the relevance of the sexual history to an issue in the trial. But in a series of cases, the Court of Appeal also made it clear that it was prepared to oversee such decisions and to impose its own broad view of what was relevant (Temkin, 1993). Relevance, however, is to some extent in the mind of the beholder and, as Justice L'Heureux-Dubé explained in the Supreme Court of Canada's decision in *Seaboyer*, all too often in this area of law it has been swayed by stereotypical assumptions, myth and prejudice.[8]

Empirical studies into the operation of section 2 revealed that unnecessary questions about sexual history were continuing to be asked in cross-examination and that for barristers defending in rape cases, questioning about sexual history in order to discredit the complainant was frequently part of the repertoire (Adler, 1987; Lees, 2002; Temkin, 2000). A similar situation prevailed

---

[5] See s 120 (5), (6) and (7).
[6] *Viola* [1982] 3 All ER 73, 77. See also *Lawrence* (1977) Crim LR 492; *Mills* (1978) Cr App R 327.
[7] [1982] 3 All ER 73 at 77.
[8] *R v Seaboyer* (1991) 83 D.L.R (4th) 193 at 228. For a different view about the relevance of sexual history, see eg Redmayne (2003).

in Scotland (Brown, Burman and Jamieson, 1992). In other jurisdictions, legislation similar to section 2, in that it gives full scope to the judge to determine when sexual history evidence should be admitted, was also passed without much success (Heenan and McKelvie, 1997; Woods, 1981). Henning and Bronitt (1998: 85) have pointed out that 'the principal structural flaw of such legislative schemes is their failure to define the key concepts for determining admissibility leaving the judges free rein to apply their "common sense" assumptions'.

Youth Justice and Criminal Evidence Act 1999

Dissatisfaction with the section 2 regime (Home Office, 1998a: para 9.64) led to its repeal with the passing of sections 41–43 of the Youth Justice and Criminal Evidence Act 1999 (hereafter 'the 1999 Act') which provide as follows:

41 Restriction on evidence or questions about complainant's sexual history

(1) If at a trial a person is charged with a sexual offence, then, except with the leave of the court—

   (a) no evidence may be adduced, and
   (b) no question may be asked in cross-examination, by or on behalf of any accused at the trial, about any sexual behaviour of the complainant.

(2) The court may give leave in relation to any evidence or question only on an application made by or on behalf of an accused, and may not give such leave unless it is satisfied—

   (a) that subsection (3) or (5) applies, and
   (b) that a refusal of leave might have the result of rendering unsafe a conclusion of the jury or (as the case may be) the court on any relevant issue in the case.

(3) This subsection applies if the evidence or question relates to a relevant issue in the case and either—

   (a) that issue is not an issue of consent; or
   (b) it is an issue of consent and the sexual behaviour of the complainant to which the evidence or question relates is alleged to have taken place at or about the same time as the event which is the subject matter of the charge against the accused; or
   (c) it is an issue of consent and the sexual behaviour of the complainant to which the evidence or question relates is alleged to have been, in any respect, so similar—

      (i) to any sexual behaviour of the complainant which (according to evidence adduced or to be adduced by or on behalf of the accused) took place as part of the event which is the subject matter of the charge against the accused, or

(ii) to any other sexual behaviour of the complainant which (according to such evidence) took place at or about the same time as that event, that the similarity cannot reasonably be explained as a coincidence.

(4) For the purposes of subsection (3) no evidence or question shall be regarded as relating to a relevant issue in the case if it appears to the court to be reasonable to assume that the purpose (or main purpose) for which it would be adduced or asked is to establish or elicit material for impugning the credibility of the complainant as a witness.

(5) This subsection applies if the evidence or question—

(a) relates to any evidence adduced by the prosecution about any sexual behaviour of the complainant; and

(b) in the opinion of the court, would go no further than is necessary to enable the evidence adduced by the prosecution to be rebutted or explained by or on behalf of the accused.

(6) For the purposes of subsections (3) and (5) the evidence or question must relate to a specific instance (or specific instances) of alleged sexual behaviour on the part of the complainant (and accordingly nothing in those subsections is capable of applying in relation to the evidence or question to the extent that it does not so relate).

(7) Where this section applies in relation to a trial by virtue of the fact that one or more of a number of persons charged in the proceedings is or are charged with a sexual offence—

(a) it shall cease to apply in relation to the trial if the prosecutor decides not to proceed with the case against that person or those persons in respect of that charge; but

(b) it shall not cease to do so in the event of that person or those persons pleading guilty to, or being convicted of, that charge.

(8) Nothing in this section authorises any evidence to be adduced or any question to be asked which cannot be adduced or asked apart from this section.

42 Interpretation and application of section 41

(1) In section 41—

(a) 'relevant issue in the case' means any issue falling to be proved by the prosecution or defence in the trial of the accused;

(b) 'issue of consent' means any issue whether the complainant in fact consented to the conduct constituting the offence with which the accused is charged (and accordingly does not include any issue as to the belief of the accused that the complainant so consented);

(c) 'sexual behaviour' means any sexual behaviour or other sexual experience, whether or not involving any accused or other person, but excluding (except in section 41(3)(c)(i) and (5)(a)) anything alleged to have taken place as part of the event which is the subject matter of the charge against the accused; and

(d) subject to any order made under subsection (2), 'sexual offence' shall be construed in accordance with section 62.

43 Procedure on applications under section 41

(1) An application for leave shall be heard in private and in the absence of the complainant.

In this section 'leave' means leave under section 41.

(2) Where such an application has been determined, the court must state in open court (but in the absence of the jury, if there is one)—

(a) its reasons for giving, or refusing, leave, and

(b) if it gives leave, the extent to which evidence may be adduced or questions asked in pursuance of the leave, and, if it is a magistrates' court, must cause those matters to be entered in the register of its proceedings.

(3) Rules of court may make provision—

(a) requiring applications for leave to specify, in relation to each item of evidence or question to which they relate, particulars of the grounds on which it is asserted that leave should be given by virtue of subsection (3) or (5) of section 41;

(b) enabling the court to request a party to the proceedings to provide the court with information which it considers would assist it in determining an application for leave;

(c) for the manner in which confidential or sensitive information is to be treated in connection with such an application, and in particular as to its being disclosed to, or withheld from, parties to the proceedings.

The new law offers the advantage of a more structured approach to decision making. Many American states, most notably Michigan,[9] together with New

---

[9] The Michigan legislation is far stricter than s 41 in its exclusionary intent. But American legislation needs to be interpreted against the backdrop of the Constitution and, in particular, the Sixth Amendment, which guarantees the right to confront and cross-examine witnesses. It has been interpreted by the judges to permit evidence in certain limited situations which are not included in the legislation itself (see, eg *People v Wilhelm* [1991] 190 Mich App 574.). However, this is not the same as 'restoring judicial discretion' to Michigan, as is claimed by Kibble (2004: 8–9, 169).

South Wales, Australia, have similar structured regimes, as had Canada although the law there has since been changed (Temkin, 2002a: ch 4). But the new provisions have been the object of criticism and controversy. On the one hand, it is considered that the circumstances in which sexual history is permitted have been drawn too widely to make a significant difference (Hall and Longstaff, 1999). On the other hand, there are those who believe that a structured regime of this sort cannot do justice to the many different situations which in practice may arise and that the provisions are so restrictive that they may prevent the court from hearing relevant evidence and hence fall foul of Article 6 of the European Convention on Human Rights (Birch 2000; 2002). Some commentators believe that a complainant's sexual history may not infrequently be relevant and that it was wrong to deprive judges of the discretion to admit it. The Criminal Bar Association has supported and helped to fund the research of Neil Kibble who takes this view (see Kibble, 2004).

The Rule of Exclusion

Section 41 of the 1999 Act provides a rule forbidding evidence to be adduced or questions to be asked in cross-examination about any sexual behaviour of the complainant but it allows certain exceptions to this rule. The exclusionary rule expressly applies only to defence evidence. Thus, the prosecution is free to adduce such evidence or ask such questions as it pleases. The rule of exclusion covers evidence of previous or subsequent sexual relations between the complainant and the accused as well as between the complainant and third parties. It was considered that there was a need to place some control on the use of both types of evidence.

Exceptions to the Rule of Exclusion

There are four express exceptions to the rule of exclusion under the 1999 Act. These are wide enough to encompass a range of behaviour and are broader than the range of exceptions in similar regimes elsewhere. The first exception (section 41(3)(a)) permits evidence of the complainant's sexual behaviour where it relates to a relevant issue in the case which is not an issue of consent. This covers a number of different situations including where the defendant alleges that the complainant's sexual history is relevant to his *belief* in consent or where, as may be the case with children, consent is irrelevant (section 42(1)(b)). The second exception (section 41(3)(b)) applies where the issue is consent and where there is evidence of the complainant's sexual behaviour at or about the same time as the sexual activity in question. The third exception (section 41(3)(c)) applies where the complainant's previous sexual behaviour was so similar to her behaviour during or at about the same time as the event in question 'that the similarity cannot reasonably be explained as a coincidence'. Finally, since the

1999 Act does not prevent the prosecution from introducing sexual history evidence, the fourth exception (section 41(5)) permits the defence to challenge any such prosecution evidence.

Under section 41(6), for the purposes of all four exceptions, the evidence must relate to specific instances of sexual behaviour. Moreover, under section 41(4), evidence will not be regarded as relating to a relevant issue in the case and coming within the exceptions contained in section 41(3) if it appears to the court to be reasonable to assume that the purpose or main purpose of adducing it is to impugn the credibility of the complainant.

Admission of evidence falling within one of the four exceptions is not intended to be automatic. The judge must, under section 41(2)(b), also be satisfied that a 'refusal of leave might have the result of rendering unsafe a conclusion of the jury or the court on any relevant issue in the case'.

R v A and the Human Rights Act 1998

The rule of exclusion covers evidence of previous or subsequent sexual relations with the accused as well as with third parties. While there is considerable scope to have evidence of sexual behaviour with the accused admitted by way of one or other of the four exceptions, there is no exception which specifically permits evidence of sexual behaviour with the accused, before or after the events in question, where this is relevant to the issue of consent.

In *R v A* the defendant, A, was charged with rape (for comment see Kibble, 2001; Nicol, 2006). He alleged that he had had a sexual relationship with the complainant, C, before the alleged rape and he wanted to have C crossexamined about this alleged relationship in order to support his claim that he had not raped her and that she had consented to sexual intercourse with him. The problem was that section 41 did not permit such a cross-examination simply on this basis. The question was, therefore, whether the exclusion of this cross-examination for this purpose would amount to a contravention of A's right to a fair trial under Article 6 of the European Convention on Human Rights (ECHR). The House of Lords considered that if such a crossexamination had to be excluded as a result of section 41, this represented a likely flaw in the law but it was not prepared to hold that the new sexual history provisions were, as a whole, incompatible with the ECHR. It decided instead to exercise its interpretative duty under section 3(1) of the Human Rights Act 1998 with a view to achieving compatibility between the new law and Article 6. It therefore read into section 41(3)(c) (the similarity exception) an interpretation that the test for determining whether questioning about an alleged relationship should be allowed was whether this was 'so relevant to the issue of consent that to exclude it would endanger the fairness of the trial under Article 6'.[10] Lord

---

[10] [2001] 3 All ER 1, para 46, p18. The use of s 41(3)(c) as the vehicle for admission of such evidence is not entirely appropriate: see Birch (2000: 549).

Steyn, who gave the leading speech, entered the caveat that due regard should always be paid to the importance of seeking to protect the complainant from indignity and humiliating questions, and made clear that a prior relationship with the accused would not always be relevant. However, no firm statement was made as to when it would be irrelevant, leaving the way open for such evidence generally to be admitted for fear of a successful appeal.[11]

The decision in *R v A* has engendered a degree of uncertainty. Strictly speaking, the rule of precedent should ensure that the new formula the House of Lords has tacked on to section 41(3)(c) applies only in the case of a previous sexual relationship with the accused. Indeed, Lord Hope did not consider that it was possible to read into section 41 'a new provision which would entitle the court to give leave whenever it was of the opinion that this was required to ensure a fair trial'.[12] However, there is clearly a danger that, relying on various statements made by the Law Lords in their speeches in the case,[13] it will be applied more broadly than this to admit evidence in any case where the judge takes the view that an Article 6 breach could otherwise result.

In *R v Andre Barrington White*[14] the Court of Appeal held that unless evidence that C was a prostitute fell within one of the exceptional categories, it could not be admitted. It went on to state that the substantial focus of the decision in *R v A* was the introduction of evidence of a previous sexual relationship with the accused himself. Where sexual behaviour with third parties was concerned, it would 'take a very special case to accommodate evidence of such acts' (para 35) where they cannot already be accommodated by an ordinary reading of the section. This decision leaves open the question of what is meant by 'a very special case' but it does at least make it clear that departures from the scheme set out in the Act are to be in exceptional cases only.

Procedural Requirements

Applications to admit sexual behaviour evidence are to be made and heard pre-trial. Rule 36 of the Criminal Procedure Rules 2005[15] contains precise instructions as to the exact timing of applications and how they are to be made and heard or decided by the judge without a hearing. They do allow for applications to be made at trial at the judge's discretion. Under section 43 of the 1999 Act, applications to the court for permission to introduce sexual history evidence must be heard in private. This means in the absence of the public, the press, the jury and all witnesses including the complainant. The accused, however, may be present (see Home Office, 1999a: para 152).

---

[11] For an example of such an appeal see *R v R (2) H* [2003] EWCA Crim 2754.
[12] See [2001] 3 All ER 1, para 109, p 35.
[13] See, eg [2001] 3 All ER para 161 and Lord Steyn's speech.
[14] [2004] EWCA Crim 946.
[15] As amended by the Criminal Procedure (Amendment No 2) Rules 2006, SI 2006 No 2636 (L 9).

THIRD PARTY DISCLOSURE

In sexual assault cases, the defence may desire to have access to records held by third parties, eg social services records, counselling or medical records (see Archbold, 2007, Supplement No2, N-59, Hoyano & Keenan, 2007: 558–568 and Temkin, 2002b). The reason for doing so will be to have access to material which may discredit and undermine the credibility of the complainant or shed doubt on her claims. Where such records are in the hands of the prosecution, then the disclosure regime which applies to all prosecution material applies here as well.[16] But where such records are not in the hands of the prosecution, a separate procedure applies if the defence seeks to have access to them and it cannot obtain voluntary disclosure. This requires an application to be made for a witness summons under section 2 of the Criminal Procedure (Attendance of Witnesses) Act 1965[17] which the court may grant where the document is 'likely to be material evidence'. Under the Attorney General's Guidelines of 2005 (Archbold, 2007, Supplement No 2, A-252), the prosecution too must take appropriate steps to obtain material in the hands of a third party if the material might reasonably be considered capable of undermining its case or assisting that of the accused, and this might also entail such an application.

At the hearing of the application for a witness summons, the critical issue will be whether the documents concerned contain evidence which is 'material' to the case. There is no statutory definition of this term but it has been the subject of some judicial exegesis. In *R v Derby Magistrates Court ex parte B*,[18] the meaning of the word 'material' was discussed in the context of section 97 of the Magistrates' Court Act 1980 which deals with disclosure applications in the magistrates' court. It was decided by the House of Lords that section 97 was not to be used to obtain discovery of documents for use in cross-examination.[19] A firm distinction was drawn between documents in the possession of the prosecution where there is a stringent duty of disclosure, and those in possession of a third party where this is not the case.[20] Their Lordships upheld the decision of Simon Brown LJ in *Reading Justices, ex parte Berkshire County Council*[21] in which it was held that to be 'material evidence', documents must not only be relevant to the issues raised in the criminal proceedings, but admissible as such in evidence.[22] Documents which are

---

[16] See Criminal Procedure and Investigations Act 1996 (CPIA) as amended by Criminal Justice Act 2003, pt 5.

[17] S 2 has been amended by subsequent legislation including s 66 of the Criminal Procedure and Investigations Act 1996 and the Criminal Justice Act 2003, sch 3, para 42.

[18] [1996] 1 Cr App R 385.

[19] At 393 confirming the decision in *Cheltenham Justices, ex p. Secretary of State for Trade* [1977] 1 WLR 95.

[20] At 394.

[21] [1996] 1 Cr App R 239.

[22] Archbold states erroneously that this case is authority for the proposition that evidence is material if it is relevant to an issue in the case: see Archbold, 2007, para 8–6a.

desired merely for the purpose of a possible cross-examination are not admissible in evidence and thus are not material. The jurisprudence on section 97 has been held to apply equally to section 2 of the 1965 Act.[23]

There is a further dimension to the disclosure issue. A third party, for example, a doctor or a local authority, may seek to resist a witness summons by claiming public interest immunity (PII)[24] on the ground that 'a confidential relationship exists [. . .] and disclosure would be in breach of some ethical or social value involving the public interest'.[25] In *R v Azmy* it was stated that PII applied to counselling records.[26] PII is also commonly claimed where, for example, social service records are at issue. Indeed, in *R v Higgins*[27] in which Higgins was charged with the indecent assault of a young boy and the defence sought disclosure of local authority files,[28] the Court of Appeal held that the local authority had a positive duty to apply for PII.[29]

Where PII is claimed, the court must perform a balancing exercise 'balancing on the one hand the desirability of preserving the public interest in the absence of disclosure against, on the other, the interests of justice'[30] in the sense of fairness to the defendant. However in *R v Reading Justices* Simon Brown LJ established the important principle that it is not necessary for the court to engage in this balancing exercise until it has first decided whether the document is material.[31]

In a laudable new development, it was held by Lord Justice May in *R. (TB) v Stafford Combined Court*,[32] following an application for judicial review, that the disclosure of medical records of a prosecution witness, in this case a child who was the alleged victim of sexual abuse, engaged Article 8 of the ECHR and that a court considering disclosure of such records in breach of confidentiality could only do so if it was proportionate, in accordance with law, and necessary. Moreover, notice of the witness summons should be given to the party whose records were being sought and such person had the right to make oral representations (see Temkin, 2002b, for a recommendation to this effect). The duty to ensure this was on the court. Rule 28 of the Criminal Procedure Rules has now been recast and goes some way towards allowing those whose records are sought to have their wishes expressed to the court and taken into account.[33]

[23] See eg *R v Clowes* [1992] 3All ER 440.

[24] Some material is well known to be covered by PII, eg information relating to children and state interests, but in *D v NSPCC*, Lord Hailsham held that 'the categories of public interest are not closed'; see [1977] 1 All ER 589 at 605.

[25] See Lord Edmund-Davies, *ibid* at 618.

[26] (1996) 7 Med LR 415 at 420. This was not part of the *ratio* of the case.

[27] (1996) 1 FLR 137.

[28] These contained statements of special educational needs and reports from teachers, social workers, and psychologists.

[29] At 140.

[30] *R v Governor of Brixton Prison ex parte Osman* [1992] 1AllER 108 at 116.

[31] See [1996] 1Cr App R 239 at 246.

[32] [2006] EWHC 1645(Admin); [2007] 1All ER 102.

[33] The rule change was introduced by the Criminal Procedure (Amendment) Rules 2007 and came into effect on 2 April 2007. See on this, Department for Constitutional Affairs (2007).

Appendix 2

Schedule for Semi-Structured Interviews with Judges and Barristers

(see Chapters Six and Seven)[1]

I. TRYING RAPE CASES

I.1   How many rape trials have you tried?

I.2   What proportion of your work is made up of sexual offences?

I.3   Are rape cases different from other criminal trials? Do you deal with them in exactly the same way as other cases?

I.4   As you know, there are concerns about low conviction rates in rape cases – what the government is now calling 'the justice gap'. Do you share these concerns?

    —Why do you think the conviction rate continues to fall?
    —Do you have concerns about juries in these cases?
    —Do you think that judge-only trials would be a good idea in sexual cases?

I.5   Do you think there is a problem in the way we categorise rape cases?
    —What is your view of so-called date rape?

I.6   Do you have any other concerns about how the criminal justice system is currently dealing with rape cases?

I.7   Have changes in the law in recent years made any significant difference to the way rape is dealt with in the courts?
    —Corroboration warning

1.8   Do you have any suggestions for improvements?

II. SECTION 41

II.1   As you know various efforts have been made to limit sexual behaviour evidence, what is your opinion of this approach in general?

II.2   In what proportion of rape trials do you think that evidence of the sexual behaviour of the complainant is relevant outside the actual commission of the offence?

---

[1] This version was used for interviews with judges. The same schedule with slight adaptations was used for the interviews with barristers.

—Can you suggest situations when it might be relevant. Can you provide examples?

II.3   Were there problems, in your opinion, with section 2?

II.4   What is your view of the new law contained in section 41?

II.5   Do you find it clear?

II.6   What is your understanding of how section 41 was intended to operate? How is the judge supposed to deal with a section 41 application?

II.7   What is your opinion of the impact of *R v A*?

—Did the House of Lords' judgment clarify matters?
—Are there other judgments you use to guide your decision-making in this area?

II.8   Do you think the section 41 regime as it now is could be improved? If so, how?

II.9   When ought the defence to make its application under section 41?

—Knowledge of the procedural rules

II.10 When do applications generally get made?

—Is there a problem with the procedural rules not being followed?

II.11 In your experience, in what proportion of cases are sexual history applications made?

II.12 Are there any situations not covered by the exceptions to section 41 which ought to be covered? Where C and D have had a previous sexual relationship, in what circumstances should such evidence be allowed?

II.13 Do you think that defence counsel sometimes evade the law by asking questions about sexual history without making an application?

II.14 How effective are prosecution counsel in arguing against admittance?

—Are there ways prosecution counsel could be more effective?

II.15 How effective has section 41 been, in your view, in limiting sexual history evidence?

—Is it admitted less often?
—Are judges more willing to intervene to limit the questions?
—Are there problems with the law which could be tightened up?

II.16 What is your opinion of the law in Scotland – that if sexual history evidence is allowed, then this opens the door to evidence of previous convictions of the defendant?

II.17 Do you think that controls on sexual history and special measures will have any effect on conviction rates?

II.18 Do you think they have any effect on the experience of giving evidence for the complainant?

Author Index

Subject Index